D0995456

BETWEEN NAIVETY AND HOSTILITY

BETWEEN NAIVETY AND HOSTILITY

Uncovering the best Christian responses to Islam in Britain

Editors Steve Bell and Colin Chapman

Authentic

First published 2011 by Authentic Media Limited
Presley Way, Crownhill, Milton Keynes, MK8 0ES
www.authenticmedia.co.uk

British Library Cataloguing-in-Publication Data
A catalogue record for this book is available from the
British Library
ISBN 978-1-85078-957-4

Cover design by David Smart
Printed and bound by CPI Group (UK) Ltd, Croydon, CR0 4YY

Contents

Foreword

It is not just for the sake of formality that I have to say how privileged I feel in being asked to write this foreword. The subject of this book is very important and its publication is timely. It is crucial for Christians to reflect upon and engage with the reality of Islam in Britain today, and who better to do it than the contributors to this volume. Among them, they have much and varied experience of Islam and of working with Muslims in many different parts of the world, including of course in this country. Their work reveals a number of different approaches to Muslims and to the world of Islam. This experience provides a depth and a dimension to the discussion of the difficult issues that is not always found in publications on this topic.

The contributors have variously been active in witnessing to Muslims about all that God has revealed and done in Jesus Christ; but they have also been engaged in a deep and sustained dialogue and in humble and loving service to their Muslim neighbours. We need therefore to listen carefully to what they have to say to us.

One matter which is immediately obvious is the need to maintain a proper balance between witness, service –

and, of course, dialogue. As can be seen from some of the chapters, serving the needs of our neighbours can also lead to dialogue with them about what is of ultimate value to them and to us. Provided that service is not an unworthy inducement for people to become Christians, it can be and should be an opportunity for witness.

Dialogue is about listening to our Muslim friends and learning more about their faith, but it also provides us with an opportunity to share our faith with them. It is also about cooperating in the building of community in a specific place and ensuring peaceful and all-round human development. At the national and international levels in particular, dialogue can be about the recognition and strengthening of fundamental freedoms. Within the bounds of civility (Col. 4:6; 1 Pet. 3:15) we must discuss the importance of freedom of expression, of belief, and of the freedom to change our beliefs. Whilst governments and other authorities may be interested in the content and the results of dialogue between Muslims and Christians, we must be careful not to be co-opted into the political agenda of parties or of states. It is particularly vital too not to think that engagement with Islam and with Muslims is a kind of capitulation and the adoption of a *dhimmi* mentality.

There is a welcome emphasis in this book on the 'wholeness' of mission and we need to make sure that witnessing to Christ and bringing people to faith in him is held in tension with the other aspects of mission such as being a voice for the voiceless, engagement in education and healing and action for community cohesiveness and development.

Whatever the approach, we must make sure that, in due course, 'the whole counsel of God' (Acts 20:27, NKJV) is brought to bear on our many and complex relations with Muslims and with the world of Islam. As Christians, we are called to love Muslims, to seek the best for them and to cultivate friendly relations with them. We owe this to our common humanity, but also so that the gospel may be seen to be at work in what we do and are, as well as in what we say.

Islam is, of course, a system of belief which may seem to have some features in common with the Christian faith, but there are basic and crucial differences as well. Central biblical doctrines such as original sin, incarnation and atonement find no place in Islam and, I believe, in the end we find a different doctrine of God. Whatever the differences, we must treat them respectfully. It is no part of Christian mission to be disrespectful about our neighbours' beliefs.

We must, however, also distinguish between Islam – as it is traditionally understood – and the ideology of Islamism (perhaps we should say, ideologies). Islamism is a comprehensive political, social and economic system based on a narrow and literalistic interpretation of the fundamental documents of Islam. It has had the effect of reducing the basic freedoms of many wherever it has had influence and has given birth to extremism, which in turn has produced terrorism in many forms. We must take note that these ideologies are attractive to many, even in the West. They are, therefore, not only a security issue, but also a threat to the building of community and to the proper participation of Muslims in national life. Loving Muslims and being respectful to their beliefs is one thing, but dealing with Islamist ideologies must be quite another.

We should not underestimate the extent to which radicalization has affected Muslim populations, including those in Great Britain. At the same time, it is important to encourage those Muslim scholars and leaders who are seeking in Islamic sources interpretations of the *shari'a* which make for an exercise of compassion, and contribute to the common good (*maslaha*).

In this connection, it is worth saying that whilst there should be no nostalgia for a past 'Christendom', it remains important for us to acknowledge the Judeo-Christian basis of British institutions, laws and core values. A common commitment to human dignity, to equality and freedom has arisen from such a world view. It remains important in helping us to make moral decisions in the public sphere today. Indeed, if those arriving from elsewhere had been welcomed on the basis of Christian hospitality, we might have been in a better place than the isolation and fragmentation created by well-meaning but misplaced secular doctrines of multiculturalism and the like.

The legal tradition in this country owes everything to the Christian faith which not only mediated the values of the Bible to society but also Christianized Roman Law and the Canon law of the Church itself. While most Muslims will want to order their lives by the precepts of *shari'a* (however that is understood), there can be no compulsion, and for very weighty reasons it is inadvisable to recognize a system of law which has completely different origins, in terms of public law in this country.

The contributors of this book have tackled a host of difficult issues and problems from a variety of angles, but with the grace and gentleness which they claim for their network. These go hand in hand with a firm commitment to truth and with the task of making Christ known to the whole of creation. I pray that this work will lead others also to commit themselves to an engagement which is arduous, but where fidelity has its own reward.

Michael Nazir-Ali, January 2011

Introduction

Colin Chapman

We don't need to look far to see evidence of hostility towards Muslims. The media and recent polls in Britain have reflected some very harsh and ungenerous attitudes towards Muslims, and there have been striking examples of the demonization of Islam in the Western world – especially in the USA and on the continent. If these feelings of hostility are fed by racial, cultural, social and political factors, Christians are likely to share them to a greater or lesser degree. They may have additional reasons to express hard feelings when they hear Muslims challenging fundamental Christian beliefs and when they see how Christians are treated in some Muslim countries. So the word 'hostility' is not too strong a word to sum up the attitudes of many – both among the wider public and among Christians – towards Muslims and Islam.

But if the hostility is obvious, where is the naivety? It's there in the political correctness which suggests that there's absolutely nothing in the religion of Islam which should raise any concern either for Christians or for the citizens of the UK. It was there very soon after 9/11 when a senior Anglican bishop said publicly, 'This has nothing to do with Islam.' Were there not traces of it in the popular concept of multiculturalism, which was used for many years to emphasize the diversities of culture and to downplay the importance of religion? When many in our secularized public sphere and in the media know little about Islam, it's inevitable that they don't share enough of the world view or the language of Muslims to be able to enter into a meaningful dialogue with them. Naivety in these areas makes us unable to discern the big issues and see what is really at stake.

A middle path?

The middle path that we're exploring isn't the result of a delicate political balancing act between two extremes. It is based on the conviction that, as the introduction to the *Gracious Responses* statement in Appendix 1 suggests, the best way to address the fears in the minds of many Christians is 'to learn more about Islam, to relate to Muslims with genuine respect and friendship, to recognize the many different kinds of Muslims and forms of Islam in Britain today, and to wrestle with the complexities of the political and social issues raised by the presence of Muslim communities.'

Each chapter of this book is intended to suggest how it may be possible to find a middle way between naivety and hostility by addressing some of the reasons why many Christians feel fearful of Islam and hostile towards Muslims. In Part 1, therefore, which deals with Assumptions and Starting Points, we begin with Steve Bell's description of his own personal journey from suspicion and fear to what he has called 'a grace response' (chapter

1). Ida Glaser recognizes that some Christians use the Bible to arrive at very negative views of Islam, but goes on to suggest a much deeper and richer way of interpreting it in relation to both Muslims and Islam (chapter 2). Addressing approaches to power, Bryan Knell reminds us that while Muslims consciously and deliberately seek to follow the example of the Prophet Muhammad, Christians are called to model themselves just as deliberately on Jesus (chapter 3). Richard McCallum is very aware that there is a wide spectrum of views among evangelical writers and analyzes the main areas where there are very significant differences among them (chapter 4). It's fortunate that we don't have to start our enquiry from scratch – as if we are the first generation to ask these difficult questions – and Martin Whittingham concludes this section by highlighting some of the most significant things we can learn from 1,400 years of Christian-Muslim relations (chapter 5).

Part 2 addresses Crucial Issues in Britain Today and begins with a scrupulously fair analysis of the dynamics of change within the Muslim communities in Britain by Philip Lewis (chapter 6). Tim Green and Ziya Meral write about some of the issues faced by Muslims who want to become Christians and are regarded by their communities as apostates, and draw attention to some of the serious human rights questions which are crying out to be addressed (chapters 7 and 8). Anthony McRoy seeks to understand how Islamic Radicalism sometimes turns to violence in our cities, and John Azumah suggests how Christians should respond to these harsher expressions of Islam (chapter 9). John Ray brings a lifetime of immersion in schools both in Muslim Kashmir and inner-city Birmingham to explore issues related to education (chapter 10). Some of the sensitive issues relating to Muslim women are explored by Emma

Dipper (chapter 11). And Julian Rivers, a professor of law in the University of Bristol, responds to the Archbishop of Canterbury's controversial lecture in 2008 about the place of *shariᶜa* law in Britain (chapter 12).

Part 3 explores Models of Positive Relationships. Thus Richard Sudworth and Bill Musk describe in different ways what can happen when a local church turns itself inside out and begins to serve the whole of the multi-faith community around it (chapters 13 and 18). Andrew Smith demonstrates that there's no substitute for finding natural and creative ways to bring Christians and Muslims – and especially young people – face to face with each other (chapter 14). And responding to Christians who use the *Shiᶜite* concept of *taqiyya* (dissimulation) to send the message 'You can't ever trust Muslims!', Toby Howarth explains the limited use of this concept among Muslims and describes his own frank but respectful and ongoing relationships with Muslim leaders in Birmingham (chapter 15). One of the sharpest tensions among evangelical Christians is over the place of polemics in Christian witness. So Jay Smith argues strongly for a more confrontational approach – especially with radical Muslims (chapter 16) – while Chawkat Moucarry sees no place for polemics and commends a more eirenic and dialogical kind of engagement (chapter 17).

Who are 'we'?

Who are the contributors and how have we come to work together to produce this book? All of us have specialized in different areas in our relationships with Muslims, and have therefore recognized the need to get beyond the headlines of the tabloids. Of the nineteen contributors, fifteen have lived and worked for considerable periods in the countries in the Indian subcontinent or the Middle East from which many of the Muslim communities in Britain trace their origins. This ought to help us to see the bigger picture and understand how Christian-Muslim relationships in one context can influence those in another. Eleven of us have doctorates or other post-graduate qualifications in areas related to Islam, and five are presently working on doctorates – which suggests that we have all recognized the need for serious academic study of Islam. Two of the contributors were brought up as Muslims and became Christians as adults.

All of the contributors have been associated in one way or another with CRIB (Christian Responses to Islam in Britain), an informal network which came together in 1998 to create a forum for Christians working among Muslims in Britain. This network developed out of the De Bron Group, named after the conference centre in Holland where in 1991 the Evangelical Alliances of Europe brought together around two hundred people to address issues related to Islam. Thirty of us from the UK who were present at the conference decided that we needed to start meeting regularly to learn from each other's experience and share resources.

In recent years, CRIB has organized annual or bi-annual conferences, and in September 2009 the conference, which was held at the London School of Theology, was attended by around two hundred people. The overall theme was the title of this book, and many of the authors presented drafts of their chapters which thay have subsequently revised.

Those of us who have been involved in the different stages of these two networks have shared an interesting journey together. Individuals working with para-church organizations, for example, have developed more confidence in people working directly within the churches – and vice versa. Those who set out with the sole aim of 'evangelizing Muslims' have begun to take seriously the need to relate to communities as well as individuals and to see that the gospel must have something to say about political and social issues. We've all concluded that there need not be any tension or contradiction between evangelism and dialogue or between proclamation and social involvement.

What's 'Christian' about these responses?

Some of us who have contributed to this book may have started out on our journey in response to the Great Commission, in which the risen Christ commissions his disciples to 'go . . . and make disciples of all nations' (Matt. 28:19, NRSV). But somewhere along the line it has dawned on us that Muslims are not only people with whom we want to share the good news about the crucified and risen Jesus, but our neighbours whom we're called to love, fellow-citizens living in the same street. We still want Muslims to have the opportunity to know 'the mystery of the gospel', the open secret of how God has revealed himself in Christ (Eph. 6:19,20). But addressing some of the difficult issues relating to Muslims and Islam in Britain has become part of our obedience to the Great Commandment in which we're told 'you shall love the Lord your God . . . You shall love your neighbour as yourself' (Mark 12:29–31). The Great Commandment and the Great Commission have therefore come to be seen as two sides of the one coin and provide the basic starting point for all that we have tried to cover.

We very much hope that these chapters will help Christians to work through their fears and prejudices about Islam, to understand better who our Muslim neighbours are, to go out and meet them and know what it means for us as Christians to live alongside them. There is no suggestion at any stage that we need to water down our beliefs in order to make them more acceptable to Muslims. We want to go on building meaningful and lasting relationships in our increasingly secularized society, recognizing the many areas of common ground shared between Christians and Muslims as well as the very significant differences. We're also aware of the need for 'hard talk' on some of the most controversial and painful issues.

In working through the difficult issues explored in these chapters, we will want to be as 'wise as serpents and innocent as doves' (Matt. 10:16). And in order to do this we will need to be listening to the one who invited people to follow him with the simple, yet profound words 'Follow me!'

Part 1:
Assumptions and
Starting Points

Chapter 1

Approaching Muslims with Grace and Truth

Steve Bell

In their book *Metaphors We Live By*, George Lakoff and Mark Johnson show how we use what they call 'conceptual metaphors' to think about things. They say that such metaphors pass into our culture and shape our attitudes, e.g. they use the conceptual metaphor 'argument is war' and show how the language we use to talk about 'argument' does actually reflect the combative terminology of war.

> Your claim is *indefensible*.
> He *attacked* every weak point in my argument.
> His criticisms were right *on target*.
> I *demolished* his argument.
> I've never *won* an argument with him.
> You disagree. OK, *shoot*!
> If you use that *strategy*, he'll *wipe you out*.
> He *shot down* all my arguments.[1]

Lakoff and Johnson are attempting to demonstrate that language is the repository of our ideas. The words we use as 'conceptual metaphors' articulate our attitudes and values about the world around us. If this is true, then perhaps we ought to pay more attention to what we say.

Islam and its adherents (i.e. Muslims) have become 'conceptual metaphors' in Britain, partly because we are so media-saturated and the public is encouraged by unenlightened media people to lump Islam and Muslims together as one amorphous mass. To many Anglo-Saxon Britons, Islam has thereby become a hostile metaphor for 'repression', 'hatred', 'violence', 'defiance', 'bigotry' and 'cunning'. For others in the media and – more worryingly – political circles, Islam has become a naive metaphor for all that is benign assuming that almost all Muslims are well-meaning towards British society.

This state of affairs makes it easy to see-saw between naivety and hostility. A case in point is the introduction to a report that was launched in November 2010 called 'Islamophobia and Anti-Muslim Hate Crime: UK Case Studies 2010'. Academic John Esposito said 'the exclusive Judaeo-Christian tradition of the West is an unhelpful false doctrine that should be jettisoned.' Boris Johnson, Mayor of London, went further to suggest that Islam should be considered as a replacement. Jenny Taylor brings balance when she comments that, while the 'Islamophobia' report rightly highlights the unacceptable 'hate crimes' against ordinary Muslims in Britain, it also ignores the 'islamo-facism' of a growing minority of British Muslims who are being welcomed onto the political landscape as 'cuddly newcomers'. She goes on to say:

> We must not lump all Muslims together. God forbid. But by what mental sleight of hand can we dissociate altogether the violent ones from the texts and teachings that

comprise the religion itself, and that keep so many in thrall to obscurantism and fear?[2]

We are greatly in need of such balance in order to develop a more realistic metaphor for Islam and the Muslims who were born into its traditions. To do this there are many issues to be taken into account – not least that Islam and its people are a complex reality due to a plethora of theological variation within the religion; there are many strains of Islamic practice; there is a huge variety of ethnicities and backgrounds among Muslim peoples who remain divided by the contrasting cultures, histories and nations they come from.

Against this backdrop it seems almost inevitable that Christians too are deeply unsettled and divided – to say the least – about what Islam is; how to think and act in relation to Muslim people; what are the appropriate 'missional' responses to them?; and what to do when Muslims who have changed their allegiance to follow Jesus Christ attach themselves to our local church.

A similar thing happened in the early church where 'sharp dispute and debate' broke out about how pagan Gentiles could be saved, and the terms by which they could be included in a predominantly Jewish Church (Acts 15:2,7). Today a largely Anglo-Saxon church in Britain is arguing about how Muslims can be saved and the terms on which they may be included. Within the British church there is a diverse spectrum of views about Islam. At one extreme of the spectrum, Islam is seen as a positive enriching influence in a secular society, which provides a 'missional' opportunity. At the other extreme, Islam is seen as a negative and destructive influence that poses a political threat, which is viewed by some Christians through a 'hermeneutic of suspicion'.

The divergent opinions about Islam provide very different answers to the following important questions:

1. 'What is the origin of Islam?' – i.e. Is it demonic, divine, human, or a mixture? Why did God in his sovereignty allow it to come into being?
2. 'What is the nature of Islam?' – i.e. Is Islam inherently violent? Are there any redeeming features in its Judaic aspects? Are there any elements of Islam that are biblical but in need of reorientation into the way of Christ? Alternatively, is it all demonic?
3. 'What is Islam's destination?' – i.e. Where is it going? What do assertive Muslims want? Will Islam be like European communism, ending in worldwide demise? Will the reforming influences end in a more malleable Euro-Islam? Will Muslims out-birth Caucasians until a fascist form of Islam takes over Britain? Will the present trickle of Muslims coming to faith in Christ escalate into a sovereign move of God that ushers in the redemption of the house of Islam?

Whatever conclusions we may reach about Islam, if we take the Bible seriously, we cannot escape the big question: how does our conclusion affect our attitude to the fulfilling of the Great Commission among Muslim people? This is the point at which many Christians become stuck and do not know how to proceed and so either walk away, and close their minds to the thought of Muslims coming into the kingdom of God, or else adopt a strident position.

As a rule of thumb, I find that Christians born during the second half of the twentieth century are at the end of the spectrum where it is easier to see the 'missional' opportunity presented by the Muslim presence. On the other hand, those born in the first half of the twentieth century are more prone to see Muslims as a threat. It seems to me that these people – all of mature years – have a greater attachment to the Christendom mindset, which sees Europe as essentially 'Christian', even if only culturally so. This age bracket is prone to a sort of grief, for the loss of the mono-racial Britain of a bygone era. Of course throughout our history, the river of the British population has been fed by multi-racial tributaries. What has changed is that today immigrants are, on the whole, not Caucasian and so more noticeable. Of course the visible minorities are now bringing their religion with them; hence the profound sense of unease. This book is written to address some of the serious issues that are posed by Islam, and hopefully to help readers to make up their own minds based on the facts presented.

Where accurate information ends, imagination takes over and misplaced fear begins. Such hearsay about the difficult issues posed by Islam is rife in secular and Christian media. It is therefore the attitude you bring to the facts about Islam that will determine whether you 'react' or 'respond' to individual Muslims. It therefore follows that our attitude to the Muslim will determine not only what we think about the best way of conveying the gospel to the Muslim, but also what is required when it comes to his or her discipleship, expression of worship and the way they follow Jesus. Of course these issues too are causing Christians to disagree. For example we must decide on questions such as:

1. In the Western practise of Christianity, how do we tell the difference between what is biblical and what is merely cultural?
2. Why should a Muslim accept the gospel communicated in precisely the way we received it in a British context?

3. Is the conservative evangelical tradition (birthed as it was in response to papal dogma in western Europe) divine writ or a contextualized application of the Bible?
4. What might a biblically faithful 'eastern telling' of the gospel look like?
5. When is it appropriate for a believer from Islam to be extracted – 'Come out from among them and be separate' (Isa. 52:11; 2 Cor. 6:17, NKJV) – and when is it right for them to be imbedded – 'Go home to your own people and tell them how much the Lord has done for you' (Mark 5:19, TNIV)?
6. Why should a Muslim change his name from Ahmad to Peter, adopt Western culture, attend Western church and worship in Anglo-Saxon ways, to follow Jesus? Are we insisting on more than the Bible does?

Returning to the church council at Jerusalem, the dispute about the inclusion of pagan Gentiles prompted them to 'contextualize' the gospel by applying it to the context of the recipient. Their conclusion was that 'it [seems] good to the Holy Spirit and to us not to burden [Gentile believers] with anything beyond' what was core and non-negotiable in the gospel (Acts 15:28, TNIV). We face the same responsibility to think through the issues with Muslims today. Our answers will be driven by underlying assumptions that are based on our answers to the questions above.

I was invited to contribute to this book because, as the author of *Grace for Muslims*,[3] I am identified as a proponent of the term 'grace approach' towards Muslim people. So I am attempting to set the scene for this phrase, give it context and define its terms.

The full expression is 'a grace and truth approach to Muslims' – an expression that is barely grammatical but thoroughly biblical. It is not intended to be a sentimental appeal for a trusting relationship with a Muslim at the expense of biblical truth. On the contrary, the aim is to encourage Christians to relate the gospel to a Muslim (in any one of a variety of ways) with humility, confidence and a Christlike attitude.

The so-called 'grace approach' is rooted in the person of the Lord Jesus Christ who uniquely came into the world as 'the One and Only . . . from the Father, full of *grace and truth*' (John 1:14, NIV, emphasis added). 'Grace' and 'truth' validate each other and we separate them at our peril. Yet evangelicals seem to be polarizing towards one or the other – a telltale sign that the enemy of all of our souls is at work. Christians are being offered an either/or scenario which wrongly sees 'grace *or* truth' rather than 'grace *and* truth'. So whether Christians relate to Muslims combatively or relationally – or with a mixture of both – it must be with both grace and truth.

There is a spectrum of opinions among Christians about Muslims. For example, some Christians think that Islam – and therefore Muslims – is intrinsically violent. They cite the Islamic source texts such as the Qurᶜan and Hadith – as well as the more recent Islamic thinking of *fiqh* and *kalam*. The fatwas and pronouncements of radical Islamic clerics – particularly in the post-colonial era of the past fifty years – also lend considerable weight to this argument. The result is that such Christians distrust Muslims, suspecting them of presenting Islam in a 'softer' light when in the minority in the West, while planning to take over by stealth through deceptive means such as the practise of a *Shiᶜite* doctrine called *taqiyya*, or dissimulation in order to further the cause of Islam. They also fear that Muslims are using immigration as a form of jihad and that they are intent on out-birthing Anglo-Saxons in Britain where they do not intend to integrate and, as such, they are a growing threat to British society and the Judeo-Christian heritage.

These Christians conclude that it is Christians – not politicians – who alone can 'defeat' Islam through prophetic warning and public discrediting of its teaching. Some Christians base their strident and even combative style on the challenge to pharisaical legalism by Jesus and the apostle Paul (Matt. 23:1–36; Gal. 3; 5); they see this as an appropriate way to relate to Muslims.

At the other end of the spectrum are Christians who accept that there are references condoning violence in Islam's mediaeval texts. Such Christians maintain that there are diverse schools of Islamic interpretation, which act as a block on violence being formalized in Islam and, as a result, most Muslims do not accept violence as a modern expression of Islam. These Christians are aware of a parallel 'narrative of supremacy' which runs through Christian history (contrary to the teaching of Jesus); and that it is counter-productive to react to vociferous Muslims with the same attitude.

Such Christians also see the shortcomings of Islamic and Western civilization and see the kingdom of God as the only valid third way. For these Christians, while Islam must be engaged with politically and theologically, they believe that the primary responsibility of the church is the Great Commission. They therefore opt for an 'eirenic' approach to Muslims involving genuine friendship and the encouragement of Muslims to explore Jesus Christ; as a result of which, they may decide to change their spiritual allegiance to him.

These Christians point to sociologists who say that the fertility rates of immigrants tend to drop over the generations and that secular influences are already eroding the Islamic values of younger Muslims and creating a 'Euro-Islam' as opposed to a 'fascist Islam'. This means that the era of prophetic warning is largely over since 9/11 which made the authorities aware of the danger of radicalization.

Thirty years ago I held a more 'polemic' position until I embarked on a voyage of discovery, which took me into 'eirenic' territory where I began adding 'grace' (to my attitude) when relating 'truth' (with my mind) to Muslim people. This transition has taken me through 100 countries on three continents over thirty years. It included Middle Eastern culture which became my adoptive home where I lived in the Arabic language among Muslims for a decade. I started out believing that Islam was spawned by the devil; Allah was an ancient moon god; Muhammad was the false prophet (Rev. 16:13; 19:20; 20:10) and the antichrist was likely to be Muslim.

My friends included local Christian leaders of churches that were systematically oppressed by the government. I was made angry about human rights violations against friends who were converts to Christ. I was beaten by border guards, nearly pinned to a wall by a knife attack, interrogated by the secret police and eventually expelled.

As a mission leader I have worked with the African church where I witnessed firsthand the horrors of south Sudan, the poverty of the Sahel and the community violence in Nigeria. During my time I have been spat at in the street, lied to as well as lied about – all by Muslims.

In spite of all this, God moved me from seeing the issues in crude black and white to a more nuanced understanding of the complex set of issues involved in Islam and the cultures into which it has become embedded. I was led to repent of my cultural and theological superiority, and from a condescending compassion for Muslims to a place where I related to them out of the same grace that I had received from God. The journey led me from fear of Muslims to faith for them; from sniping at them in private Christian meetings to a concern for integrity in what I said to Christians and Muslims.

After cultural immersion in the Muslim world, I moved back to Britain where I became involved with the immigrant Muslims communities. I have spoken to hundreds of thousands of Christians in Britain and around the world about the grace and truth approach to Muslims – a position that is gaining momentum.

It is not easy to put my finger on why, but it seems a fundamental change in the Christian psyche came about in the aftermath of the attacks of '9/11' and '7/7'. I began running Muslim awareness seminars in 1991 when there was little interest. British Christians were content to send mission partners to the Muslim world while ignoring Muslims living across the road. They seemed oblivious to the fact that the Muslims pictured in mission presentations had come to live in their postcode. Within a month of 9/11, I was speaking to packed venues at major Christian events where I found that Christians are looking for a more constructive way forward than has been on offer.

Although there is no direct parallel to Muslims in Jesus' ministry, the closest counterpart to Islam in Jesus' day was probably the pharisaic system. This enforced Mosaic Law in the same way that some Muslims enforce *shariʿa* law. Jesus challenged (not ordinary Jews but) the religious professionals who were manipulating the Scriptures as a form of social control by stealth (Matt. 16:5–12). However, although Jesus cleared the temple (Luke 19:45,46), he also took care not to break the proverbial 'bruised reed' (Isa. 42:3; Matt. 12:20) in his gentle interaction with the pharisee Nicodemus (John 3:1–21). It also seems significant that Jesus never actually denigrated Judaism itself, either publicly or privately. So truth can be robustly presented with the restraint of grace.

This book makes this a live option because it provides a reasoned account of the difficult issues, which need addressing without demonizing all Muslims. Even if everything negative we hear about Islam were proved to be true, Christians who take the Bible seriously would surely agree that any conclusion we come to which suggests Muslims do not 'deserve' the gospel (i.e. due to the wicked things some Muslims do) would be as biblically questionable as the view that Muslims do not 'need' the gospel (i.e. as though there were salvation in Islam). We have a responsibility to Muslims regardless of their beliefs, agenda or behaviour. May these pages help us to become a greater part of the answer than we are part of the problem.

Chapter 2

Thinking Biblically about Islam

Ida Glaser

Christians differ about how they understand Islam. Far more important, however, than any assessment of Islam is that we learn how to honour the Lord Jesus Christ in our relationships with, and our speaking about, Muslims. Whether we look at what we might judge the best of Islam or the worst of it, at the most friendly Muslims or the most hostile ones, at the rich or poor, this is the crucial question.

To find out what honours Christ, where should we go but the Bible? This paper does not address the complex issues of later chapters, but offers a framework for reading the Bible with such issues in mind. As we seek to engage biblically with the multifaceted subject of 'Islam' – addressing questions of faith, worship, ethics, power, politics, law and culture, along with Islam's specific dealings with Jesus and critiques of Christianity – we are setting an agenda for one of the most important theological tasks facing the church today.

Christians go to different parts of the Bible to justify their responses to Islam and to Muslims:

- to Elijah and the prophets of Baal as a basis for ruthless challenge to Islam
- to Joshua as a basis for dealing with struggles over land or as a picture of spiritual warfare
- to Daniel and Revelation as frameworks for understanding the place of Islam in the unfolding of history
- to John the Baptist's and Jesus' confrontations with the Pharisees as a basis for polemics
- to Paul at Ephesus as a basis for apologetic debate
- to Peter's sermons to Jews as a basis for starting dialogue from the Qurᶜan
- to Cornelius and the woman at the well as bases for personal evangelism
- to the Sermon on the Mount as a model for dealing with law-based religion
- to Hagar, Tamar, Leah or Rachel as a basis for understanding Muslim women
- to Jesus' dealings with the Samaritans as a basis for challenging prejudice
- to passages about false prophets and the antichrist as a basis for dealing with Islam's denials concerning Jesus.

Who is right and who is wrong? I believe that we need all these passages – the whole Bible in fact – if we are to think biblically about Islam and, perhaps more importantly, about how we relate to the people who live out Islam in so many different ways. For God has given us the whole Bible to help us understand human beings and how we relate to him and to each other.

However, we cannot simply jump from a biblical passage to something that we think is equivalent in today's world. It is dangerous, for example, to jump from Elijah and the prophets of Baal to the conclusion that we should set up competitions with Muslims. How should we distinguish this from the opposite conclusion – that, as Muhammad opposed idolatry, he was just like Elijah? We need to look at the story's background of Baal religion, and to consider the passage in its context, as part of the history of Israel's failures that led to the exile, recognizing it as a call to Israel to repent rather than a recipe for inter-faith relations. Most importantly, we need to look at it in the light of the New Testament, and in the fulfilment of Elijah in God's purposes of redemption in Jesus and in his cross. Only by asking such questions can we discern what any passage is saying to us about our relationships with Muslims today.

We cannot look at the whole Bible in such depth in this chapter.[1] What I am going to do is, firstly, offer a framework for understanding religions in general and Islam in particular; secondly, suggest how we can use the Old and New Testaments to think about Islam; and, thirdly, show the importance of keeping the cross at the centre of our reading. These will offer ways of relating biblically to Muslims and will be followed, fourthly, by some pointers for thinking biblically about Islam as a system.

A biblical framework for understanding religions

Genesis 1 – 11 offers a powerful framework for understanding the world, both then and now, as a multi-religious place:

a) Humans are religious beings (Gen. 1 – 3)
Genesis 1 addresses a religious world whose creation stories featured many gods. In contrast, Genesis has no warring, jealous, lustful or hungry deities; the one God

is good, and in control of everything. As human beings are made by God for relationship with him, we are naturally religious and can expect to find some awareness of the Creator in everyone.

God puts human beings in a beautiful place, with authority to tend it, fill it and to care for its inhabitants. But people took things into their own hands, abusing the fruit of the land. Their relationships with God, each other, the animals and creation were spoilt, their power had to be limited and they lost their land.

b) The world outside Eden continues to be full of religion (Gen. 4 – 11)
Human attempts to approach God: The first thing recorded of the first people born outside Eden is a 'religious' act, followed immediately by a 'religious' argument and murder. The story suggests both positive and ambiguous aspects of 'religion':

- Human beings are likely to seek relationship with God through forms of sacrifice.
- God accepts some sacrifices and sacrificers. Genesis 4 brilliantly, if frustratingly, leaves open the question of what makes Abel's sacrifice acceptable and Cain's sacrifice unacceptable. Is it the nature of the sacrifice or the attitude of the sacrificer, or is it simply God's sovereign decision?
- God speaks – not to the accepted sacrificer, but to the angry, rejected, violent one.
- Return to God is open to the Cains of the world; but they are judged if they choose not to take the opportunity offered.

From this point on, the biblical authors describe a world in which all sorts of people offer all sorts of sacrifices, assuming that God can and does speak to all sorts of people.

Religion as a dangerous human construct

The story of the tower of Babel is a vivid analysis of the common phenomenon of the building of a power base in a particular place, fusing the god and the temple with political power and the conquest of land. Such religion does not reach God, and its gods do not represent the One Creator – he has to come down even to see its tower. It is dangerous for humankind and for God's creation purposes, and has to be judged and limited. From this point on, we see a world in which much religion is linked with power. On the one hand, gods are linked with particular peoples; on the other hand, Israel is constantly tempted to use both Yahweh and other gods for power purposes.

Dealing with evil

At the heart of Genesis 4 – 11, the flood story offers two ways of dealing with pervasive human wickedness: flood or sacrifice. The wickedness of human hearts after the flood is described in similar terms to that which necessitated the flood in the first place (6:5 cf. 8:21). God's heart-reaction to this wickedness is described in 6:6 as 'pain' (NIV) – the word implies a powerful emotion, and echoes the pain of 3:16,17 and 5:29. The result of this reaction in chapter 6 is destructive judgement – a reverse of the very act of creation. However, the creator God preserves one family to start a new creation. In the new creation, he smells the sacrifice and, despite the persistent evil in the human heart, chooses the very different option of covenant.

As in Genesis 4, the question of why the sacrifice leads to a different response from the heart of God is left open. However, the repeated covenantal commitments of 8:21 – 9:17 insist that the way opened by the sacrifice is God's preferred option. The Noahic covenant represents God's commitment not only to all humanity but also to his whole creation. The tension between judgement and salvation as ways of dealing with persistent evil can be traced throughout the Bible, and is resolved only on the cross, where God's pain opens a new creation.

A biblical framework for understanding Islam

If we accept Genesis 1 – 11 as the Bible's diagnosis of the human condition, we can expect today's world – our world – to exhibit similar characteristics. Islam is no exception:

Muslims are human beings: they are made in the image of God, with the same desires for God and potential for communication with God as any other people. Muslims are also fallen, despite the fact that Islam removes the Fall from the Adam story and deals with the problematics of human nature through *shari͑a* – the classification and regulation of human actions – rather than through redemption.

Islam exhibits both seeking after God and dangerous religion: from the time of the *hijra*, Islam has had a political dimension. As Genesis 11 shows, a fusion of religion and power is so potentially dangerous to creation that God himself will not let it happen beyond certain limits. It is not surprising that the political dimension of Islam has been one of its greatest challenges to Christians since its inception.

Many dimensions of Islam, however, reflect Cain and Abel's attempts to reach God through sacrifice – from some popular understandings of the *Eid* sacrifice as in some way substitutionary to more orthodox teaching about the Hajj wiping out sin. Ritual prayers, fasting, almsgiving and pilgrimage can all be considered offerings to God, and it is not surprising that there is not only debate, but also violence, associated with different Islamic understandings of what is acceptable to God. Is it possible that some sacrifices offered by Muslims might be acceptable to God from a biblical perspective? The Bible includes stories of individuals outside Israel whose prayers are heard by God, as well as stories of people within Israel whose sacrifices make God sick. Can we not expect God to respond to the agonies of some Muslims as he did to Hagar (Gen. 21:15–19), or to the prayers, fasting and almsgiving of others as he did to Cornelius (Acts 10)? Might he not speak also to those who are inclined to violence, as he did to Cain and to Saul of Tarsus?

Dealing with evil

The Qur'an and other classical writings recognize human and satanic evil and seek to deal with them. However, they do it on a different basis than does the Bible, since they see the human problem as weakness, ignorance and stubbornness rather than as a Fall. This is a key to understanding and engaging constructively with the differences between the framework and details of the Bible and the Qur'an. We can ask, for example, how the biblical authors deal with people who do not see themselves or others as fallen – both those who think that they are 'OK', but that others are weak, ignorant or stubborn; and those who know they are sinners, but do not know the root of their problem or that it can be dealt with.

Genesis 1 – 11 presents a God who will not overlook any evil, but will judge it or deal with it by sacrifice. We know, therefore, that God will deal with any evil associated with Muslims and with Islam, whether directed towards, or by, Muslims or non-Muslims. However his preference will always be to delay judgement and offer salvation. It is helpful to remember this tension when reading through the Bible with Islam in mind, allowing the tensions in our world to drive us to the cross.

Using the Old and New Testaments to think about Islam

Islam and Muslims are then part of the world of which and into which the whole Bible speaks. The task of thinking biblically about Islam is not only to understand both Bible and Islam, but also to move from Islam to the Bible and from the Bible to Islam as we develop our understanding of both. In more technical terms, we set up a hermeneutical spiral that moves between text and context in order to build an increasing understanding both of the text and of its contextual application. This section can but offer pointers for so doing.

The Old Testament

The Qur'an sees history in terms of God sending a series of prophets with a repeated message and developing laws, culminating in the final prophet with the final law for all peoples. It is accepting the prophets and following the law that enables people to approach God, and the Muslim community is the people governed by the law. The Bible sees a history of God's covenant commitment to his creation, then to a particular people called for the purpose of blessing all other peoples, culminating in salvation through Christ. It is within this history that the law, the land, the nation and the prophets find their place. The aspects of creation that are so easily distorted into 'dangerous religion' are, in Israel, to be put to the service of God's priority for enabling human beings to approach him through covenant and sacrifice. This analysis points towards resources for thinking both about Islamic theory and practice relating to law and society and about how Christian views might differ.

The problem is that Israel constantly reverts to the fallen state, seeking her own interests and to be governed, even to worship, like the nations. She seems not to understand the judgement/salvation tension in God's dealings with evil, and is therefore unable to maintain the apparent paradox in her relationship with other peoples – that, on the one hand, she is to guard against pollution from their idolatry to maintain her own holiness while, on the other hand, her very existence is for their sake. Despite this, God's covenant commitment triumphs throughout. This analysis points towards resources both for understanding the conflicts into which Christians as well as Muslims can fall, and for keeping focus on God's priority for salvation.

The Old Testament records not only the establishment of the covenants and law, but also the prophetic exhortation, rebuke and promise that deal with wrong sacrifice and abuse of power – primarily within Israel, but also within the surrounding nations. It also records the whole range both of human attempts to approach God and of dangerous religion – again, primarily within, but also without, Israel – not only through narratives but also in passionate poetry and reflective wisdom.

Whether, then, we are looking at the plight of threatened minorities (as in Esther or Daniel) or at the responsibilities of communities towards foreigners (as in Ruth or the sojourner legislation), at polygamous families (as in those of Jacob or David) or oppressed women (too numerous to mention in the OT), at those who have committed atrocities (such as Babylon and Nineveh) or at their lamenting victims (as in Lamentations or Psalm 137), the Old Testament offers immense resources. However, it never allows us to over-simplify the complexities of the human condition or to suppose that sin will be on only one side.

The New Testament

In its dealings with legal, nationalistic, philosophical, political, mystical and magical aspects of religion, the New Testament offers further rich resources for a response to Islam in its varied forms, and for mission and ministry amongst Muslims.[2]

Throughout the Gospels, for example, Jesus is faced with the complex world we have explored above – a world of tensions, pluralism and tyranny – and much can be learnt from his wise dealings with all these. However, his priority throughout was the purpose for which he had come – salvation on the cross – a purpose which he pursued in spite of opposition and temptation. In terms of our Genesis analysis, Jesus on the cross was offering himself as the acceptable sacrifice to which all other acceptable sacrifice points. He was God's way of responding to evil with both justice and salvation. It follows that this was God's path to dealing with dangerous religion as well as answering personal seeking after himself. The acceptability of the sacrifice was demonstrated by the resurrection.

The rest of the New Testament explores the tensions and triumphs as the good news of salvation goes out to the nations. As in the Old Testament, we meet both political and religious powers, but also people seeking God, and we see how God's people grapple with all the issues raised. In every page, we can see situations and people that parallel Muslims that we might meet. Here, we have space to focus on one thing only: Jesus' priority, which should also be ours.

Keeping the cross at the centre

The cross is at the centre of biblical history and of Christian thinking; but is almost universally denied by Muslims. A focus on the cross should therefore take us not only to the centre of what it means to think biblically about Islam, but also to the heart of how Christian thought and action should be different from Islamic thought and action. This paper has aimed to show that 'thinking biblically about Islam' is a complex and multi-faceted task; the ultimate test of our thinking, however, is simple: does it reflect the cross of Christ? Do our actions, then, truly follow Jesus?

As Jesus' focus was on saving others rather than on saving himself, just as Israel was called for the sake of others, so our focus needs to be on the eternal welfare of Muslim people rather than on showing Christian superiority or limiting Islamic rule. This makes evangelism and all that goes with it a priority, but it also determines how we relate to Muslims at every level. In particular, in the context of current debates about Islam, it is important that the cross is the way that Jesus faces the worst of the fallen human world. It should therefore guide our

response to what we might see as the worst as well as
the best aspects of the world of Islam; and it should
remind us how much potential there is for sin in us as
we relate to Muslims.

The cross is the result of Jesus' dealing with political
and legal religion, and of his confrontation with falsehood and evil; but how should it guide us in relating to
opposition and to power? The Crusaders based their
thinking on the Bible and put the cross at the centre of
their responses to Islam.[3] Here, we have space for but
one key to thinking about Islam in the light of the cross:
the account of the transfiguration in Luke 9, where
Jesus meets Moses, the leader and lawgiver, and Elijah,
the zealous prophet, and talks with them about the crucifixion to come. There is plenty of discussion about
how the cross transformed earthly ideas of kingship,
fulfilled all that Moses was pointing to, and changed
understandings of law. Elijah's presence suggests that
the cross also fulfilled all that Elijah was pointing to,
and thus changed the prophetic confrontation with
power and idolatry.

Interwoven into Luke 9 are predictions about the
cross. Jesus repeatedly tells the disciples that he must go
to the cross, and that they must follow him in taking up
their cross. It is the cross that will be the final confrontation with evil. However, the transfiguration in Luke is
immediately followed by three areas of specific confrontation that echo some of Elijah's concerns: firstly, the
confrontation with the unclean spirit alerts us to spiritual opposition and the challenge to prayer and faith (cf. 1
Kgs. 18, especially vv. 36,37); secondly, a confrontation
with the disciples' ambition and jealousy which demonstrates the need for God's servants to be humbled in
preparation for confrontation with religious and political powers (cf. 1 Kgs. 19); and, thirdly, a confrontation

with the Samaritans (cf. 1 Kgs. 16:23–32 as the context for Elijah's ministry).

In this final confrontation, while Jesus is at the receiving end of the ethnic and religious prejudice between Jews and Samaritans, the incident is presented primarily as a confrontation with the disciples, who are rebuked for wanting to emulate Elijah by calling down fire from heaven on the heretics. Here we have a representation of the national dimension of religion that Jesus had already challenged in his reference to Elijah and the widow of Zarephath in Luke 4, and that will be challenged again through the parable of the Good Samaritan in the very next chapter. In the context of Islam, we see parallel rejections of Jesus and of his followers amongst some Muslims; but the passage challenges us first to deal with our own tendencies to exclude and judge Muslims, and then to see that what Jesus wants for them is their salvation.

The key to the transfiguration of confrontation is this attitude of Jesus that is leading him to the cross: people may show enmity towards him and all that he stands for; but whether they are his disciples or the religious and political enemies of his people, he does not show enmity towards them but offers himself for their sake. He is the embodiment of his own teaching in Matthew 5:43–48; and if you act in love towards your enemies they may kill you. But that is Jesus' way to resurrection power. It comes as no surprise, then, that the transfiguration is preceded by the call to take up the cross (Luke 9:23–27), and that Luke 9 finishes with the cost of discipleship (vv. 57–62). The Crusaders were right about following Jesus even to death; the problem is that they were doing it for the sake of themselves and their civilization, and not for the sake of the people they saw as their enemies and Christ's.

Thinking biblically about Islam

We have, to this point, been mainly thinking about
Muslim people. Because they are human beings, it is relatively easy to see them in various places in the Bible,
and to consider our reaction to them. What about how
we think biblically about Islam as a system? Even here,
we must repeat the caveat that Islam is not a single system, and that we need careful study and observation to
understand what it is we are trying to think about.

How then does the kind of Bible reading explored so
far help us to think about Islam? I would like to suggest
our analysis of the transfiguration as a starting point.
The Gospels indicate that Jesus transforms and fulfils,
and therefore supersedes both Moses the community
leader and lawgiver, and Elijah, the paradigm of zealous
prophetic confrontation. We might argue that Islam
reverses this transfiguration. First, it equalizes all the
prophets, since Jesus is no longer greater than Moses or
Elijah. Second, it raises another prophet who supersedes
all and who combines the leadership and lawgiving of
Moses with the prophetic confrontation of idolatry of
Elijah. In the Gospels, the transfiguration signals the
movement towards the cross. In the Qur'an, the merging
of the Moses and Elijah paradigms in Muhammad signals the removal of the cross from Islamic thinking.

The law in Islam

When asked what the difference is between Islam and
Christianity, I sometimes answer, 'Christianity has no
shari'a!' Where *shari'a*, at least in theory, classifies all
human actions on a scale from compulsory to forbidden,
Christians are more likely to base their actions on categories of right and wrong, love and hatred, or building

relationships. This brings into sharp focus the difference in Christian and Islamic views of how human beings relate to God and what they need.

In brief, the idea of *shari͑a* is based on the understanding that what people need is guidance on how to act so that they will gain success in both this world and the next. This guidance is believed to be available through the Qur͑an, the *Sunna*, and the accepted deliberations of scholars. From a biblical perspective, however good such guidance might be, it cannot deal with the fundamental human problem: fallen nature.

The focus on judging activity by law gives, I think, one of the most important clues to thinking biblically about Islam: Islam can be seen as similar to the Judaism of New Testament times. And this suggests an overall way into thinking biblically about Islam as a whole. While it is popular to speak of Islam, alongside Judaism and Christianity, as an 'Abrahamic faith', and while it is true that the Qur͑an sees itself as preaching the religion of Abraham, the biblical figure most mentioned in the Qur͑an is not Abraham but Moses; and, unlike the biblical and qur͑anic Abrahams, the biblical and qur͑anic Moses' are remarkably similar. It might, then, be most appropriate to think of Islam as a Mosaic faith – a development of Judaism. This seems sensible historically as well as theologically, since the Qur͑an exhibits far more interaction with the Judaism than with the Christianity of its time.

This, of course, is a development that differs significantly from other current Judaisms:

• It accepts Jesus as Messiah
The Qur͑an repeatedly emphasizes the title 'Messiah' and castigates the Jews for rejecting him, raising the question, 'what kind of Messiah is Jesus?'

- It puts law before covenant

The Qurʿan speaks of covenants, but these are essentially agreements taken by God from human beings in order that they should acknowledge him and keep his laws, rather than promises given by God to human beings. Where biblical covenants start with God's commitment to people and then lay out what people should do in the context of their relationship with him, the Qurʿan implies that it is by keeping laws that we become God's people.

- It universalizes

It recognizes that the one God of the Jews is the God of the whole world; but, where Jesus called the Jewish people to repentance in order to invite all peoples into a kingdom unlike the Roman kingdom, Islam seeks to extend the rule of God to all peoples through the spread of *shariʿa*. Where the rule of God is equated with the rule of Muslims, the result can be very 'dangerous religion' which is more parallel with the Roman rule than with the Jewish struggles of New Testament times.

- It loses the pain in the heart of God

The biblical tension between the holy requirement for justice and the loving longing to save is missing from Islamic views of God because, to put it simply, most Muslims see God as above emotions. With such a view of God, the sharing of the human state in incarnation is unthinkable and the bearing of the consequences of sin on the cross is unnecessary. Further, while the Bible holds together both justice due and love given to each individual as well as each society, Islam has no problem in dividing people into the good and the bad – those who receive judgement and those who receive mercy.

Such an analysis gives a way of thinking about the Qur⁵an as a book that builds a new version of Judaism and about *shari⁵a* as having many parallels to Jewish law. It also offers a way of finding aspects of Islam in the New Testament as its writers deal with the Judaism and with the imperial religion of their times.

The prophet: thinking about Muhammad

As Christians historically have sought to understand Muhammad in the light of the Bible, they have seen him in a range of biblical models. Early records[4] view him as a political rather than as a religious leader, like the leaders of the beastly kingdoms of Daniel, while others have seen him as God's instrument of judgement on corrupt churches and Christian regimes, like a Nebuchadnezzar or a Cyrus. Another response was to consider him as a prophet to the Ishmaelites, with a genuine message to prepare idolatrous Arabs for the gospel, while John of Damascus lists Islam among Christian heresies, seeing Muhammad as a heretic and hence a false prophet. One of the cleverest answers to the question, 'What do you think of Muhammad?' comes from the Nestorian patriarch, Timothy. Face to face with the powerful Caliph al-Mahdi, he responded, 'He walked in the way of the prophets,' and listed ways in which Muhammad was similar to Old Testament prophets.

The problem in making a Christian assessment of Muhammad is the question of who we are assessing. One of the reasons for the range of Christian thinking has been that some judge him by the traditional Islamic accounts of his life, while others seek to get behind them to a historical figure. While it is helpful to try to understand and discuss Muhammad as Muslims see him, it seems to me that Christians can best understand Muhammad as someone of his time – a time in which there was not only division between Jews and Christians, but also division between Christian power blocs that favoured different christologies. This would mean seeing him as someone who started out thinking he was preaching the same as the Jews and Christians (and maybe even wanted to unite the Jews and the warring factions of Christians) but ended up pleasing none, and taking power into his own hands.

Our Genesis framework offers a way of analyzing this complex character.

A person attempting to approach God

Muhammad's mission was based on calling people to the one God and, at least in the Meccan years, he appears to have been driven by a genuine desire for a monotheism continuous with that of Jews and Christians. How acceptable his attempts were to God is not, I think, a question that we can answer, but I think we can be sure that, as with Cain, God was speaking to him at some stages, quite possibly through dreams or visions. At the very least, he was getting the opportunity to hear God through the biblically based material that he evidently knew.

A person who originated a power-linked religion

The move from Mecca to Medina signalled the development of Islam as a political identity, together with the power implications that have been part of most manifestations of Islam ever since.

Dealing with evil

Muhammad was clearly aware of evil, and understood the possibilities of judgement or clemency. He does not, however, seem to have made the link between sacrifice and forgiveness. The nearest he got to the biblical idea of sacrifice is the commemoration of Abraham's sacrifice of his son, which signified for him not atonement, but obedience. The Qur'an has a pattern of dividing the world into good and bad people. After death, the bad go to hell and the good go to paradise; in this life, the good distinguish themselves from the bad and may even fight and kill them. It is not surprising, then, that as Muhammad developed political power, he also took on the role of administering judgement, moving towards the position where he saw it as the role of the believers even to kill unbelievers in some circumstances.[5]

Where then might we see Muhammad in the Bible? As a human being, I suggest that we see different aspects of him in different places: a preacher of monotheism in an idolatrous world, like Elijah or Jonah; an Esau-figure wanting to follow the God of Israel outside the covenant; a false prophet, claiming new revelation; an Apollos defending the messiahship of Jesus but not his divinity; a great leader like Nebuchadnezzar who was reckoning with, and used by, the God of Israel; a Jeroboam who believed in the one God but wanted to set up his own way of worship; a prominent leader like David with family struggles; or a ruler like Saul who took on the role of both prophet and priest. It is difficult to find in the Bible someone who combines the various aspects of Muhammad because, from the inception of Israel, the roles of prophet, priest and ruler were deliberately distinguished. Perhaps the closest comparison is with the figure most mentioned in the Qur'an: Moses.

Many Muslims claim that Muhammad is the prophet like Moses of Deuteronomy 18:18, and certainly Muhammad is presented as being like Moses in many ways – not only as the leader of the people, but also as prophet and lawgiver.

Thus as we return to Islamic views of Muhammad, what do we make of the claims that he is the final prophet bringing the final book of God, and the perfect example for humanity? First, from a biblical perspective, Moses, like all other people, finds his place in relation to God's supreme action in Jesus Christ. Deuteronomy 18:18 is fulfilled in him, and there is no need for another Moses figure – indeed, another Moses would be a regression. Second, the nature of prophetic revelation as understood in the Qurᶜan differs significantly from biblical ideas of revelation: even if we were to allow another revelation after Christ, this could not be it. Third, but not least, all the biblical characters in whom we have noted parallels to Muhammad were, like all human beings, fallen. They were also, like Muhammad, people of their times, and what might have been appropriate in those times might not be appropriate now. The elevation of Muhammad to a model to be followed for all times is, from a biblical perspective, one of the most problematic aspects of Islam.

Conclusion: Seeing ourselves in the mirror of Scripture

After all this reflection, where do we now see *Islam* in the Bible? Everywhere and nowhere! There is no one biblical model that will fit all Muslims or all of Islam. But, because Muslims are human beings, there is no part of the Bible irrelevant to our thinking about them. Readers may be frustrated that I have not used the limited space in this chapter to explore the raft of questions about, for example, where Islam might fit into God's providential ordering of history, or its role in keeping people from or pointing them towards Christ. This is partly because answers depend on wider frameworks for understanding the Bible, but more because I believe that the most important question is not, 'What does God think of Islam?' but 'What does he expect of us?'

Where then do we see *ourselves* in the Bible as we seek to relate to Muslims? Do we share God's pain in seeing things that need judging while longing for people's salvation? Do we share Jesus' focus on the needy exemplified by his reference to the widow of Zarephath? Do we, like him, rejoice in the good in people as seen in his parable of the Good Samaritan? And, in our concerns about things that are wrong, do we prioritize confrontation with Satan or dealing with our own faithlessness, ambition and desires for revenge? Elijah challenged the Israelites as to which god they would follow. I trust that this brief biblical reflection will challenge readers as they go on to consider various aspects of Islam, to ask whose example they will follow as they make their response. We cannot follow both the way of Muhammad, who established Islamic rule in Arabia, and the way of Jesus, who went to the cross in Jerusalem. There is a choice to be made.

Chapter 3

Approaches to Power – Muhammad and Jesus

Bryan Knell

I suppose it is inevitable that when Christians come face to face with Muslims they have to make comparisons. It is one of the helpful ways by which we understand and learn. The danger is that we compare the good of what we understand and support with the worst of the things we oppose and want to criticize.

There is no doubt that Jesus and Muhammad are two of the greatest and most influential men that ever lived. Because they are the founders of two of the greatest and often competing religions they are often compared. 'What do you think of Muhammad?' is a question that Christians are often asked by Muslims, and the way they answer it can be a defining moment with regard to future conversations and indeed to any developing friendship. Often the same question comes with more point and some hostility: 'We accept Jesus as a prophet; why do you not accept Muhammad as a prophet?'

Comparisons of Jesus and Muhammad are often based on their personal lives. But I want to concentrate more on the decisions they made which shaped the course of their ministry and the characteristics of the religions that they founded. They both developed very distinctive approaches to life, success and their destiny.

There are twenty references in the Gospels to Jesus saying to people, 'Follow me.' Obviously some of the Gospel writers are reporting the same occasion, but even so, for the Holy Spirit to preserve so many instances in the Gospel accounts is significant. I know of more and more people in Muslim contexts who choose to call themselves 'followers of Jesus' rather than Christians. The Qurʿan tells Muslims to 'Obey God and the Messenger' (Sura 3:32) and the Hadith literature is full of descriptions of the way Muhammad did things, which devout Muslims will follow as closely as possible. So who are we following?

The early years

Both Jesus and Muhammad started life in less than salubrious circumstances. No one would choose to start life as they did. Jesus was born away from the parental home, forced to go there because of a government decree over which his family had no control. Not only was he away from home but the maternity delivery room was probably the living room of a peasant dwelling, and the cradle, the manger used by the animals. Muhammad was born in very sad circumstances. His father had died weeks before he was born and his mother, Amina, had to face the future as a single mother in a society where women in any position were not treated with respect.

Within a couple of years of Jesus' birth, the family had to leave for Egypt, where they lived in a foreign land with strange customs as refugees. By the time Muhammad was 6 years old, his mother had died and he was an orphan.

Both Jesus and Muhammad grew up therefore in simple and poor circumstances. After his mother had died, Muhammad was looked after initially by his grandfather, but when he died, he was taken in by an uncle who struggled to make a living by trading across Arabia. Jesus' family may not have been the poorest of the poor because Joseph was a carpenter; but it was still a peasant family. Tradition has it, and the Bible seems to suggest it, that Joseph died when Jesus was a teenager and if that is so, it must have put extra economic pressure on a family with several children.

Jesus started his ministry at about the age of 30. When did Muhammad's ministry start? When he was 25 and married Khadija? He already had a deep concern for his community and the moral state of Meccan society, but his marriage to wealthy Khadija gave him the time to concentrate his attention on the things that really mattered to him. It was a time of preparation for his life's work which started after he received the first Sura of the Qurʿan in the cave outside Mecca at the age of 40.

Both Jesus and Muhammad had few followers at the beginning and were rejected by their hometowns. When Jesus went back to Nazareth and preached in the synagogue, his contribution was not well received. 'All the people in the synagogue were furious when they heard this' (Luke 4:28, NIV). Muhammad had a similar experience. When he started preaching in Mecca that there was only one God, it was the last thing they wanted to hear. It was an attack on the fundamentals of their economy because the wealth of the city was based on pilgrimage and the worship of the 360 idols that were housed in the *Ka'aba*.

As a result of this unpopularity, there were attempts on the lives of both Jesus and Muhammad. The citizens of Nazareth took Jesus to a cliff top with the intention of throwing him to his death. There were also attempts on the life of Muhammad. The number is unclear, but some Muslims claim that there were several.

So there were many similarities in the early years of Jesus and Muhammad. Difficult circumstances at birth, problematical early years, family poverty, few initial followers and opposition from their hometowns characterized both of them. But if their early lives were similar, that is where the similarity ended. They chose very different paths and lifestyles.

Decision time

As the year 622 approached, Muhammad made a crucial decision which changed his life and shaped the religion of Islam. He had already faced years of opposition and persecution, and 619 was a specially difficult year for him. Not only did he lose his wife, Khadija, the love of his life, but his uncle, Abu Talib, also died. Abu Talib, as a senior member of the Hashimite clan, had been able to provide Muhammad with some protection against the many in Mecca who opposed his teaching. The death of these two family members must have had a major effect on Muhammad's emotional composure and his personal security.

In the year 620, six visitors from Medina tried to persuade Muhammad to leave the pressures of Mecca and relocate in Medina, where all the pressures that he faced would be removed. In 621, twelve visitors arrived with the same sort of message. In 622, apparently seventy-five visitors from Medina, including two women, arrived and met with Muhammad at night, promising that they would not only accept his teaching but also fight on behalf of God and his prophet. Finally, Muhammad was persuaded to leave his hometown and the most significant event in Islamic history, the *hijra*, took place. *Hijra* is the Arabic word for 'flight' or 'emigration.' Muhammad left Mecca in a hurry by night on a camel for the 200-mile journey north to Medina. He had suffered in Mecca for his outrageous monotheistic views, and may have seen his departure as a temporary failure. But the prospect of leaving persecution behind and the promise of success, status and power and the opportunity to establish an Islamic community would have been very attractive. It was a decision which determined the future and ethos of Islam.

If the *hijra* marks the decisive event in Muhammad's life that determined the way that Islam developed, then for Jesus, his temptation in the wilderness was the decisive period which characterized the sort of life he was to lead, and defined the basic lifestyle that he asked his disciples to follow (Matt. 4:1–11).

The devil waited until Jesus was physically weak through hunger and considering the implications of his role as the Messiah, and then tempted him with a very reasonable suggestion: 'Why don't you turn these stones here in the wilderness into bread?' What could be wrong with that? Why should not the creator of the universe, the maker of stones and bread, perform another little miracle? The devil's attack is clever. 'If you are the Son of God,' he questions, 'what would be the harm in making life a little easier for yourself? You are here by yourself in the desert – no one would ever even know, anyway.' But this is the great temptation. Will Jesus use

his power, authority and position to reduce some of the
stresses and difficulties that make up his life? Jesus cate-
gorically refuses.

If the first temptation is for Jesus to make life easier
for himself at the physical level, the second temptation
(in Matthew's record of the occasion) is for Jesus to make
his ministry more successful and effective. Again, in
human terms, it is perfectly reasonable: 'You have a message, Jesus. You want people to take notice. You need to
create some publicity to market your message. Why not
create a spectacle – throw yourself off the pinnacle of the
temple?' Again Jesus refuses outright to take the easy
path and to go for immediate success.

The last of the three temptations at this time also
encourages Jesus to avoid pain, humiliation, seeming
failure, and claim what is rightfully his – but through the
easy way. The devil shows him 'all the kingdoms of the
world and their splendour. All this I will give you' he
said, 'if you will bow down and worship me' (Matt.
4:8,9, NIV) Could this be the temptation to win political
power? If so, Jesus rejects this as a satanic temptation.

The invitation to go to Medina and the temptation in
the wilderness were the two destiny-defining moments
in the lives of Muhammad and Jesus. These decisions
determined their lives and shaped the religions that they
were to found, and Muslims have followed the lead
given by Muhammad more closely than Christians have
followed the lead given by Jesus.

In 1940 Muhammad Marmaduke Pickthall translated
the Qur'an into English and called it 'The Meaning of the
Glorious Qur'an'. In the introduction to his translation
he describes the *hijra* in these words:

> Such was the *hijra*, the flight from Mecca to Medina,
> which counts as the beginning of the Muslim era. The

thirteen years of humiliation, of persecution, of seeming failure, of prophecy still unfulfilled, were over. The ten years of success, the fullest that has ever crowned one man's endeavour, had begun. The *hijra* makes a clear division in the story of the Prophet's mission, which is evident in the Qurʿan.

Till then he had been a preacher only. Thenceforth he was the ruler of a state, at first a very small one, which grew in ten years to the empire of Arabia.

These words communicate forcefully the passion that Muslims feel for the 'success' of Muhammad's post-*hijra* life. The time before the *hijra* is described as 'humiliation . . . persecution and seeming failure', and for Muslims the significance of the *hijra* is that it brought success and the establishment of the first Islamic state.

In complete contrast, Jesus rejected success and power. He said 'no' to the chance of satisfying his hunger and making his personal circumstances more bearable. He said 'no' to the opportunity of making a spectacle and giving himself an immediately responsive audience. He said 'no' to the idea of exercizing political power.

Continuous temptation

We read that, after the devil tempted Jesus with those three questions while he was alone in the desert, 'the devil left him' (Matt. 4:11, NIV). It cannot have been long, however, since throughout the rest of Jesus life, the temptation to compromise his stand and make life easier for himself was constantly with him. The devil introduced the same thoughts into his mind through all sorts of different people.

Firstly, the temptation came to Jesus from his own family. At the beginning of John 7, we read that the Jewish Feast of Tabernacles was about to happen. What a brilliant opportunity for someone with a message to get it across to a large number of people! Jesus' family certainly thought so:

> You ought to leave here and go to Judea, so that your disciples may see the miracles you do. No one who wants to become a public figure acts in secret. Since you are doing these things, show yourself to the world. (John 7:3,4)

Yet Jesus refuses and goes 'in secret' several days later.

Secondly, the same temptation came from the words of his own closest followers – especially from Peter, who had just made one of the greatest affirmations of the truth about Jesus' identity: 'You are the Christ, the Son of the living God' (Matt. 16:16, NIV). Was this not the breakthrough in understanding that Jesus was looking for? It seems it may have been so, because he immediately started to explain to the disciples about the cross and how much he would have to suffer.

Peter then reminded Jesus that there is another way. '"Never, Lord!" he said. "This shall never happen to you!"' (Matt. 16:22, NIV) Here was the devil tempting Jesus with the thought that he did not have to suffer in this way. There was another way. He was the King of the universe, after all. But Jesus immediately saw this as the temptation that it was, and recognized the devil's devices through Peter's words as he said, 'Get behind me, Satan!' Jesus went on to explain that to seek the easy path of avoiding suffering, the strategy that would bring immediate success, was not to 'have in mind the things of God, but the things of men' (Matt.16:23, NIV).

Thirdly, the same temptation came to Jesus when he was struggling most seriously with the consequences of the path he had chosen – when he was in the Garden of Gethsemane. When those around tried briefly to defend Jesus and themselves with force, he said, 'Put your sword back in its place, for all who draw the sword will die by the sword. Do you think I cannot call on my Father, and he will at once put at my disposal more than twelve legions of angels?' (Matt.26:52,53, NIV).

As Jesus faced the greatest trial of his life, he was very aware of a way out. The devil made sure his mind never forgot that there were thousands of angels who could be summoned by the flick of a finger and all the pain, suffering, persecution and humiliation would be over. The temptation was so powerful and real. Was he going to choose the easy way? The choice had been made, the commitment was unwavering and the answer was 'no'.

Fourthly, the same temptation came to Jesus while he was on the cross. On this occasion it came through the words of the religious leaders:

> In the same way the chief priests and the teachers of the law mocked him among themselves. 'He saved others,' they said, 'but he can't save himself! Let this Christ, this King of Israel, come down now from the cross, that we may see and believe.' Those crucified with him also heaped insults on him. (Mark 15:31,32, NIV)

Not only did they suggest a way out of the suffering that he was going through, but they even suggested they would believe. No one in excruciating pain thinks as clearly as they do normally, and that is why torture works by forcing people to say things they would never say in normal circumstances. So the temptation that Jesus faced could not have been more acute and challenging.

And yet he still resisted the opportunity to take the easy path.

Jesus had the power

The fact that Jesus did not act powerfully to ease his circumstances or to stimulate a greater response to his message, should not lead us to assume that he did not have the power or had surrendered his authority. It was not that Jesus did not have the power. He was well aware that at any moment he could completely change his circumstances. Although living as a man, he was the King of the universe. It was through his Word that creation had come into existence. 'Through him all things were made; without him nothing was made that has been made' (John 1:3, NIV).

Jesus was very aware that he had the power. Indeed, it was the aim of the devil not to let him forget it for a moment. Yet Jesus used the power that was his not to avoid suffering, rejection, insults, humiliation and abuse, but he used the power to go to the cross. Jesus himself said, 'The reason my Father loves me is that I lay down my life – only to take it up again. No one takes it from me, but I lay it down of my own accord. I have authority to lay it down and authority to take it up again. This command I received from my Father' (John 10:17,18, NIV).

The commitment not to use his power for his own ends was so extreme that even after death, when it was over and he had uttered those words, 'It is finished' (John 19:30, NIV), Jesus did not abuse his power to bring himself back to life. Instead we read in the New Testament that he committed his spirit into the hands of God the Father who raised Jesus from the dead (Acts

2:24; Gal. 1:1; 1 Pet. 1:21). In other words, even though he had the power to bring himself back to life, it was the power of God the Father that raised him. Jesus therefore had the power to raise himself, to avoid going anywhere near the cross and to summon the angels at any moment. But he laid that power aside and went to the cross, and it was the Father who raised him.

Jesus and Muhammad – power and glory

From similar beginnings, Muhammad and Jesus deliberately choose very different paths. Muhammad left Mecca for Medina and the promise and prospect of wealth, authority, status, influence and power. His life became more and more involved with military might, bloodshed, political success, marriages of convenience, and brutality. Islam has always accepted that military might and suppression are a legitimate means of spreading the message. Islam thrives when it is dominant and struggles at being second, or when Muslims are in a minority.

Jesus, on the other hand, taught us most clearly through his words, his actions and his lifestyle that God is a suffering God and that he is pained and hurt by sin. After the introduction of sin into his beautiful and perfect world, God involved himself through the incarnation of Jesus and suffered to restore and rescue a rebellious world. Power is not God's way – love and sacrifice are.

So Muhammad built a religion based on power, status and military might. Jesus founded a church which should thrive on love and sacrifice. Glory for Muhammad was the conquering of Arabia, the domination of Islam and the establishing of Muhammad as the most important prophet. Jesus talked about glory in very different terms. Following his traumatic time facing up to the suffering to come in the Garden of Gethsemane, Jesus was meeting with his disciples in an upstairs room. His personal anguish must have been heightened as his friend Judas left to go and betray him, and yet it was in that situation that Jesus talked about glory: 'Now is the Son of Man glorified and God is glorified in him. If God is glorified in him, God will glorify the Son in himself, and will glorify him at once' (John 13:31,32, NIV).

We think of Jesus now in his glory at the right hand of the Father in heaven, but that was not what Jesus was thinking about. His glory was most clearly revealed when things were most difficult, when the pain was intense, when his heart was broken, when his followers were failing him, when the authorities were against him and when he was about to face death as a common criminal.

Jesus' teaching about power

Jesus was constantly trying to teach his followers that following him was not about power and authority. He must have been aware of the temptation – from friends and opponents alike – to take a political role and particularly to lead a military campaign to throw out the Roman occupation. This was the role expected of any leader, but Jesus rejected any plans to force him into a role of power.

In Mark 10:35–45 we read how James and John asked Jesus about their own position, status and influence in his future kingdom. They wanted to be the most important and to sit in the places of honour. Not only was this incompatible with Jesus' teaching and approach, but it is not surprising that it resulted in tension and conflict between his disciples. The Gospel record tells us Jesus called them together and said:

> You know that those who are regarded as rulers of the Gentiles lord it over them, and their high officials exercise authority over them. Not so with you. Instead, whoever wants to become great among you must be your servant, and whoever wants to be first must be slave of all. For even the Son of Man did not come to be served, but to serve, and to give his life as a ransom for many.
>
> (Mark 10:42–45, NIV)

The church and power

For the last 1,700 years, the message of the gospel and the command to follow Jesus has been compromised by the church's relationship with, and demand for, power. For three centuries, the church remained separated from the power of the state because it was a persecuted minority. But the Roman emperor Constantine changed all this with devastating results. Stuart Murray Williams writes:

> Constantine's invitation to the church to become the religious department of the Empire revolutionised its missiology. This is particularly evident in the evangelistic dimension of mission. From being a powerless and sometimes persecuted minority that nevertheless could not refrain from talking about Jesus and his impact on their lives, the church had become a powerful institution able to impose its beliefs and practices on society. Evangelism was no longer a winsome invitation to a

deviant and dangerous way of living and into a puzzling and yet strangely attractive community. Mission now involved ensuring doctrinal conformity, enforcing church attendance, enshrining moral standards in the criminal law and eradicating choice in the area of religion. Methods used included education, persuasion, inducement and coercion.[1]

Following Constantine, Christianity took on an ethos and a structure which made it much more like what Islam later became. Constantine linked Christianity to the power and authority of the state. Physical, military or institutional power has always been a temptation to Christians and has created acute problems for the followers of Jesus. Paul is eloquent about the value of weakness when he writes to the Corinthians: 'God chose the weak things of the world to shame the strong. He chose the lowly things of this world and the despised things – and the things that are not – to nullify the things that are, so that no one may boast before him' (1 Cor. 1:27–29 NIV).

Bernard Lewis writes: 'The founder of Islam was his own Constantine, and founded his own state and empire. He did not therefore create a church. The dichotomy of regnum and sacerdotium (church and state), which is so crucial in the history of Western Christendom, had no equivalent in Islam.'[2]

The church for much of its history has followed the ways of Muhammad and Christendom and constantly ignored the teaching of Jesus and the emphasis of the New Testament. Jesus calls us, not to the Islamic spirit of victory and dominance or even the Judaic spirit of retaliation with 'an eye for an eye', but the Christlike spirit of turning the other cheek and loving our enemies.

Clearly it isn't possible for Christians today to put the clock back and return to the situation of the first three centuries. But in the different contexts in which we find ourselves in Britain and the West today, what would it mean to resist the very natural human inclination to counter force with force, and get back to following Jesus' example rather than that of Muhammad? What would it mean for us to attempt to be more faithful to the spirit of Jesus? It would take an unlikely change of Christian culture, a show of humility which would be regarded by many as weakness, and a huge miracle.

Chapter 4

The Spectrum of Evangelical Responses to Islam in Britain

Richard McCallum

In 2008 the BBC broadcast an episode of the archaeological detective drama *Bone Kickers* entitled 'Army of God'. It portrays the fictional 'Brother Laygass', a TV evangelist and head of a 'philanthropic, right-wing Christian alliance', who declares that Britain is 'at war for its Christian soul . . . the day is coming when St Paul's Cathedral will be the grand mosque of London'. Inspired by his rhetoric, 'James', a mentally unstable devotee of Laygass, dresses as a Crusader knight, goes out and is shown in gruesome clarity decapitating a Muslim with a broadsword.

Far-fetched? Hopefully. Evangelical Christians in Britain, however, are clearly disturbed by the presence of an increasingly visible Muslim minority, and feel the need to respond. Recently, during a conference of mainly older evangelical Anglicans, a lady said to me, 'I know I should love them, dear, but if I'm honest, I'm afraid of them. What should I do?' Another lady joined the conversation.

She agreed and felt not just fear, but anger. 'It's not right what's happening. Should we just let them get away with it? This is our country . . . isn't it?' The answers to these questions are immensely important but not straightforward.

This chapter maps out the spectrum of evangelical responses to Muslims today by reviewing some of the books published by evangelical authors in the British context in the early part of the twenty-first century.[1] It is not a comprehensive review, but sketches the breadth of approaches amongst evangelicals, highlighting some of the key theological, missiological and socio-political issues raised. It is not my intent in this chapter to pass judgement or even to give the 'right answer.' Rather it is to outline the spectrum of views held by these authors, who all sincerely want to be obedient to God, true to the gospel, and love their Muslim neighbours – and yet sometimes come to very different conclusions!

The authors come from a wide range of backgrounds. Some are in church leadership, others are lay Christians; some have studied Islam formally, others have no specialist knowledge; some are academics in educational institutions, others are members of mission organizations; some have lived and worked amongst Muslims, others have no contact at all with Muslims; some are Westerners, others are not, including some from a Muslim background. They are, however, all seeking to inform the reader about Islam, and hope to influence how people think about Muslims in this country today. They have been chosen and arranged to illustrate the range of opinion within the evangelical public sphere. Of course each author says much more than can be highlighted here, and the best way to access their full thought is to read their books! Following the review, the second section of the chapter identifies some of the underlying tensions that are illustrated by the approaches these authors take towards Islam and Muslims.

A spectrum of evangelical authors

Stephen Green is the national director of Christian Voice. His pamphlet, *Understanding Islam* is combative in style and sounds a warning of what Green sees as the dangers of Islam. It is a call to action, particularly to prayer. Theologically he demonizes Islam, claiming that Allah is 'Lucifer or Satan himself' and strongly criticizes the character of Muhammad. There can be no place for Islam in Britain, which is a country founded on Christian principles and for which he feels multiculturalism has been a disaster. The only answer is a return to being a 'Christian nation'. It is the government's responsibility to reassert 'Britain's Christian heritage and Constitution', and to 'rely again on the wisdom of the Bible in framing law'. If immigrants to this country object then, 'anyone who does not like that state of affairs is free to leave'.[2]

The Challenge of Islam to Christians by David Pawson, a well-known freelance Bible teacher, demonstrates similar approaches. The book caused quite a stir in the evangelical community when it was first published, as Pawson reports having a 'premonition that Islam will take over the country' which came to him whilst he was listening to Patrick Sookhdeo speak. However, whilst he suggests that Islam is supernaturally inspired by demonic powers, he stresses that Muslims 'are not our enemies'. He does not want his book to stir up hatred or fear, but does feel that some Christians are already 'too intimidated' by Islam. Pawson's answer to this is not that Christians should seek political power or expect the government to oppose Islam. To do that would be to play by the same rules as Islam and seek a theocracy. Rather Islam is a challenge to the church to pray, to seek revival and to put its own house in order. Otherwise he suggests that it may not survive at all.[3]

Another book that addresses itself mainly to the church regarding the danger of the apparent Islamization of Britain is Patrick Sookhdeo's *Islam: The Challenge to the Church*. Sookhdeo is a prolific author on the topic of Islam and has authored or sponsored some ten books since 2001, all of which in some way address the problems posed by Islam. One of his distinctive concerns in his capacity as director of the Barnabas Fund is the treatment of Christian minorities and apostates (those who choose to leave Islam) within the Muslim world, particularly under *shariᶜa* law. He highlights how under *shariᶜa* Jews and Christians are accorded 'an inferior second-class status as *dhimmi* and are sometimes deprived of rights. Apostates from Islam suffer even more and, whilst 'the death penalty is not often implemented nowadays', they are often persecuted or socially excluded. He offers advice to Christians seeking to build relationships with Muslims, warning that they are likely to be rebuffed by Muslims, and counselling against trying to work on projects together. He also highlights the Islamic doctrine of *taqiyya*, meaning 'dissimulation or permitted deceit', whereby he explains Muslims are permitted to deny or conceal their faith in order to advance the cause of Islam (see chapter 13). Consequently, he suggests that Muslims cannot be believed or trusted as they frequently use this principle to defend Islam, misrepresent motives, rewrite history and further *daᶜwa* (Islamic mission). For Sookhdeo this is a key strategy being used in the Islamization of Britain today.[4]

The West, Islam and Islamism by Caroline Cox and John Marks also addresses the problem posed by political

Islam in Britain. The authors are careful to distinguish between traditional Islam and Islamism, and are very aware of the danger of provoking Islamophobia (fear of Islam). However, they see moderate Islam as lacking resonance for the majority of Muslims as it 'cherry-picks' peaceful verses from the Qurʿan whilst ignoring violent ones. Cox and Marks also see *taqiyya* as a real issue and legal moves, such as the outlawing of incitement to religious hatred, as a thinly disguised attempt by Muslims to shield Islam from legitimate criticism and to restrict freedom of speech on religious issues. The authors challenge Muslims to embrace human rights and take a stand against slavery, oppression of women and restrictions on religious freedom in Muslim countries. They point out that reciprocity is often sadly lacking and that 'there are few Muslim countries that offer Christians, Jews or those of other religions the freedom to practise their religion that Muslims enjoy in Western societies'. Despite their misgivings about even moderate Muslims though, they do advocate the setting up of inter-faith organizations to 'promote peace and mutual respect between people of different faiths and cultures.'[5]

Holy Warriors written by Frog and Amy Orr-Ewing takes a closer look at violence within Islam. After an engagement with the concept of fundamentalism, they focus particularly on the issue of *jihad*, suggesting that violence is normative in Islam as the more peaceful statements in the Qurʿan are mainly early Meccan verses that have been abrogated (replaced) by later more belligerent Medinan ones. Their central argument is that the Qurʿan's emphasis on eschatological judgement is not accompanied by any assurance of salvation – apart from martyrdom in battle. Therefore, for them, it is not socio-political issues that drive Islamist violence, particularly suicide bombings, but rather it is theology. That said, they do also clearly acknowledge the diversity of Islam and try to 'avoid making generalizations about all Muslims'. The main thrust of the Orr-Ewings' writing is clearly 'missional' and the book comes across with a compassionate tone, including a critique of the West for its decadence, greed and lack of religious life.[6]

As an academic, Peter Riddell in *Christians and Muslims* also focuses more on the diversity of Islam and avoids definitive interpretations. He counsels that 'Christians should avoid passing judgement in intra-Muslim debates' about the interpretation of qurʿanic texts and the sanction of violence. He recognizes that the 'Islamic texts offer the potential to be interpreted in both a peaceful and a militaristic way' and that there is a 'titanic (internal) struggle taking place between moderates and radicals for the hearts and minds of the Muslim masses in the middle'. He does not ignore difficult questions but feels that they call for 'diverse approaches' including dialogue (the talking together of Christian and Muslim representatives) as well as apologetics (the defence of the gospel) and polemics (the combating of Islam). So 'those committed to dialogue should not delegitimize the efforts of the debaters, nor should the reverse occur'. In this way, whilst it is often difficult to reconcile the world views of Islam and the West, a clash of civiliszations is not inevitable and 'rivalry need not turn to conflict if carefully handled'.[7]

This more open approach is reflected in the writing of Michael Nazir Ali, who, in addition to being a scholar and senior clergyman, has a Muslim family background and ongoing relationships with Muslims. In his book *Conviction and Conflict*, he draws on both theological and sociological resources to illustrate the role religion has to play in peacemaking. To this end, a dialogue between the religions is 'almost indispensable for world peace today' and indeed governments should be able to draw on the fruit of such dialogue in their policy-making. At the same time, Christians must come to such 'robust dialogue' as realists, and Nazir Ali does not hesitate to raise problematic issues such as religious freedom, apostasy, reciprocity and the *dhimmi* status of minorities. However, he does so in a non-judgemental style that does not demonize Islam, and indeed recognizes the role that the West itself has played in 'assisting in the emergence of an internationally linked Islamist movement'. Neither is he as pessimistic as other authors and he believes that Islamism is actually losing the support of many young people, and has in some cases led to increased pragmatism and 'demonstrations for greater popular participation in affairs of state'.[8]

This optimism is also evident in the relational emphasis of Steve Bell's *Grace for Muslims*. Bell lived in Egypt for several years, and this book tells some of his story including his concern on returning to Britain to discover that 'most Christians tend only to see the negatives, which leads to an attitude problem towards Muslims'. For Bell, 9/11 acted as a 'trigger' to start a new ministry called Friendship First, which seeks to counteract some of the 'un-grace' of Western Christians by educating them about Islam and promoting a 'grace response' to Muslims (see chapter 1). This book embraces the idea that Muslims might present a 'missional' opportunity for the church, and may even be here in Europe as part of God's purposes at a time when society is becoming increasingly secular.[9]

As a Syrian Arab Christian who grew up living amongst Muslims and had many Muslim friends before he came to live in France and then in the UK, Chawkat Moucarry knows what it's like to be a new arrival in Western countries. His book *Two Prayers for Today: The*

Lord's Prayer and the Fatiha engages in a serious comparison between two texts from the Bible and the Qur'an. He strongly rejects the demonization of Allah and feels that those who hold this view have 'little meaningful interaction if any with Muslim people' and that 'their perception of Islam is often based on ignorance or even prejudice'. He suggests that there is common ground and that Christians and Muslims 'should not merely tolerate each other but should work together, actively cooperating for the common good'. For Moucarry, Christians should be less critical of Islam and be more self-critical. Terrorism and violence are not problems limited to the Muslim world, and he – not uncontroversially – points to unquestioning Western support for the state of Israel and the so-called 'war on terror' as examples of Western 'state terror'.[10]

This critique of Western foreign policy is also a major consideration for Colin Chapman, who spent many years in the Middle East and is best known for his writings on the Israeli-Palestinian situation. In a completely revised second edition of *Cross and Crescent: Responding to the Challenges of Islam*, he gives serious consideration to Islamist grievances and suggests that 'terrorism itself is not the root of the problem; it is usually a reaction to a perceived injustice, and therefore needs to be seen as a symptom of other underlying problems.' Chapman examines the questions and concerns that Christians have about Islam and Muslims, but also recognizes that 'Muslims often think the same' about Christians – Western 'Christian' support for violence in Israel, Afghanistan and Iraq being among the prime examples. For Chapman personal relationships are the 'absolute priority'. It is vital for Christians to get to know and build relationships with Muslims. They must be approached first and foremost as fellow human beings.[11]

Finally, the title of Bill Musk's *Kissing Cousins: Christians and Muslims Face to Face* reflects the 'ambiguous' and 'provocative' nature of the relationship between the two faith communities. Musk insists that 'in any relating of cousins it is important that each be true to his or her own faith'. However, whilst they are distinct and are sadly quick to demonize one another, this does not negate the truth that the cousins have much in common and indeed even need to stand together against secularizing trends. This sort of shared experience is reflected in the critical, internal wrestling for the 'soul' of both Islam and Christianity. It is not so much the texts themselves but the often fundamentalist interpretations of them by both sides that cause the problems. So if Christians want to defend their own text against accusations of violence and literalism, then the Muslim too must be allowed to 'make reply on his own behalf, from within his own view of his faith'.[12]

Some underlying tensions

Islamization, terrorism, *shariᶜa*, *taqiyya*, Islamophobia, suffering minorities, Israel-Palestine, war on terror. Dialogue, peacemaking, friendship, the common good, love your neighbour. It is easy to see how the issues raised above can fall into caricatured categories. Unfortunately in any discussion of this kind it is very easy for the debate to become polarized – even amongst well-meaning Christians! Such polarization is rarely helpful and so it is important to be aware of the tensions and tendencies of the debate within the evangelical community. Few of the authors above would find themselves exclusively at one end or other of the spectrum on all of these issues, and many would not be at either of the extremes, but most clearly lean one way or the other.

Tension 1: Criticism of Islam v. self-criticism

One extreme is to focus solely on the dangers and problems posed by Islam today. Given the current climate and the threat posed by some Muslims, a critical assessment is understandable and indeed needed. As citizens we should be concerned about extremist radicalization, oppressive practices and the possibility of parallel communities and legal systems. However, if Islam is portrayed as being purely problematic, then this will make our relationships with Muslims very difficult. The opposite tendency is a self-abasing critique of the role the West has played in the current poor relations with Muslims. From the Crusades, through the colonial period, to the contemporary 'war on terror', some Christians have felt the need to accept responsibility and apologize for the shortcomings of the nominally 'Christian' West. Of course, to see it as entirely 'their' fault or entirely 'our' fault is unhelpful. There has to be a full and frank recognition that there is fault on both sides. Only as this is accepted can damaging mutual antagonism and conflict be resolved.

Tension 2: Demonization v. sanitization

Another tendency is to demonize everything about Islam and to see it as totally bad. The opposite approach is to whitewash some of the less attractive aspects and even to see Islam as being almost Christian. This raises some very difficult questions that stretch us theologically, any one of which merits a whole book on its own!

Firstly, there is a concern to decide where Islam came from. Some suggest it has purely human origins, others that it is demonically inspired, and still others discern a mixture of these. This is reflected in different views as to whether Muslims may ultimately be saved. Some evangelicals take an *exclusivist* stance and fear that no Muslim can be saved unless they explicitly renounce Islam and convert to the Christian religion. Others adopt a more 'inclusivist' approach and feel that God may well save some sincere Muslims despite their ignorance of the gospel. These two positions are reflected in the discussion about whether or not a Muslim can remain 'inside' Islam and yet still be a follower of Christ.

Secondly, are the God of the Bible and the Allah of the Qurᶜan the same God? Some Christians are happy to use the word Allah (for instance all Arab Christians, Arabic translations of the Bible and the majority of converts from an Arab background). As we have seen, others are vehemently opposed to this and believe that the Allah of Islam is actually a demonic being. Who is right? It may be helpful to ask some slightly different questions. For instance, who are Muslims *seeking* to worship? Are they seeking to worship the one, true creator God of the universe? What have Muslims been taught about the *character* of the God they are seeking to worship? Does it sound like the character of the God of the Bible?

The analogy is sometimes used of two sons who have the same father. It goes like this: 'If one son says his father is kind and loving, and the other son says he is violent and cruel then they cannot possibly be describing the same father.' Maybe another way of looking at this would be to imagine that two sons share the same father, but neither has seen him for a long time and they live apart. One is told that his father is kind and loving to all, but the other son is told the opposite. How will the two sons then describe their father? Do they have the same father? What will they discover when they are reunited with their father?

Lastly, there are different thoughts on the degree to which the teaching of the Bible and the Qurʿan can be reconciled, particularly on subjects such as the nature and Lordship of Christ, the cross and the Trinity. One stance is that they are completely incompatible and teach diametrically opposed positions. The other extreme suggests that it is possible to reconcile many of the texts but it is rather the traditional Muslim (and Christian) 'misinterpretations' of the texts that produce the oppositional readings.[13] This by no means exhausts the theological issues but does demonstrate some of the areas of difficulty.

Tension 3: Over-generalization v. over-specialization

Everybody over-generalizes. I just did! It makes life a lot easier. We like to put things in neat boxes so that we can make sense of the world. We often want clear statements like 'Muslims believe . . .' but, of course, life and particularly belief are not so clear-cut. Just as there is huge diversity amongst the Christians of the world, there is huge diversity amongst Muslims. One extreme of this tension totalizes and says 'all Muslims . . .' This is extremely unhelpful as Muslims are clearly not all the same and have very different practices and interpretations of their beliefs. The other tendency, however, is to present so much diversity that the ordinary lay person cannot get a handle on it. Not everyone will be able to remember the differences between *Sunni*, *Shiʿi*, Kharijite and Ismaili thought, or read the *Sufi* mystics and the Hanbali jurists. So whilst it is important for some to gain a specialist grasp of these things, the majority of people do need some amount of generalization. The challenge, particularly to those who write and teach about Islam is to emphasize the diversity of Muslims without making it so specialized and complicated that most people just get confused.

Tension 4: 'True Islam' v. 'Lived Islam'

Some writers focus on the system of Islam. By deciding what Muslims 'should' believe and do according to *their* reading of the Islamic religious texts, they attempt to essentialize what 'true Islam' is. The trouble is that this tends to preclude listening to what Muslims say *they* think Islam is, because we already know the answer! So for instance, when some Muslims say that they interpret violent texts as being only applicable to the specific historical context, we don't believe them, tending rather to insist on the radical Islamists' literal understanding of such verses. The other tendency is to focus on Muslims as people. It asks how Islam is lived and understood by Muslims, allowing them to interpret their own scriptures and explain them to us. The dangerous extreme here is a gullible naivety that accepts everything that is said and fails to ask Muslims the difficult questions that sometimes need to be sensitively raised.

Tension 5: A 'Christian' Britain v. a secularized, plural Britain

The final tension exhibited by these authors surrounds the character and identity of Britain as a country. One tendency is to look back to a 'Christendom' model and say that Britain has been and should still be a 'Christian country'. The church should in some way be established at the centre of society, and Christianity should inform and guide the making of laws and policies. This is often linked with a nostalgia for a lost past and resentment at the cultural changes that have accompanied wide scale immigration. The opposite tendency is an embracing of 'post-Christendom' and the opportunity for the church to be resituated on the margins of society as a prophetic voice amongst many voices and faiths.[14] The loss of power and prestige is seen as a healthy thing for the church and a catalyst for a return to the purity of its roots. The presence of other faith communities is accepted as being part of the purposes of God, even bringing a new cultural richness, a timely criticism of Western culture and an opportunity to share the gospel. These are huge issues which lie at the heart of not just the current tension in evangelical thinking about Muslims in Britain, but also the church's understanding of its wider role and mission in the nation.

Most of the issues and tensions identified here cut across all the themes of this book. Almost certainly the authors in this volume – some of whose books I have mentioned above – would find themselves holding widely varying positions on these different spectrums. Regrettably the sort of tension that this produces within the evangelical community occasionally spills over into rancour and unedifying public disagreement. Part of the challenge of the Muslim presence in Britain today is whether we as Christians can show grace, not just to Muslims, but also to one another. It is by our love for one another that others will know that we are followers of Christ (John 13:35). Learning to disagree and yet still be faithful to the One who is both 'full of grace and truth' (John 1:14) is difficult but surely crucial in our response to Muslims in Britain today.

Chapter 5

Christian-Muslim Relations in Britain in Historical Context

Martin Whittingham

If you are drinking a cup of coffee as you read this, then you are affected by the history of Christian-Muslim relations. Coffee, thought to have originated in Ethiopia, travelled from coffee houses in Yemen via Istanbul. The coffee house arrived in Oxford in 1650, where I write this. But beyond contacts based on trade and cultural habits, what can people in twenty-first century Britain learn from the long history of Christian-Muslim relations? Quite a lot, I would argue.

The context of Christian-Muslim contacts in the modern world may look new, but often the issues turn out to be old ones in new settings. Is it possible to co-exist peacefully when one community is the majority and the other a minority? How can Christians form authentic relationships with Muslims when they themselves are troubled by fear, indifference or even hostility? How do Christians and Muslims negotiate the real and unavoidable differences in beliefs about Jesus? People in previous centuries were aware of these questions. This is not surprising since Christians and Muslims have been impacting each other's lives since long before such well-known developments as British rule in nineteenth-century India and the post-World War 2 immigration movements.

There are limitations to what historians can uncover. Written works from centuries past can reflect the bias or interests of the writer. It can also be difficult to uncover the feelings and experiences of ordinary people from past ages, especially women, as predominantly male writers often discuss ideas or beliefs, or concentrate on (predominantly male) rulers or elites. So historians offer what they can, recognizing their limitations, but also hoping to help others focus on real priorities, rather than wasting energy on secondary issues, or worse, on complete red herrings. The hope here is to avoid both, and to identify some critical points for reflection.

Some readers might want to protest that some of the people involved in what follows were not 'real Christians'. Since Muslims, however, perceive that they were Christians, at least in the sense of representing a state or power based upon Christian claims and rituals, they are still relevant to our survey of Christian-Muslims relations.

This brief chapter cannot hope to do more than open some windows onto the world of Christian-Muslim interaction. After setting out some of the historical contexts in which Muslims and Christians have interacted with each other, I shall then offer some instructive snapshots from some of these encounters. The question of the quality of the information which Muslims and Christians circulate about each other is also discussed, and in closing I consider the possible nature of Muslim-Christian relations in the twenty-first century.

Some historical encounters

Muslim tradition records that Muhammad himself met Christians who came in a delegation from Najran in modern Yemen, and there were other Christians present in the Arabian peninsula during his lifetime. Muslim-Christian interaction therefore dates back to the very beginnings of Islam. In the century after the death of Muhammad there was an astonishing military spread of Islamic power, extending as far west as Spain, with brief forays into France, and east into Persia and India. Here we find encounters because of conquest, with Christians forced to recognize a new and powerful religious presence. In the following century there was a period of generally more peaceful consolidation. Conquered Christians, still in a majority, began the process of gradual conversion which eventually led to countries such as Egypt becoming majority Muslim a few centuries later. One example of a dynamic situation of co-existence was Islamic Iberia – Spain and Portugal – where Christians, Jews and Muslims co-existed in varying patterns of control for centuries.

In 1099 the First Crusade seized Jerusalem from Muslim power, ushering in centuries of crusading in the Middle East and elsewhere. At the time these conflicts were regarded by Muslims simply as one war amongst many in the Muslim world, and the motives of the Crusaders were not always understood to be specifically religious. But since the nineteenth century, attention has been refocused on the Crusades as a painful insult to Muslim pride and a potent symbol of Christian domination and untrustworthiness. Christian responses today vary: while some bemoan the violence involved, others see them as a regrettable but unsurprising reaction to earlier Muslim conquest.

Powerful Muslim empires began to emerge following the Crusades. The Ottomans, based in modern Turkey (c.1300–1924), the Safavids in Persia (1501–1722), and the Mughals in India (1526-mid nineteenth century). These empires meant that most Muslims looked on Europeans, when they did so at all, from a position of strength rather than weakness. But then Western empires arose, with European colonial powers gradually taking various degrees of control over the whole of the Muslim world (with the exception of Arabia, Turkey, Iran and Afghanistan). This created the new kind of power balance, both political and cultural, which exists today, in which Muslims feel oppressed and victimized by Western forces which are seen to be as unstoppable as the Ottoman Empire at the height of its power.

One of the most significant twentieth-century developments has been the establishment of the state of Israel in 1948. The repercussions of this have affected Muslim and Christian perceptions of each other for decades. During the same period, as a result of immigration into Western nations, Muslims and Christians have developed new levels of contact, in schools, colleges and places of work. Many Muslims therefore live as minorities, rather than under a government at least nominally Muslim. This raises a host of questions which Islamic law has traditionally not addressed.

Learning from the past

The early spread of Islam

In the earliest years of Islam, Christians in Arabia and in the wider Near East were busy dealing with the rise of Islam long before any Europeans developed well-informed responses. Some of these are described in Philip Jenkins' book, *The Lost History of Christianity*, which gives an invaluable background survey of the combination of violence and tolerance involved in Islam's relations with Eastern church leaders. Christian theologians and church leaders wrote lengthy responses to Islam in both Arabic and Syriac, in which they tried to give explanations appropriate to the Islamic context for core Christian beliefs such as the crucifixion, the Trinity, and the reliability of the Bible. Mar Timothy, patriarch of the Nestorian Church from 780–823, for example, was based in Baghdad for most of his long period in office, and as the leader of the church he needed both to write to the Abbasid Caliphs (also in Baghdad) and also to meet them personally. In one of these meetings he had a long discussion about Christian and Muslim beliefs, and we can read a detailed account of this discussion today. Realizing that such efforts were occurring can help Christians today to move beyond simple assumptions about East-West divisions being equivalent to Muslim-Western divisions. Eastern Christians were responding to Islam and Muslims centuries before European Christians began to be aware of Islam. And in today's Britain an Eastern-background Christian could easily be talking with a Western Muslim who has converted to the faith.

Al-Andalus

It is important for Christians to remember that they will disagree over responses to Islam. If this is a feature of modern Britain, it also clearly existed under Islamic rule in Spain. The Muslim conquest of Spain began in 711, when soldiers under Tariq invaded (via a certain well-known peninsula which became known as the 'Mountain of Tariq' or in Arabic 'Jabal Tariq', leading to the name Gibraltar). In 851 a movement lasting around ten years began amongst certain Christians in Cordoba in southern Spain, who became known as 'the Martyrs of Cordoba'. Around fifty people, many of them monks, provoked the Muslim authorities by deliberately insulting Islam in order to seek martyrdom. This was not, however, a simple story of Christians against Muslims. Many Christians at the time disagreed with the martyrs' confrontational approach to Islam and preferred more relaxed relationships. They did not approve of the martyrs' actions because they caused the Muslim authorities to put pressure on the Christian community as a whole. The point here, therefore, is not to defend the martyrs as a faithful remnant standing up against compromise, or to criticize them as aggressive hot-heads choosing the wrong approach. The story of the Cordoba Martyrs should remind Christians not to be surprised when they disagree with one another. Sometimes a commitment to truth is used as an excuse to criticize or even abuse other Christians who are seen as too compliant towards Islamic or other non-Christian teachings. Alternatively, Christians committed to grace in relations with Muslims can also criticize or abuse Christians who, in their view, seem to lack that grace. How Christians handle disagreements in relations with one another matters as much as how these disagreements are discussed before the wider public.

The Crusades

In 1095 Pope Urban II summoned the first Crusade, and the serious Crusader threat in the Middle East ended with the fall of Acre in 1291, although the crusading phenomenon continued there and elsewhere for many years to come. What kind of Christian convictions created such a prolonged belief in the need to fight Muslims for control of places understood as holy? It is easy for Christians today to assume that the Crusaders simply forgot biblical teaching about love and wisdom in their appetite for battle and power. It would be more accurate, however, to recognize that they did appeal to certain different biblical themes: taking up the cross, for example, was interpreted as denying self by fighting people regarded as enemies of Christ. This is a graphic demonstration of the far-reaching consequences of misinterpreting biblical teaching, and the need to recognize that we can never say that 'all interpretations are equally valid'. Interpreting taking up the cross as a call to arms may seem an obvious error today, but was a sincerely held view amongst some significant Christian leaders at the time.

As in other areas of Christian life, Francis of Assisi (d. 1226) went against the standard approaches of his age. Rather than writing in a hostile tone of the wickedness or threat of Muslims, he decided to get involved in face-to-face relationships. He went on the fifth Crusade to Egypt in 1219 to join the huge force besieging Damietta on the Nile Delta. Francis made this journey, however, not in order to fight but to mediate between the two parties in the fighting and to convert the Muslim leader, Malik al-Kamil, Sultan of Egypt. Francis may also have been deliberately seeking martyrdom. It is unfortunate that Francis himself did not write down what he discussed, nor what the outcome was; but contemporary accounts show how unusual his approach was, and how much courage it took to cross a boundary – not just literally, by walking across the 'enemy' lines at huge personal risk, but metaphorically, by reading the texts of the other. Neither of his goals – of mediation and conversion – was fulfilled, and in the end many thousands perished in the siege of Damietta. But Francis had the vision to seek not just information, but human contact.

Muslim empires

Both Christians and Muslims need to be reminded from a study of history that power relations between the two religions have been more varied than has been played out in the last two centuries of Western domination, which has been perceived as 'Christian' domination. In the Muslim empires already mentioned, the Ottomans, Safavids and Mughals, and also before them, in situations of Muslim control, Christians (and Jews) were traditionally given *dhimmi* status in Islamic law, signifying protected status. This was formalized under a document known as The Covenant of Umar, named after the second Caliph Umar (634–44), but often thought to have been devised much later than this. *Dhimmi* status gave a certain kind of protection, offering freedom to continue being Christians in return for accepting restrictions prohibiting the building or repairing of churches, requiring distinctive dress, and a range of social limitations adding up to a 'second-class' status. These regulations were applied with great inconsistency in practice, and the formal concept of *dhimmi* status persisted until it faded from use in the nineteenth century with the onset of legal systems influenced by colonial rule.

The famous reformer Martin Luther (1483–1546) wrote about Islam in the context of a potentially unstoppable Muslim power approaching Europe. In 1528–29 the Ottomans under Suleiman the Magnificent moved northwest through the Balkans and into Central Europe before besieging Vienna. It is therefore hardly surprising that Luther, living in Germany, wrote about Islam. Nor is it surprising, given the context of possible invasion, that one of the issues he wrote about was whether a Christian is allowed to fight. He concluded that while it was legitimate to fight to defend one's land against invasion, such fighting should never be linked to advancing or defending Christian faith. Luther condemned fighting in the name of religion, and was scathing about anything which confused defending territory with defending the gospel. He wrote that if he saw a military banner on the battlefield bearing a cross, 'I would run as though the devil of hell were chasing me'.

Western empires

During recent centuries of Western imperialism, it has proved all too easy for Christians to mingle political and military advance with advancing the Christian message – exactly the type of confusion against which Luther warned. One example which reveals Muslim perceptions of those they saw as Christians is the British conquest in 1903 of the Sokoto Caliphate, based in what is now northern Nigeria. Once this sudden conquest had occurred, Muslim leaders decided that it was legitimate for Muslims to stay and live under non-Muslim rulers, rather than choosing the other options of fighting or flight to another area. Staying under non-Muslim rule was traditionally a point of contention amongst Muslim scholars, and needed some justification. The Sokoto leadership justified its decision through emphasizing that the conquering Christians were not a religious threat, since they were not trying to eradicate Islam as a religion. Instead, as one Muslim wrote at the time, 'Their goal is seeking for territory and overlordship in worldly matters'. So it appeared to the Muslims that the Christians were not a danger to faith, because they were more interested in land and power than in beliefs. Many sincere Christians were involved in different ways in this period, but the colonial project as a whole has contributed to Muslims linking Christianity to a power-seeking agenda.

It could also be added that this is a natural inference given the traditional expectations of *Sunni* Muslims that power would accrue to righteous Muslims.

One surprising example of Christian-Muslim interaction during centuries of Western domination can be found in Napoleon's invasion of Egypt in 1798, which is often regarded as the beginning of Christian-Muslim relations in the modern period, at least in a Western context. While Napoleon is not most modern Christians' idea of a role model, he was regarded by Muslims as the leader of a Christian nation. He issued decrees, displayed in public places and designed to make the Egyptians feel happier about his sudden arrival, in which he stated that he served God, and revered 'his Prophet Muhammad and the glorious Qur'an'. The Egyptian historian al-Jabarti, an eyewitness of the invasion, responded to these statements of professed reverence for Muhammad by saying that 'if he respected him he would believe in him, accept his truth, and respect his nation'. As for the reverence expressed for the Qur'an, he adds that, 'this too is a lie, because to respect the Qur'an means to glorify it, and one glorifies it by believing in what it contains'. Napoleon's statements were made in the context of an invasion which would naturally make subject people suspicious. Butal-Jabarti is clearly confused by statements revering Muhammad and the Qur'an which come from a power which he knows not to be Muslim. He thinks that these statements are not worth the paper they were distributed on, because truly revering the Qur'an means putting one's faith in its message. In Britain in recent years, however, there has been a shift towards greater recognition that the honest and respectful airing of differences, alongside discussion of common ground, can be a constructive way of building trust.

Information and misinformation

Both Christians and Muslims need to be encouraged to
spread accurate rather than false or misleading information about each other. Christians have been no strangers
to spreading false ideas about Islam, as Norman Daniel
famously documented in his book, *Islam: the Making of an
Image*. One striking example from the Muslim side is the
continuing popularity of the so-called 'Gospel of
Barnabas'. This document is widely available amongst
Muslims in many countries and is presented as representing or distilling the genuine gospel – in contrast to
the Gospels of the New Testament. Its appeal to Muslims
derives from the fact that it is regarded as agreeing with
the teachings of Islam. In reality, however, it contradicts
these too, describing Muhammad as the Messiah,
despite the Qurᶜan giving this title only to Jesus. It also
includes geographical errors such as descriptions of sail-
ing to towns which are in fact located inland.

This 'Gospel' has only ever been known in Italian and
Spanish manuscripts, an Italian medieval original being
most likely. The Italian version was first published in
English translation in 1907, and the translators' introduction gave ample evidence for the view that the work
was a medieval forgery, on the basis of doctrines and
historical details. Serious historians differ over which
community or century gave rise to the Gospel of
Barnabas, but all agree that it was not a first-century
document. Yet one year after its appearance in English it
was published in Arabic by the famous Muslim reformer
Rashid Rida under the title *Al-Injīl al-Sahīh* ('The
True/Sound Gospel'). It is also widely circulated today
by Muslims in its 1907 English translation, but without
the critical introduction mentioned above. By contrast,
Sura 29 'The Spider': 46 of the Qurᶜan says regarding

Jews and Christians, 'Do not dispute with the People of the Book save in the best manner'. Although a few Muslim writers have expressed their view that the Gospel of Barnabas is not authentic, in general its profile remains high. Given the overwhelming evidence for it being a forgery, its wide dissemination seems far from the 'best manner' for conducting argument with Christians.

By way of a contrast, in the early centuries of Muslim-Christian interactions, few people stand out for their willingness to use accurate information about the faith and textual sources of the other. Amongst Muslims, the historian and geographer al-Yaʿqūbī (d. 897 or later) is one example. His work, entitled simply The *History*, is typical of its time in attempting to outline history from Adam right up to the period of the author. But al-Yaʿqūbī is highly untypical of his time in quoting the Bible, or paraphrasing it fairly, many times in the section on biblical history. Some other Muslim writers also attempted to give accurate summaries of Christian beliefs, including differences between various Christian groups. The fact that they did this with the aim of demonstrating the falsity of the beliefs should not detract from their effort to report correctly what others believed. One modern example is 'Abbas Mahmud al-ʿAqqad (d. 1964), author of *The Genius of Christ*. Although a Muslim, his account of Jesus is largely based on the New Testament Gospels. The significance of this is not that he believes all their teachings, but that he uses and defends the Gospels as reliable sources for the life of Jesus.

Peter of Cluny (d. 1156) provides a parellel to al-Yaʿqūbī since he was one of the first to advance knowledge of Islam amongst European Christians (as opposed to Eastern Christian leaders already familiar with Arabic and/or the Qur'an). Known as Peter the Venerable, he was elected abbot of Cluny in France in 1122, and was invited to visit Spain in 1142 by the emperor Alfonso VII. The reason for the invitation seems to have been the prospect of a large donation to the famous abbey. But Peter's fundraising trip produced something even more significant than swelling the abbey's coffers: it yielded a project to study Islam from its original sources. These had become more readily available to Europeans following the reconquest of parts of Spain which had previously been under Islamic rule.

The idea that crusading was not the way to treat Muslims and that salvation in Christ was available to Muslims as much as to others was far more obvious to Peter than to most of his contemporaries. He initiated a project which led to the 'Toledo Collection', a group of translations and writings named after the Spanish city at the centre of the enterprise. The Latin translation of the Qur'an which resulted from Peter's efforts was itself championed by Martin Luther some four hundred years later. Luther pressed for its publication in the face of opposition, for the same reason that Peter of Cluny had promoted such work in the first place – because fair comment on the faith of others, even when given with the aim of disproving that faith, must be based on accurate information. Al-Ya'qūbī, Peter the Venerable and Luther were all staunch defenders of their own faith. Yet this was no bar to their wanting to promote accurate information as part of what could be termed better quality disagreement.

This brings us to the modern world, with all its complexities and griefs. It is sufficient here to note that there are both challenges and opportunities on a grand scale. Political problems surrounding Christian and Muslim views of Israel/Palestine, and the recent events in Iraq and Afghanistan, continue unresolved. On the other hand, never before have so many Muslims and Christians lived alongside each other in situations of work, school and neighbourhoods as in modern Europe. Alongside this development the rise of the internet also increases potential understanding greatly; but it also greatly increases the capacity of believers on both sides to insult or alienate each other. All this raises an obvious final question, to which I now turn.

Conclusion

What might good Christian-Muslim relations look like? What is the goal towards which Christians and Muslims might aim? Some place the emphasis on peaceful coexistence, while others are primarily concerned with reaching out as a witness to the truth they consider that they have discovered. But is it possible to combine these two? Historically, coexistence has tended to be bought at the price of not presenting or declaring one's faith to the other. This was how Christian communities traditionally maintained a stable presence during the early Islamic empire and under the Ottoman Empire. Perhaps as the new century unfolds there will be some parts of the world where this delicate balance of constructive coexistence and faithful witness can be achieved. In fact it is possible that the relative lack of power of either Christians or Muslims in modern Britain, in comparison to the secularizing forces at work, may help that balance to occur. As an historian is bound to say, time will tell.

Part II:
Crucial Issues in
Britain Today

Chapter 6

Making Sense of Muslim Communities in Britain

Philip Lewis

The contributors to *Contextualising Islam in Britain: Exploratory Perspectives, 2009* – twenty-six Muslim academics, religious scholars and community activists – insist that a long-term goal for Muslim communities in Britain is 'to be seen as an integral part of society, not as something oriental or exotic that could be regarded as alien to society'. This aspiration captures a major shift in attitudes among an ever-widening circle of British Muslims from isolation or opposition to majority society, towards one of engagement.[1]

This chapter will identify obstacles to such engagement which continue to generate alienation among sections of the Muslim communities, and review some attempts to address them. I have deliberately spoken of 'Muslim communities' rather than 'Islam' in the title of this chapter. No one is a Muslim-in-general, any more than a Christian-in-general. If one is to make sense of English evangelicals, Italian Catholics and Serbian Orthodox Christians, an understanding of the Old and New Testament would not be enough! To speak of European Christianity would not obscure the need to enter into the complex and specific histories and memories of such Christian communities.[2] So it is with Muslim communities in Britain.

No one is a Muslim-in-general

Muslim communities carry radically different histories and diverse cultural baggage with them into Britain. There are, for example, some 100,000 Muslims from Turkish backgrounds in London, who have little public profile and seldom feature among the faces of angry young radicals protesting against this or that issue. As a people, the Turks were never colonized; indeed, they were the colonizers and carriers of a huge empire, including much of the Arab world. Further, they have had more than seventy years of uncompromising, doctrinaire secularism which Ataturk borrowed from the French. Finally, many define themselves as European, and Turkey is not only part of NATO but wants to join the European Community.

This is in marked contrast to many Muslims from South Asia who, according to the 2001 census, comprised more than 70 per cent of the 1.6 million British Muslims. Of these, 42 per cent have roots in Pakistan, 17 per cent in Bangladesh and 7 per cent, India. South Asia was colonized by the British. The majority communities come from Pakistan and they consider British policy has invariably favoured India. They are often referred to as 'the new Irish'. As with the Irish, they carried into

Britain negative stereotypes of the British and vice versa. This is very evident in the content and ethos of specific, imported religious traditions, as will become clear later when we consider the world of the imams in the mosques.

Algerians, Egyptians and Saudis – from whom were drawn the 'Arab Afghans' who comprise the backbone of al-Qaʿida – have never been numerically significant in Britain. Most Arabs in London either fall into the category of international commuters – London has been dubbed 'Beirut-on-Thames' by journalists – or are well-educated students who have chosen to stay, or political exiles with their home country remaining as their focus of engagement.[3]

Ethno-religious clustering and socio-economic profile of Muslims in Britain

Notwithstanding the ethnic diversity of Muslim communities in Britain, it is Pakistanis (70 per cent of whom have roots in Azad Kashmir, one of the least developed areas in Pakistan) who tend to shape the public profile of Islam in Britain. Their traditionalism is kept alive by substantial exchanges of religious leaders, politicians and investment, as well as high levels of transcontinental marriages – for Kashmiris, some 80 per cent of all marriages. Just over half of the Muslim communities are under 25 as against a third in wider society. Since the average number of children born into Pakistani and Bangladeshi families is 4.7 and 4.2, compared with 2.3 nationally, this suggests that the Muslim communities could almost double within the next twenty years.[4]

If Muslims are to be equitably incorporated within British society, policy makers will have to focus on the

cities where Muslims are disproportionately concentrated. These are cities, especially in the north, where the
industries, especially textiles, which attracted migrant
labour, have collapsed. Since most young Muslims are
from 'a working-class with the majority . . . living in
neighbourhoods considered to be the most deprived
wards in England . . . [this is] reflected in statistics as
underachievers, anti-school rather than pro-school and
generally displaying signs of disengagement with
school authorities.'[5] Despite narrowing the educational
gap in the last few years, as with all communities, the
gap between male and female success remains wide. A
further 35 per cent of Muslim families are growing up
within households where no adult is in employment (17
per cent the national figure) and unemployment levels
are three times higher than the national figure. 68 per
cent of Muslim women are economically inactive, as
compared to less than 30 per cent for Christian women
and approximately 35 per cent for Hindu and Sikh
women.[6]

Class and cultural differences, in part, explain some
educational and employment differentials across the different Muslim communities. A distinguished historian
of Muslims in Britain, noted that

> Not only was a higher proportion (75.4%) of men from
> the Middle Eastern, predominantly Muslim, groups
> more economically active than white males, but the per-
> centage of economically participating females from this
> group was higher than their white counterparts . . . Local
> variations have also been striking. According to the 1991
> census, while 11.8% of Bangladeshis were unemployed
> in Brent, a colossal 47.3 % were out of work in Tower
> Hamlets.[7]

The five largest Muslim population clusters are: London with 607,000; Birmingham with 140,000; Greater Manchester 125,000; Bradford 75,000, and Kirklees with 39,000.

Brent is not Leicester is not Bradford

Different cities have quite distinct profiles. Brent, for example, is one of the most ethnically diverse Muslim communities in UK and is the place to which the upwardly mobile British Bengalis move from Tower Hamlets. A recent localized study indicated that there are some thirty ethnic groups in Brent.[8] This ethnic diversity has generated huge creativity and Brent has become the home of Islamic human rights groups, pioneering Muslim women's groups such as An-Nisa, and the home of British Muslim magazines in English such as *Q-News* and *Emel*. Further north, in the east Midlands, a majority of Leicester's Muslim communities are 'twice migrants' with origins in East Africa. They fled brutal Africanization under Idi Amin, and arrived with considerable 'cultural capital'. They had learned to live as a minority in East Africa over the previous fifty years, were English speakers and had generated commercial and professional networks. In the UK they have contributed greatly to the local economy.[9]

It is from such communities in Brent and Leicester that the YUMMIE phenomenon has emerged: Young Upwardly Mobile Muslims who provide a market for the beautifully produced Muslim lifestyle magazine, *Emel*. They also are the pool from which activist Muslim groups are drawn, including young professionals who have pioneered the *City Circle*, a space in London where Muslims working in the city can debate what it means to

be a British Muslim, and the young adults in their twen-
ties who founded the Muslim Youth Helpline, a counselling service which created an institutional arena
where issues of sexuality, relationship and mental health
can be discussed – issues which are frequently taboo
among elders and religious leaders. They provide the
twenty plus 17–25 year olds whom government depart-
ments have identified as a 'critical friend' for policy
makers, the Young Muslim Advisory Group (YMAG).[10]

In contrast to Brent and Leicester, Bradford – like
many northern cities – has suffered massive deindustri-
alization, with high levels of unemployment. Some
60,000 textile jobs were lost between 1960–90. The majority of the city's growing Muslim communities have roots
in rural Kashmir and are a very young community: in
the 2001 census, 16 per cent of population had roots in
Pakistan and Bangladesh, but some 28 per cent of the
school population.

The Pakistani communities include a growing 'under-
class', with a significant section of young men under-
achieving in schools, joining an intractable white under-
class on outer estates. This opens the door to extremists
in both communities intent on capitalizing on a widespread feeling of malaise, whether the BNP or *Hizb at-
Tahrir* (Party of Liberation), a radical movement with
roots in Palestine. Both are carriers of a supremacist ideology, one based on a selective interpretation of
'Englishness', the other an equally tendentious interpretation of Islam. Alas, YUMMIES are involved in such
radical, anti-Western movements as well as constructive
movements such as the Muslim Youth Foundation.

Youth alienation amongst sections of British
'Pakistani' and white communities translates into major
problems of crime, drugs and anti-social behaviour. The
prison population now includes a disproportionate

'Muslim' component.[11] This then accelerates the flight of the affluent in *all* communities and can threaten business conduct. Relations between British Pakistanis and English communities are rendered difficult by a number of factors: a measure of residential segregation of communities which is even more apparent in schools which have become ever more ethnically homogeneous, and high levels of youth unemployment which mean that there is little interaction at work. This means that all too often there are neither opportunities, institutional spaces, nor a common vocabulary to talk openly and honestly about problems within and between communities. There is also fear of being labelled racist if wrongdoing is challenged, and fear of confronting the gang culture, the illegal drugs trade and growing intolerance, harassment and abuse that exist across communities.[12]

Identity and belonging: Not easy being Muslim after 7/7

In the 1990s there was a new emphasis by British Muslims on 'identity politics' which was apiece with multiculturalism and the pluralization of interest groups – whether the basis was race, gender, sexuality or regional. Wherever one could argue that one's identity needed recognition, resources and representation followed. As one acute social scientist noticed, Muslim identity politics became

> integral to local community politics and thrives through romantic, global solidarities as wars and massacres in Palestine, Bosnia, Kosovo, the Gulf, Chechnya, Kashmir, India and so on fill our newspapers and television screens and lead some young, British-born Muslims to

reinvent the concept of umma, the global community of
Muslims, as global *victims*.[13]

Such politics persisted in the new millennium with
Afghanistan, Iraq and Israel/Palestine being added to
the list of grievances. While educated Muslims would
organize aid to stricken areas or join radical groups,
among working-class Muslims in the inner cities, most
young men did not involve themselves in Muslim
organizations. Instead, they used Islam in the construction of an assertive identity which was little more than a
tribal badge of identity.[14]

There is a satisfying and seductive allure about self-
representation as victim. It relieves communities from
self-criticism. However, this was less easy after 7/7,
which was a shock for Muslims and non-Muslims alike.
The fact that British Muslims had visited such an atroc-
ity on fellow citizens began a period of soul-searching in
sections of the Muslim community.[15] However, it also
opened Muslim communities to intense and sustained
scrutiny from the media, politicians, academics and the
intelligence services. Hardly any aspect of community
life has been spared the unwelcome glare of media attention. Specific cultural practices and abuses have been
conflated with Islam – everything from 'forced marriages', female gender mutilation, headscarves and face
coverings (*hijab* and *niqab*), to gun crime, gangs and
heroin distribution. Moreover, stoning for adultery and
amputations for theft, as practised by Saudis and
Taliban, are presented as normative for all Muslims in all
places for all time.

Many educated Muslims have begun a process of self-
education, tapping into 'Shaykh Google' to find answers
to the many questions a sceptical wider society are now
asking about Islam. This can have both liberating and

disturbing consequences. British Muslim women are finding their voice and beginning

> to question their elders by comparing what they had dis-
> covered in the sources of Islam with what their elders
> believed. This situation occurs in a range of issues from
> forced marriages to seeking higher education . . . females
> [are] particularly vociferous in discussing the topic of
> education . . . They argued that their parents' expectation
> of them and what they understood as their rights and
> responsibilities as a Muslim were, at times, at polar
> opposites . . . [This can generate] constant battles about
> topical issues or [the] leading of double lives.[16]

Young women are especially agitated by the importation from the parental homeland of the *biraderi* (literarily 'brotherhood') system, the 'traditional Indo-Pak tribal system of social order, in which kinship and age are important. The traditional tribal hierarchical system is criticized by many young Muslims [who] argue that respect and honour should be gained through diligence and hard work and not given because someone is older or of high ranking in the caste system'.[17] These clan networks, at once patriarchal and hierarchical, impact many aspects of Pakistani communities, and mosques, community centres and local politics are often the preserve of such 'clans'. Because there is a pecking order of such 'brotherhoods', the more influential and numerous embody a pattern of exclusionary politics. Yet local party bosses often find it convenient to work with such clans because they can guarantee vote banks.[18]

For many young Muslim men living in the inner city, there has been a process of multiple alienations, from wider society, mosque and home. Three vivid quotations communicate some of the reasons for the alienation of many young men in northern towns from mosque and home alike. 'Basid' speaks to a young Muslim researcher about attitudes of wider society:

> I don't know if there's a single day that I don't hear, 'Paki go home,' . . . They don't get that I was born here, I've lived here all my life. I've only been to Pakistan twice in my life cuz of a wedding and my daadi's died. I'm gonna live here . . . and I'll probably die here too.

A 22-year-old man, 'Jaleel', in reply to a question about mosques expostulates:

> Who goes to the mosque, mate? Do you? The mullah don't speak our language, yeah? They [the elders comprising the mosque committee] bring some . . . villager over here and he gets up there and tells us every Friday that we are [rubbish] and we're a bunch of [losers] and we chase birds all day long and we aren't good Muslims. Who needs it man? . . . I know how to live in the UK. That [mullah] hasn't been here for more than a few years and he thinks he knows where it's at . . .

Similarly, for many British Muslim youth, their homes are also unsympathetic places. 'Ashfaq' comments:

> Me mum loves PTV [Pakistan Television], man. She watch [sic] it all day long. All I get at home is what some [person] is doing in Lahore or Multan or some village . . . I got to call me mates to get the footie scores, man, cuz I don't get no telly time at home. I mean, I don't care [at] all what's going on in some village in [Pakistan]. I wanna know what's outside my door; me mum's only caring about what's happening over there . . .

Such young men seek sanctuary with their 'mates' on the streets.[19]

Specific intellectual challenges facing Muslims as a minority

Thus far, I have concentrated on social issues and patterns of exclusion which British Muslims face, internal and external. This is important because many young Muslims, especially in the inner city, face similar problems to white working-class lads: poor education, impoverished environment, high levels of unemployment – a situation in which young men, 'hoodies', become the new folk devils.

However, Muslims also face a new set of intellectual tasks created by being a minority in Western society. This is over and above making a multiplicity of practical accommodations to a culture and society which is very different to that which their parents or grandparents left behind. For example, in restaurants owned by Muslims there is a spectrum of positions on the provision and sale of alcohol, which is *haram* (i.e. totally forbidden) in Islam: some restaurants will not sell it themselves but allow diners to bring it in with them; others will sell it themselves; while some of the largest and most successful will not allow it on their premises.

It is worthwhile recalling that Islamic jurisprudence (*fiqh*) did not envisage minority, Muslim communities formed by voluntary economic migration from Muslim to non-Muslim lands. Over a quarter of a century ago, the late Sheikh Dr Zaki Badawi (d. 2006) lamented the fact that *Sunni* 'Muslim theology offers, up to the present, no systematic formulation of the status of being in a minority'.[20]

An Indian scholar also observes that with the exception of the recent trauma of Western colonialism, 'Sunni Muslims took power and dominance for granted. They knew how to command or to obey. They had for most of their history, rarely learned to live with others in equality and fraternity.'[21] He was so concerned with the lack of critical thinking in a world where one in five Muslims now live as minorities that he created the *Journal for Muslim Minority Affairs.*

Living in a society in which Muslims are a minority requires investment in institutions and an understanding of the imperative for new thinking. A South African scholar, now in America, has identified with unexampled clarity the enormity of the challenge this poses:

> The body of thought that the project of re-thinking . . . attempts to confront is premised on a triumphalist ideology: an age when Islam was a political entity and empire. A cursory glance at this intellectual legacy will show how this ideology of Empire permeates theology, jurisprudence, ethics, and espouses a worldview that advances hierarchy. What adds to the frustrations of millions of followers of Islam is the fact that this triumphalist creed and worldview is unable to deliver its adherents to its perceived goals of worldly success and leadership.[22]

In conversation, he told me that he was working on a book with the poignant title *After Empire*. In this, he seeks to disengage the religious disciplines from the imperial narrative in which they are embedded, since that narrative is now dysfunctional.

Nor are Muslims better equipped for inter-faith dialogue with Christians. One of the few British Muslim scholars who has actually studied Christianity regrets that 'a frank supersessionism written into the Islamic tradition leaves little need for "curiosity" about "the otherness of the other"'.[23] This has created a huge hole in Islamic training. Where Muslim scholars, especially those tasked with giving legal answers – the muftis – are required to have some basic knowledge of the local customs and practices of the people amongst whom they live, he noted that

> In Europe, I am not aware of any *madrasa* which is in the business of training ʿ*ulama* [in] even the basic concepts of the Judaeo-Christian traditions . . . Furthermore, there is an urgent need to introduce the intellectual and cultural trends of Western society into Muslim seminaries' syllabi.[24]

Imams in Britain: agents of de-radicalization?

Until 9/11 the world of the imams in Britain, their influence, training and institutions was largely a matter of indifference to the government. Subsequently, that world has become the focus of intense interest both from government and the media. Unsurprisingly, such scrutiny has intensified exponentially since 7/7.

Initially, after 9/11, the intelligence services began to identify, monitor and prosecute a few notorious individuals – often self-styled *shaikhs* such as Abu Hamza al-Misri, Abdullah El-Faisal and Abu Qatada – who had been pumping out virulent anti-Western diatribes against the *kuffar* (unbelievers), as well as romanticizing and recruiting for *jihadist* activities – often from a few mosques in London.

The temptation to see the imams through the prism of these individuals began to give way to a more nuanced understanding of violent extremism and its carriers, whether *takfiri Salafis* or violent Islamists.[25] Indeed, the government has sought to mobilize and equip imams as part of a coordinated attempt to deradicalize young British Muslims vulnerable to the siren calls of violent extremism.

They have begun to create and commend 'the good imam' as a counterpoint to the likes of Abu Hamza and Omar Bakri Muhammad. 'The good Muslim' is outward-looking, able to engage confidently with British Muslim youth, local schools, public and civic bodies, as well as being hospitable to members of other religions. It is hoped he will embody – as mainstream Christian clergy do – 'bridging' social capital; that is, enable trust and reciprocity across different communities.

Before rehearsing some of the measures the previous Labour government introduced to encourage such developments, we need to consider the provenance, status, training and social roles of imams in Britain. Given the dominance of Muslims with roots in South Asia, the majority of mosques have been created to serve these communities. The most comprehensive mapping of Britain's mosques with regard to location, ethnicity and 'school of thought' to which they belong, suggests that 600 are *Deobandi*, 550 *Barelwi*, 60 Islamists, 75 *Salafi*, 65 *Shiʿite*, along with a number of ethnic-specific mosques serving Turks, Somalis, Arabs and so on (www.muslimsinbritain.org). In short, most reflect the different traditional *Sunni* schools of thought which are active in South Asia – especially *Deobandi* and *Barelwi*. While British *Deobandis* with roots in India tend to belong to a pious and a-political tradition, some with roots in Pakistan are the same ethnic group which has gener-ated the Taliban. *Barelwis* have suffered from the 'Talibanization' of Pakistan and, unsurprisingly, are bitterly hostile to them.

In Britain, most of the mosque committees are dominated by the elders, whose experiences in rural and small town Pakistan continue to shape a limited set of expectations about the imam's status and role. Most are reimbursed well below the minimum wage and lack contractual security. Their roles are generally confined to the mosque, where they lead the five daily prayers, teach children after state school every weekday, give the Friday address, preside over the 'rites of passage', offer advice, when sought, within their competence on the application of Islamic teaching and law. Traditionalist Muslims occasionally seek amulets from them – for example, to ward off the evil eye.

In the last quarter of a century, side by side with mosque building, a new phase of institution building has begun with the proliferation of *Dar al-ʿUloom* 'Islamic seminaries'. There are at least twenty-four registered 'seminaries' in Britain: sixteen *Deobandi*, five *Barelwi*, one *Shiʿite*, one Muslim Brotherhood and one founded by the late Sheikh Dr Zaki Badawi, who had been trained at Al-Azhar in Cairo. These probably have a capacity to train about two hundred and fifty ʿulama (i.e. religious scholars) a year. This means there is already a surfeit of *Deobandi* but a shortage of *Barelwi* scholars. One reason is that in the *Barelwi* tradition the key figure is the *Sufi sheikh* – a spiritual guide – who appoints the imam, who is often considered a low-level functionary.

The training and ethos of most of these 'seminaries' indicates only minor concessions have been made to their new location in Britain. The syllabus is often a thinned down version of what is taught in South Asia. In the case of the *Deobandi* school of thought, the focus is on mastering Arabic to understand the Qurʿan and canonical collections of Hadith. There is minimal study of qur'anic commentaries and Islamic law, no Islamic history beyond the first two generations after Muhammad's death and no Islamic philosophy. The medium of instruction often remains Urdu. Further, even if students study the few 'A' levels taught in such institutions – Arabic, Urdu, ICT, law and accountancy – their knowledge of British society, its history, culture and institutions will remain minimal.

The ethos of South Asian 'seminaries' can still be characterized as rejectionist of modernity and of discourses developed outside its circumscribed world. A recent survey of Pakistani students studying at Urdu and (elite) English medium schools and universities (public and private), registered between 65 and 90 per cent across the different institutions who favoured equal rights for women – in marked contrast with 'seminarians' for whom the figure was 17 per cent. Significant differences were also evident with regard to treating non-Muslims equally and a willingness to make peace with India.[26] A cursory look at traditional websites of 'seminaries' and those of many traditional scholars in the UK evince similar attitudes, certainly with regard to gender and often negative attitudes to non-Muslims. One other worrying import into Britain from South Asia has been a ratcheting up of intra-sectarian bigotry, exacerbated alike by Pakistani governments and Saudi petrol dollars.

However, there have been a few welcome changes from within the world of British 'seminaries'. Since 9/11 and 7/7 some have begun to open up in a limited way to wider society, its civic and religious dignitaries, as well as to the police. Some of their scholars go on to study in a limited number of British universities or further afield. The best are beginning to find jobs as religious education teachers, chaplains in prisons, hospitals and further education, where they are developing new intellectual and social skills. One or two are even barristers.

Unfortunately, many mosque committees still seem reluctant to employ such British trained imams – perhaps because they press for realistic salaries, contracts and pension rights. In the ten years after 1997, some 420 imams from Pakistan have been granted visas to come to Britain to discharge the duties of an imam. A survey of 300 mosques in 2008 indicated that 92 per cent of the imams were foreign born and trained with only 6 per cent speaking English as their first language. This creates a significant disconnect between many mosques and the 52 per cent of British Muslims under 25 years old, most of whom were born and educated in the UK.[27]

It is this disconnect which is seen as a major factor in a process of radicalization. British Muslims who are unable to get answers to their questions, often look outside the mosque altogether. There is an emerging consensus that radical anti-Western ideas do not translate into violent extremism without the presence of three combustible factors: a Manichean world view (Muslim versus the infidel); Islam understood as a supremacist, political ideology; and a commitment to violence to achieve goals. Research into violent extremists in Britain suggests an additional nuancing of these variables: a sense of moral outrage at crimes committed against Muslims globally and locally, such grievances being interpreted as part of a larger war of the West against Islam; and a perspective which resonates with personal experience of discrimination, real or imagined. A few individuals are then mobilized through extremist networks, whether face to face or online.[28] Insofar as imams embody a rejectionist, anti-Western stance, they can be seen as part of the problem.

To address these issues, the Labour government adopted a twin track policy. It excluded some seventy-nine 'preachers of hate' between 2005-08 while seeking to enhance the capacity of imams to build more resilient cross-community links and to de-legitimize the extremist narrative. It raised the bar for imams to get into Britain: they now have to speak the same level of English as would be expected of a foreign student applying for a postgraduate course of study, and supported the creation in June 2006 of the Mosques and Imams National Advisory Board (MINAB) – inclusive of most sectarian traditions – to improve the governance of mosques and the training of imams.

Most significantly, it funded a flagship project, the Radical Middle Way (www.radicalmiddleway.co.uk) which organizes visits by prominent Muslim scholars from across the world to preach against extremism and to urge engagement with mainstream society. Further, the Foreign and Commonwealth Office's 'Projecting British Islam' was designed to undercut the narrative of 'Islam versus the West' by showcasing British Muslims as an integral part of the UK. Between 2005-09, over thirty trips were organized to Muslim countries, in which younger imams and religious leaders participated. The Labour government also funded an innovative Islam and Citizenship Education (ICE) project which had an advisory board of Islamic specialists drawn from most of the different Muslim schools of thought. This is being piloted in a range of mosques across the country.

These welcome initiatives, along with some imams moving out of their comfort zones to become chaplains and teachers, may in the long-term equip a new generation to engage with wider society. The Radical Middle Way, however, has unwittingly exposed the paucity of front-rank British Muslim scholars at ease with wider society. There was only one British, male, scholar of Pakistani ethnicity, Dr Usama Hasan, and he did not belong to either majority *Barelwi* or *Deobandi* tradition. As a result the *Deobandis* responded with their own road show.

Peering into the future

It is clear that a new generation of young British Muslim leaders and celebrities is emerging: in the media the likes of the feisty Saira Khan of *The Apprentice* fame; in sport, the boxer Amir Khan and the cricketer Sajid Mahmood. In the social sciences, younger academics are emerging, such as Dr Tahir Abbas at Birmingham University and Dr Tufayl Choudhry at Durham University. In the present coalition government, there are five MPS – three of whom are women; of the two men, one is in the Shadow Cabinet, Sadiq Khan. Of the twenty plus Muslims in the House of Lords, one – Baroness Sayeeda Warsi – has a seat in the coalition cabinet, the first Muslim woman elevated to such a position. At a local level there are more than two hundred councillors, including a few who have been Lord Mayors.

The previous Labour government had invested in imam training and the development of women's and young people's networks. This is to be commended. However, the gender equality assumption underlining such initiatives may well run up against the quiet resistance of traditional *Sunni* networks.[29] In all, British Muslims have generated a huge amount of creativity: there are websites for progressive Muslims, secular Muslims, even ex-Muslims, as well as an explosion of traditional *Sunni* sites. What counts as Muslim identity will continue to be constructed, contested and agonized over for the foreseeable future. The Cambridge University project – 'Contextualising Islam in Britain: Exploratory Perspectives' – with its refreshing self-criticism bodes well for the future.[30]

So long as the 'war on terror' continues and conflicts in Afghanistan, Pakistan and Israel/Palestine drag on, however, relations with sections of the Muslim communities will remain fraught, especially those who share the same ethnicity and sectarian identity as the Taliban.[31] In the long-term, the most important work will often go on unnoticed. There could be significant developments, for example, as British institutions open their doors to Muslims and are willing to negotiate reasonable accommodations to Muslim-specific needs, whether in Housing Associations, the Scouts or churches.[32]

Chapter 7

Conversion from Islam to Christianity in Britain

Tim Green

Today in Britain and worldwide, more Muslims are turning to Christ than at any time in history.[1] What explains this extraordinary growth? Is it causing Muslim scholars to question Islam's traditional theory of apostasy? If so, has this yet changed attitudes on the ground in Muslim communities? How should British Christians respond, and how may they best support converts? This chapter examines these questions in particular, while recognizing that religious conversion is a multifaceted phenomenon which cannot be fully explored in the space available.

Religious conversion, a growing trend

From a human perspective, globalization has played a big part in opening up conversion as a realistic option. Travel and migration provide more face to face contact between Muslims and Christians than ever before, and thereby the opportunity to explore each others' beliefs and to observe each others' practices. This also leads to intermarriage, which (probably for the couple concerned and certainly for their children), has implications for religious allegiance. Pluralizing societies challenge the old assumed alliance of faith, ethnicity and nationality, thus creating space for new hybrid combinations. And even within mono-cultural societies, the internet and satellite dish allow people more freedom of religious choice than ever before.

For all these reasons and more, individuals today are no longer bound to follow their parents' religion. Rather, they can shop around in the world supermarket of religious ideas, and are choosing to do so in increasing numbers. 'The days of closed, homogeneous, unchanging societies are rapidly going and they will not come back', writes Jean-Marie Gaudeul. 'Social conformism will no longer suffice to deal with the great questions of life, every human being has to make his own choice by himself, or herself'.[2]

Unsurprisingly then, conversion to Islam and conversion from Islam are both on the rise.

Conversion to Islam in Britain

We lack reliable statistics on how many indigenous British people have converted to Islam. Estimates range from 15,000 to nearly fifty thousand.[3] Many of these converts are well educated, white, professional people; more than half are women. Most are from non-religious backgrounds, but often had investigated other religions before choosing Islam, and 10–20 per cent had been practising Christians at some point in their adult lives before converting. Their choice of Islam usually came in a careful, deliberate way rather than through any dramatic 'Damascus Road' experience. Some became Muslims for the sake of marriage, but more commonly they were introduced to Islam through meeting their partner and later making it their personal choice.

An additional and contrasting group of converts come from black urban communities, often young men who have found identity and empowerment through embracing Islam. Conversion to Islam is also taking place in Britain's prisons.

Leaving Islam: Apostates speak out

Conversely, large numbers of cultural Muslims in Britain are abandoning any personal religious commitment. Until recently this has remained a largely invisible trend, for these apostates continue to live within their Muslim communities and culture. But now the internet is giving them voice. The Council of Ex-Muslims of Britain splashes across its home page the words 'We have renounced religion!'[4]

With remarkable boldness, writing mostly under their real names and sometimes with photos attached, scores of members explain why they left Islam. Ahmed Fawad from Leeds says, 'I am an atheist and I would like to join this brave organisation along with my wife and young daughter who also do not want the burden of religion upon them.' Parsa Karimi proclaims, 'I am happy I can publicly renounce Islam.' J. Ahmad writes with a tone of relief, 'I have been living a secret life here in the UK for the last few years . . . but now I have decided to come out openly.' Marina from Sheffield announces that she is an 'ex-Muslim' who has 'come out of the closet' to her parents.

By such phrases, these ex-Muslims invite comparison with gay people 'coming out'. They seem glad to throw off at last the shame and secrecy, to stand erect as apostates and to look their community in the eye. However, they have mostly turned not to Christianity but to atheism or agnosticism. In their rejection of Islam and especially repressive or violent forms of Islam, they oppose religion altogether.

Some (though only a minority) of these former Muslims are turning to Christ. We focus on them now.

Muslims choosing Christianity in Britain

A lack of information

Back in the 1980s when I first began to meet ex-Muslim followers of Christ in Britain, they were few indeed. Today I come across them frequently. Their numbers have grown many-fold in the last thirty years.

Why, then, is this trend so little known? It is firstly because most converts from Islam, and the Christian organizations assisting them, tend to shun publicity (though Iranians have been bolder than most). Secondly, and as a result, there is almost no media coverage of Muslims choosing Christianity. This may at times be due to political correctness,[5] but when journalists have proactively tried to interview converts, they found their efforts mostly thwarted.[6]

Thirdly, in contrast to the academic studies on conversion *to* Islam in the West, there have been surpris-ingly few on conversion *from* Islam. The secular academic world seems to be unaware that this phenomenon exists at all, and oblivious to the research on conversion being done in Christian circles.[7] I know of no academic books specifically on conversion from Islam to Christianity in Britain, and almost no research at PhD level.[8] At masters level there are three useful but little-known dissertations based on interviews with converts.[9]

At a less academic level, there is printed and internet material about converts in the form of biography, auto-biography and 'testimony'. Some of them converted before or after coming to Britain, while others grew up in Britain as Muslims and later found Christ.[10]

Hazy statistics but a clear trend

In the absence of reliable coverage by academia or media, or of centralized church statistics, it is impossible to estimate accurately the number of Christians from a Muslim background in Britain.

Certainly, by far the largest group are Iranians, proba-bly numbering between two and three thousand, possi-bly more.[11] Yet there is also growth across the whole eth-nic spectrum. In one small British city, I know of more than thirty 'Muslim background believers' from many nationalities: Iranian (the largest group), Pakistani (both immigrant and British-born), Bangladeshi, Indian, Kurdish, Nigerian (several), Rwandan, Somali, Tanzan-ian, Turkmen, Ugandan and Zambian. In total, there may be at least four thousand Christians from Muslim backgrounds in Britain today, but this is only an educat-ed guess.[12] More than half of them are women. Some are former converts to Islam from among the indigenous population.

So, statistics are hazy, but the growth trend is clear. Is this causing Islamic scholars and leaders to reconsider the long-entrenched theory of apostasy?

Are Islamic scholars changing their position?

Apostasy in Islamic tradition

Islamic attitudes to apostasy developed early and hardened quickly, not to be challenged in any significant way until modern times. The consensus of the centuries was almost unanimous: apostates are traitors and deserve execution.

This stern attitude derives only in part from the Qur'an, which in fact is quite ambiguous on whether apostates should be punished in this life or only by God in the afterlife. More clear-cut were Muhammad's words, as reported in several Hadith including the well-known saying 'he who changes his religion, kill him'.[13] Attitudes to apostasy continued to harden immediately after Muhammad's lifetime, as the nascent Muslim state fought to reassert its authority over dissident Arab tribes and firmly welded together the concepts of political and religious allegiance. Loyalty to Allah meant loyalty to his ruler on earth. Rejection of one necessarily implied rejection of the other, so apostasy spelt treason.

And so down through history, Muslim societies have tended to view religious apostates as social renegades and political traitors. Far from being unique to Islam, such a stance is typical of collectivist cultures including pre-modern Christendom. Religion is not a private choice, but rather a tribal or ethnic identity label. A person switching over to the religion of a different ethnic group, especially an enemy group, is perceived as rejecting their heritage and bringing shame upon their whole community. It upsets the social order. It needs to be crushed.

Thus in all schools of Islamic law, *Sunni* and *Shi'a*, the unambiguous penalty for sane male apostates is death.

The jurists differed over who is qualified to pronounce the sentence, and on what to do with female apostates or the insane, and on how much time to allow an apostate to change their mind, and on what constitutes apostasy anyway. But the principle of capital punishment was clear-cut and almost unopposed. Not content merely with capital punishment, the jurists also applied civil penalties, such as the automatic dissolution of an apostate's marriage and the confiscation of his or her property.[14]

In practice the penalty was rarely applied down the centuries, simply because so few Muslims ever converted to Christianity.

The colonial era

From the early nineteenth century onwards, European colonial rule allowed missionaries and Christian literature to have some influence in Muslim lands. Although the numbers converting to Christianity remained small, attitudes began to change among some Muslim scholars exposed to Western education, such as Muhammad Abduh. They began to argue that rejection of Islam need not automatically imply rebellion against the government.

Others, even in the modern era, continued to argue that all apostasy is treason. Abu Ala Maududi (probably Islamism's most influential ideologue in the twentieth century), argued that freedom of religion in Islam means freedom to enter, not to leave. For him, the interests of the Islamic state take precedence over those of the individual, so 'a state has the right to use force to . . . crush those segments which insist on breaking away.'[15] Such extreme statements were perhaps an embarrassment to even Maududi's own followers, who declined to translate them into English, but he was not alone in making them.

Twentieth century human rights discourse

Pressure for change increased with the human rights provisions enshrined in the 1948 United Nations Declaration of Human Rights. Most Muslim governments assented to the UN Declaration, while harbouring doubts over article 18 which, by asserting a person's 'freedom to change his religion or belief', directly challenged the Islamic law of apostasy.

Islamic versions of human rights declarations later modified this freedom significantly.[16] For instance, the Universal Islamic Declaration of Human Rights (1981), while maintaining a studied ambiguity in its English version, is clear enough in the original Arabic that 'forsaking the Islamic community' is forbidden. However, it should be borne in mind that this and other 'Islamic Declarations' have not carried great influence in practice.

Further change in the twenty-first century

Within the last few years, internationally recognized Muslim leaders have increasingly started to state publicly that apostates should *not* be punished by death. In 2002 Sheikh Tantawi, then head of the world's foremost Islamic university Al Azhar, declared the death penalty for apostasy to be 'null and void'. Other leaders followed suit, prompted especially by the widely publicized news in 2006 that a convert in Afghanistan had been initially sentenced to death. Thereafter the views of more than one hundred notable Muslim scholars who oppose this penalty for apostasy were published on the 'Apostasy and Islam' website. Their worldwide list of names is quite impressive and includes several who are prominent in Britain.[17]

In addressing international audiences, these scholars spoke in a clear-cut way. But those of them based in Muslim-majority countries needed to perform a balancing act, as Egypt's grand mufti Ali Gomaa found in 2007 when he first informed an international forum that apostasy should only be punished if combined with treason, and then later assured irate Muslims at home that apostasy and treason are linked anyway! In Qatar in 2006, the influential Yusuf al-Qaradawi supported the death sentence for apostasy, albeit hedged around with caveats. A 2009 conference of Islamic jurists meeting in the Middle East was unable to take an agreed position on punishment for apostasy.

So, at an international level the doors of *ijtihad* (creative interpretation) are starting to creak open, though slowly and fitfully; but what about in Britain?

Contemporary debate in Britain

In 2007, Channel 4 screened a *Dispatches* documentary on Muslims converting to Christianity in Britain. On the programme, senior clerics Suhaib Hasan of the *Shariᶜa* Council of Great Britain, and Ibrahim Mogra of the Muslim Council of Britain, were confronted with evidence that some converts face violent intimidation from Muslims. Both were adamant that there should be no punishment for apostates. Afterwards Mogra reiterated to a Muslim audience that an apostate should be left alone without fear of intimidation because to choose apostasy is to choose hell-fire.[18]

In 2008, an insightful Radio 4 programme, *Could I Stop Being a Muslim?*, asked a range of Muslim leaders in Britain whether they think the death penalty still applies for apostates. Usama Hassan, an imam with a Cambridge PhD, argued that the classical law of apostasy in Islam is not right, due to being based on a misunderstanding of the original sources. He went so far as to assert that the Qurʿan and the teaching of the Prophet don't actually talk about a death penalty for apostasy. Haras Rafiq, leader of the *Sufi* Muslim Council, agreed.

However, other interviewees on the programme were equally adamant that the death penalty still applies in principle. 'There are legislations and rulings which remain eternally and they will remain up until we perish and the world itself perishes,' asserted Abu Khadijah, a Wahabi running an Islamic bookstore in Birmingham. A *Deobandi* lecturer, teaching jurisprudence at an imam's training college in Britain, similarly stated that the 'unanimous consensus among the jurists' is for the death penalty.[19]

Between these two extremes, most interviewees sought space in the middle ground. While agreeing that apostates in Britain today should not be punished, they were unwilling to sweep aside altogether the consensus of the centuries. Dr Hisham Hellyer (now a fellow at Warwick University) explained that under certain circumstances the classic punishments could be suspended, or commuted, or be technically inapplicable but it could not simply be taken off the books as this would be tantamount to saying that all the authorities that came before were misguided and wrong.

Scholars taking this middle ground seek ways to explain why the penalty for apostasy could still be valid in theory but would not apply in Britain today: either because it is not an Islamic state, or because there is no perfect Islamic ruler to pronounce sentence (a *Shi'a* view), or because apostasy should only by punished when combined with treason.

In 2008–09, the 'Contextualising Islam' project under Cambridge and Exeter universities brought together twenty-six Muslim scholars, activists, community leaders and academics to discuss what Islam means in Britain today. Their report makes the breathtakingly bold (even novel) assertion that Islam

> prohibits discrimination against apostates . . . It is important to say quite simply that people have the freedom to enter the Islamic faith and the freedom to leave it.[20]

In 2009, the Muslim Christian Forum drew up a set of 'ethical guidelines for Christian and Muslim witness in Britain'. This is a landmark document, for it was agreed by recognized leaders from both faith communities, and it tackles head-on the question of conversion. The guidelines state that 'we should recognise that people's choice of faith is primarily a matter between themselves and God', and that

> whilst we may feel hurt when someone we know and love chooses to leave our faith, we will respect their decision and will not force them to stay or harass them afterwards.[21]

In 2010 a Christian convert challenged a gathering of imams and clergy to recognize that some in Britain who convert from Islam are treated very badly by the Muslim community. Afterwards some of the Muslim leaders told her privately that they were deeply upset and shocked by what she said, and that they would go back to their communities to challenge this attitude to converts.

Thus, change is in the air. A growing number of mainline Muslim leaders in Britain are now affirming – clearly, corporately and unambiguously – the right of individuals to leave Islam without being punished or harassed.

But has this new lenient approach by Islamic scholars yet made any difference to Muslim attitudes on the street? To this we now turn.

How do British Muslims treat apostates in practice?

A startling poll result

In 2007 in a Policy Exchange poll, no less than 36 per cent of British Muslims aged 16 to 24 believed that apostates should be killed. Considering that most of these young people had been brought up and educated in a liberal society, this response was surprising indeed. It may reflect more what they feel *should* be said to an interviewer, in terms of giving the correct Islamic answer, than what they have carefully considered for themselves. Still less does it indicate any action they would actually carry out. But it seems clear that scholars' more liberal attitudes have not yet 'trickled down' to street level, at least among certain sectors of Muslim society. Significantly, this age group of British Muslims gave more radical answers than their elders across a whole range of questions in the poll, and this probably reflects their more self-consciously 'chosen Islam' in contrast to the 'cultural Islam' of the previous generation.[22]

However, individualism works both ways, and if secularizing trends among young British Muslims prove more influential in the long-term than Islamizing trends, this will favour a more moderate attitude to apostasy.

Do some converts face physical danger?

I personally know of no cases of converts in Britain being murdered for their Christian faith. However, there have certainly been recent attempts at murder. In July 2009, two Afghan converts in Heathrow's main detention centre were told by other inmates 'if we are sent back to Afghanistan on the same flight, we will kill you before we land there'. Indeed, one of them reports that during a riot in their wing, thirty angry Afghans tried to break into his room and kill him.[23] Other severe attacks on Afghan converts by fellow-Afghans took place in Canterbury in 2009[24] and on several occasions in Nottingham in 2010.[25]

Another 2009 incident took place in the Bradford area, when a Pakistani convert was very badly beaten with baseball bats by five young men, including his brother and nephews. Bricks had previously been thrown through his windows and his family threatened. Surprisingly the assailants were let off with a suspended sentence, and were later to be seen boasting of their impunity. Another Pakistani convert in Bradford, Nissar Hussein, similarly believes that the authorities made a complacent response to the death threats and property damage which he and his family endured over several years until he eventually had to move house.[26]

So, severe persecution can take place in Britain today. At risk are converts who live in solidly Muslim urban enclaves, where disaffected second generation Muslim youth adopt an aggressively Islamic identity and claim the local turf. Where Islam's 'territory' is staked out within prisons or detention centres, violent intimidation may be impossible to escape.[27] New arrivals from particularly intolerant countries such as Afghanistan may also face violence. South Asian females may also be at relatively higher risk, because of cultural codes of honour which punish them more harshly than males for bringing shame on families.[28]

Is this typical for converts in Britain?

It is important to stress that cases of violent persecution are not typical in Britain. They represent just one extreme from a whole spectrum of Muslim responses. Most converts are 'merely' (though this is still devastating) verbally abused by their Muslim families, perhaps ejected from their homes, and disowned by the community. Rather typical would be the experience of a British Pakistani friend of mine, who was scornfully told by her relative 'Don't you realize that by becoming a Christian you have abandoned your roots, your heritage and your family name?'

At the other extreme are those cases where the Muslim family is neutral or even positive towards the convert. Another British-born Pakistani lady was, by her mid-twenties, in a fearful state. Divorced and back in her family home, she was so plagued by depression and demonic oppression that she was on the verge of suicide. But after she found Christ, the changes in her life were so positive and dramatic that her Muslim family members did not object to her new faith. She continues in good relationship with them.

In between these two extremes come the more typical family reactions: almost always negative, almost always hurtful, but rarely life-threatening.

This is confirmed by two field studies. Tom Walsh interviewed sixteen former Muslims, mostly of South Asian ethnicity and all living in Britain. Their relatives expressed extreme disappointment ('in their grief they didn't eat'), anguish ('my mum cried buckets and buckets') and concern for their honour in the community (to the extent of jeopardizing siblings' marriage prospects). They reacted by condemning or isolating or ignoring or expelling their errant family member who had brought such shame upon them.[29]

Des Harper interviewed twenty-three converts from Islam in Britain. He found that family reactions, while negative, were overall less severe than in the published conversion accounts arising from Muslim majority countries. Moreover, despite the initial rupture or strain, relationships tend to improve over time. Almost half of Harper's sample reported that their Muslim community came eventually to accept or even respect them; of the others, most continued to be viewed with suspicion, some were ignored or ostracized, and only a few underwent ongoing hostility. Generally his Iranian interviewees faced less difficulty than those from the Indian subcontinent.[30]

These findings fit with my own experience, that even when initial family response is hostile, some degree of reconciliation is likely after several years.

How should Christians respond?

The number of Muslims in Britain repudiating Islam will almost certainly continue to rise, with a proportion of them turning to Christ. Christians should respond appropriately to this growing phenomenon. I venture to offer five suggestions for consideration.

1. Give a fair and balanced analysis
Though lacking accurate statistics, we know that conversion from Islam is more than a trickle and less than a
flood, and Christian agencies do themselves no service
by emphasizing either extreme. Likewise, the degree of
persecution should neither be exaggerated nor mini-
mized. Although cases of violent persecution should
certainly be reported, it is inaccurate in my opinion to
paint these as the norm. It is not the case, as some have
argued, that most ex-Muslim Christians in Britain live in
fear.

2. Engage in advocacy where appropriate
Whenever converts do face credible threats, their fears
should be taken seriously by government authorities. In
cases of assault, criminal charges should be pressed vig-
orously without pandering to multicultural relativism (a
policy which is now, belatedly, being followed with honour killings). Vigilance is needed over any trend to
accommodate, in the British legal system, any parts of
shariᶜa law which would result in converts being subject
to Muslim community rulings.

3. Support efforts by Muslim leaders to bring change
Muslim leaders in Britain have started to express a
clear consensus against punishment or harassment of
apostates. Such initiatives can be supported better
through coaxing and encouragement than through
publicly picking holes in them. It was patient cooperation between Christian and Muslim leaders which produced the 'ethical guidelines for witness'. If Muslim
scholars make such sweeping assertions as 'Islam pro-
hibits discrimination against apostates' then Christians
will want to encourage them to repeat this openly and
widely.

It is natural for Muslim communities to experience hurt and anger over any members who desert Islam, and Christians should be sensitive to this. If pastors can build strong relationships with local imams from the beginning, it will create bridges to help ameliorate tensions when conversions in the Muslim community take place later.

To be sure, any change in attitudes will be incremental, but this is better than no change at all. Muslim scholars have only a small room for manoeuvre if they are to justify, *on Islamic grounds*, overthrowing the Islamic law of apostasy. To make the case for change to a sceptical Muslim public, they will need to resort to arguments which are not based on Western human rights discourse. So be it.

4. Avoid excessive secrecy
Christian agencies working in Muslim countries have become very security-conscious. This is understandable, but for those working in Britain, a sensible balance should be drawn between necessary caution and undue secrecy.

Atheist and secular ex-Muslims in Britain are becoming more visible and vocal. As one of them proclaims, 'It's about time we ex-Muslims came together and had our voices heard. To stand up and be counted.'[31] 'Why should Christian ex-Muslims not be noticed too?', asks Dr John Azumah at the London School of Theology. When people like him and Ziya Meral are willing to be known publicly, it makes it easier for others to follow suit. Their voice needs to be heard.

5. Support and 'be family' for converts
Many ex-Muslim followers of Jesus find the 'Christian' subculture confusing at best, disappointing at worst.

Christians should be helped to understand their needs better, especially the need for *a new family*. For a church member to say cheerily to a Muslim background believer, over coffee after the service, 'Hi, bye, see you next week' is simply not good enough; being family means being available.

Moreover, new believers seek a new role model of what being Christ's follower actually looks like in practice. They want a new framework of Christian discipleship to replace Islam's detailed prescriptions for daily life. And they long for a new identity, knowing where they fit as spiritually Christian, but retaining some elements of Muslim culture and some contact with their Muslim communities.

Discipleship courses and perhaps a support website are also needed for converts from Islam in the British context. There is a need to help them link up with each other locally and nationally, and also to find marriage partners in the faith.

These needs are not yet well understood in the British churches, and they will become all the more urgent as more Muslims turn to Christ in Britain.

Chapter 8

Islam, Human Rights and 'Our Way of Life'

Ziya Meral

I remember enjoying a strong Lebanese coffee in a hotel lobby in a Middle Eastern country after a long day of research and listening to stories of persecution. My few moments of calm would soon turn into a sad panic. An email from a friend in Turkey was asking for urgent prayers for the breaking news that an office used by a Christian publishing company had been attacked and that there were fatal casualties. In a few hours the news would be confirmed that two Turkish and one German Christian – Necati, Ugur and Tilmann – had been tortured to death by a group of five young men in Malatya, eastern Turkey.

Necati had been a friend of mine for some ten years, a member of my home church in Izmir, Turkey. We had prayed and fellowshipped together in the same home group and talked at length. Two days later I was standing in tears during his memorial service alongside members of the small Turkish Christian community, and watching his coffin being buried amidst tears and prayers.

The horrendous murders shook the country, and Christian leaders and churches found themselves at the centre of attention, learning to process their pain, raise their voice for justice and represent the love and peace of Jesus Christ. The murdered men had suffered immensely, and now the body of which they were a part was bleeding. Some new believers stopped attending churches and some long lost ones emerged from shadows. And we all knew that nothing would be the same for the Turkish church again.

When the news of the murders was picked up by the Western church, the actual events were reported in ways that were disturbingly wrong. Reports painted a gory picture, claiming that each of them suffered more than two hundred stab wounds and that their fingers were cut in a way prescribed by *shari'a*. The perpetrators were said to be 'Islamist extremists' and '*jihadists*'. We were told that the murders had proved once again that Islam and Muslims do not share our values of tolerance and religious freedom and do not demonstrate civilized reactions to other religious communities. Islam was inherently in opposition to the ideals of democracy. This was why Her Majesty's government had to restrict immigration and uphold British values as it seeks to integrate Muslims into mainstream British society.

Although this reasoning seemed convincing, it had major flaws at every stage. The gory descriptions of the suffering of our brothers were grossly exaggerated, although the men did die of stab wounds and eventually had their throats cut. There was no *shari'a* pattern to their suffering and most importantly, their murderers, who were all caught red-handed, were nationalists, not Islamists. Ironically, one of the first emails I received expressing condolences and heartfelt support and prayers was from a world-famous committed Muslim writer. The same writer subsequently published one of the strongest articles defending Christians and our right to share our faith with others.

In Turkey, almost all of the physical attacks on Christians come from the nationalist groups who see non-Muslims, particularly those who engage in evangelism, as threats to national security and social cohesion. The same nationalist groups are also responsible for harsh reactions shown to Islamists in the country. The murderers in Malatya were motivated by crooked ideals of 'protecting their nation' from 'external and internal enemies'. It emerged later on that their aim in torturing Christians was to get information out of them on how they were 'working' with Western intelligence agencies and supporting terrorist activities.

It was sad to see a local incident in Turkey, caused by factors unique to Turkey, being sucked into ongoing British and European debates on Islam and faulty notions of 'a clash of civilizations'. The actual suffering of our brothers were effaced and utilized as metaphors for such debates. But, the truth of the matter was much more complicated than it seemed.

The need for self-awareness

The example of how the murders in Malatya, Turkey, have been perceived by the Western church can be multiplied many times over. It only proves the humble philosophical and theological conclusion that as human beings our knowledge is often limited. We perceive events through our own lenses, shaped by our questions, worries and limitations. We often find what we want to find and often choose a clear-cut and simple answer rather than allow the truth to remain patchy, complicated and much bigger than our particular concerns.

A significant portion of the debates around Islam in Britain and Europe today suffers from the same human limitation rather than from lack of awareness of Islamic doctrines or history. A host of unspoken anxieties leads to preference being given to faulty methodologies that confirm our fears and provide clear-cut answers to extremely complicated issues. The outcome of this is detrimental for the British church, since Islam and Muslims emerge as one block with a mystical unity, consistency and stability which have no space for change or adaptation. Thus, Islam and Muslims seem to be on an inevitable collision course with 'our way of life' and 'our values' and far from wanting peaceful coexistence and harmony.

If we want therefore to understand Islam and Muslims as they are, we must first understand ourselves and then learn to ask the right questions. Only then will our knowledge of Islamic theology and history be able to help us to make sense of events unfolding around us.

The first cluster of issues we need to reflect on is who we are and why we are interested in this subject. If Islam has been around for 1,400 years, why only now has it become one of the most talked about issues for the British and European churches? Clearly, the most straightforward answer to this is the terrorist attacks committed by Islamist extremists. The 11 September attacks in the US, the July bombs in London and a host of global explosions and military clashes have brought Islam onto the main stage of international media. Violence committed in the name of Islam, filtered through problematic media reports and exploited by politicians to win votes, has shaped our fears.

The list of worries goes far beyond the question of Islamist terror, since Britain like every other country in the world has been going through substantial social change, which creates anxiety and a host of struggles in people's minds. We see increasing numbers of Muslims in our neighbourhoods, with their strange dress, food and lifestyles. People of a different religion, who were once far-away subjects of a long-gone empire, are now equal citizens with an equal claim to be British. Panic over immigration issues and debates around 'British identity' and the role of Christianity in the UK all help to shape how we process information on Islam and how we analyze the root of the problem – and thus arrive at solutions.

Common mistakes

The second cluster of issues that we need to subject to scrutiny is the methodologies we use to make sense of Islam and Muslims. Often our wrong conclusions are caused by the use of wrong methodologies, even though the information gathered in the process might be correct in its own terms.

The most common mistake when trying to make sense of what is going on in the world is to unify a host of different issues into one single issue: Islam. I often find myself out of breath while listening to or taking part in debates on Islam in the UK or elsewhere. Speakers or audiences melt politics and tensions in the contemporary Middle East together with disconnected points in the history of Islam. The development of Islamic theology, the failures of British governments over immigration and security issues and the failures of certain groups of Muslims in adjusting to life in Britain are all bundled into the single issue of Islam. Yet, all of these issues are distinct and independent from each other.

A failure to separate these different issues automatically leads us to see the world through the lenses of a Manichean battle between light and darkness. Islam emerges as one entity and Muslims as almost a robotic, monolithic, single body. Thus our next door neighbour is not simply Ahmed, who is a kind family man and wants the best for his children and worries over his mortgage and job. Ahmed gets effaced and vacuumed into a unified narrative, becoming all that is wrong with the world and Britain. In actuality, Ahmed is only Ahmed, a Muslim living in Britain.

This mistake is mirrored in Muslim countries. When a Muslim turns on the TV, sees USA attacking Iraq and then hears about the Crusades some eight hundred years ago, he perceives a unified attack on Muslims and Islam everywhere in the world by the Christian West. A new Crusade is being fought against Muslims. The Christian living next door – George – is not just a Christian Arab or a Turk; he is a spy for the CIA, working in secret to destroy Muslim societies. But, we know that George is a Christian Palestinian, whose political views, worries and patriotism are the same as his Muslim neighbour's, and George has nothing to do with wars carried on by other countries, current or historical. Most significantly, there is no 'Christian West' and no 'united West' engaged in a 'Crusade' to defeat Muslims.

The second most common mistake is deductive theological thinking. This type of enquiry does not start with the complex reality as it is and then seek inductively to come to a conclusion as to what might be happening around us. On the contrary, it starts with a principle, a theological idea, a verse from the Qur'an or a saying from *Hadith*, and from there it proceeds to reach conclusions.

For the deductive mind, Islam might seem forever alien to democracy and secularism for one theological reason or the other. Although this logic is attractive and claims to provide a quick answer, it is far from being helpful or true. The interaction of religions with politics and individual and collective identities is complex, and can never be understood simply in theological terms.

The deductive mind, for example, is doomed to fail in making sense of the 1979 revolution in Iran and the current semi-theocracy that rules the country. It would argue that the revolution was an expression of Islam's desire to take control of countries and regimes, and how it runs the country is a textbook example of their religious beliefs being shown up in their true colours. A more sophisticated version of this argument would add that *Shi͏ᶜa* faith has always been a reactionary movement in conflict with its *Sunni* counterpart, and that it is therefore not surprising to see reactionary *Shi͏ᶜite* zeal overtaking a country.

As perfect as these arguments sound, they simply do not correspond to the reality of how and why the 1979 revolution happened and what are the dynamics of religion and politics in contemporary Iran. The revolution happened because of the serious economic and political failures of the Shah's regime and a unified reaction from all segments of Iranian society, including both communists and religious people. The clerics, especially Ayatollah Khomeini, were last minute additions and winners in a long-term power game.

Even the Ayatollah's theo-political idea of 'the rule of the righteous jurist' over the country is a brand new idea in *Shi͏ᶜite* theology, and is still regarded by other high level *Shi͏ᶜite* clerics as not being orthodox. Clerics and theologians opposing the official state theology continue to face imprisonment and ostracism.

The conflict in Northern Ireland could provide a similar example in our own region of the failure of deductive thinking. Can the tensions between Republicans and Unionists be seen only as a clash between 'Catholicism' and 'Protestantism' and understood by looking at the Bible and the writings of Augustine, Martin Luther and Erasmus? If various Irish political figures of different denominations might use religious discourse, can we honestly think that this is all because of ideas of *sola scriptura* and *sola fide*? If it was so, then why don't we see similar clashes between Catholics and Protestants all around the world?

There must be something else going on in Ireland, unique to its own context, which brings together a host of contemporary and historical socio-political issues that result in polarization, mistrust and violence. It cannot be simply an inevitable clash between the universal and timeless theological beliefs of Protestant and Catholic traditions. Yet it seems that we see no problem in making the same mistake when it comes to understanding the complex relationship between Islam, politics and violence.

Another major mistake is essentialism, which is an attempt to find an inherent and unmoving essence of Islam. The clearest example of this response was the frenzy we witnessed following 9/11 attacks on the World Trade Center in New York. For so many reasons it was only a matter of time before a major incident occurred in the USA. Since we have been sanitized from exposure to violence and made to feel that we were untouchable, the shock of witnessing destruction within the West caused a serious disorientation. Why were we under attack?

The politicians were ready to provide an easy way out which would not lead us to question the policies and actions of our governments overseas. 'Our freedom' was under attack from individuals who did not share 'our ideals'. Yet, no one was attacking Sweden, one of the most 'free' countries in the world, or the offices of Nobel prize or Bodleian library, and no terrorist was speaking about hating 'freedom'. This desire to find an easy answer was expressed by many commentators and, sadly, by the majority of Christians who argued that militant *jihad* was essential to Islam and what we were witnessing was an inevitable outcome of the core of Islam, which was a violent religion with a mandate to kill.

The arguments about how terrorist acts could be faithful to Islam hindered us from seeing the complexity of the issue. This led to a failure in understanding what we were facing and therefore what we should do. Our governments responded to al-Qaʿida terror in a conventional military and diplomatic way under the banner of 'the war on terror'. The disastrous outcome of this response was to make the world much more unsafe and terrorism much more attractive than before. Wise commentators were quoting the Qurʿan and Islamic history to provide answers and solutions, causing only a deepening of the rift between 'East' and 'West', as if both categories were fixed and clear-cut, and thus offering self-fulfilling prophecies of doom and gloom.

Meanwhile al-Qaʿida was drawing condemnation – even from fellow *jihadists* and Islamists – for not being 'faithful to Islam'. Not only was the organization causing security concerns for Muslim states and harming fellow Muslims, but it was condemned by most Muslims in the world as not being an expression of true Islam, and representing a complete break from traditional understanding of *jihad* and the use of violence.

Unlike Hamas and Hizbullah, which represent traditional understandings of the use of violence for protection, or the achievement of a geo-political victory for
Muslims within a rigid command structure which
demands theological alignment and piety, al-Qaʿida has
no definite geo-political goals, no demand for theological submission to an official ideology, no expectation of
Islamic piety, no clear dictates as to what its followers
should do and what the limits of their actions should be,
but only an appeal to harm the 'great Satan' wherever its
manifestations are found.

In this way, al-Qaʿida had not only democratized *jihad*
by reducing it to a personal act and removing the control
of a rigid hierarchy, but created something brand new by
melting a host of *Sunni* and *Shiʿite* ideas within a global
world view which was different from historical and
modern understandings of *jihad*. But of course, essen-
tialist thinking about Islam missed all of this out since it
was on a quest to find an unchangeable core of Islam.

Yes, there certainly must be a correlation between certain theological trends within the broad umbrella of
Islam and terrorism; but correlation does not mean cau-
sation. Is it simply because of a qurʿanic verse or a
Hadith that young Muslim men and women seek to kill
themselves in suicide attacks?

Theology indeed offers a strong reference point that
serves to give strength to the individual through a deep
belief in a cosmic cause; it also provides comfort and justification for seemingly destructive acts. This, however,
is only one of the variables that would lead individuals
to end their lives. Personal disillusionment, alienation,
lack of hope and future, promise of financial and social
support to remaining family members, a chance to assert
an active presence in an ever-aggressive age, anger at the
discriminatory and imperial foreign policies of Western

countries, and a host of other 'mundane' variables all play an important role in leading an individual to terrorist acts.

It is only when we become fully aware of strong currents that shape our perception, and our own failures in tackling extremely complicated issues that we can humbly proceed to scrutinize Islam. This becomes all the more evident in the central question with which this chapter is concerned: is Islam compatible with ideals of democracy and the problematic idea of 'our way of life'?

If one approaches this question along the lines of the common failures already described, the answer is simple: 'No! Islam is a static force and Muslims are zombies under its spell.'

This, of course, is not simply an intellectual failure in an abstract debate which has no real life implications. Such a premature and problematic conclusion leaves us out in the cold without any hope. We share the planet and the country with millions of Muslims, and Islam will always remain one of the biggest and strongest of all religions in the world. We simply do not have the luxury to retreat into our bubble and mourn the seemingly inevitable outcomes.

The antidote to this straight-out 'No' is not a naïve over-glorification of Islam, or an airbrushing of genuine points of concern, but a framework that can enable us to interact with all of the dimensions of the issue in a constructive manner.

Plain truths, positive and negative

We need to hold tightly to a few plain truths, which can be a source of hope for us. First of all, the relationship of Islam to politics is dynamic. All across the centuries,

Muslims have lived under a diverse range of political structures, ranging from tribes to larger emirates, empires, nation states, autocratic police states and semi-theocratic regimes.

There is not a single form of government or model of political engagement that Islam rigidly enforces. Pious Muslim movements have promoted a host of views on the engagement of Islam and its clergy with politics: some have seen this engagement as a sin and as something impure, while others have seen it as an essential obligation. What we today call 'political Islam' is a brand newcomer to Islamic thought which has sprung up since the 1960s and drawn its goals and aims not only from the Qur^can but equally from Marxist and other modernist political perspectives. There is therefore no intrinsic problem for Muslims in living in Europe under post-Christian secular democracies.

Secondly, most Muslims in the world live in secular and modern societies and want it to remain so. Today, out of some forty-four Muslim-majority nations, only around ten give some constitutional provisions relating to Islam as the state religion, and only a handful use aspects of *shari^ca* law in their legal systems, often limiting *shari^ca* to personal status matters. Even in the most radical example of Saudi Arabia, there are increasing signs of modernization – such as the development of a Ministry of Justice, an appeal system and efforts to codify Islamic jurisprudence. It is therefore extremely problematic to think that the majority of Muslims living in Britain ultimately want a *shari^ca* state.

Thirdly, human rights, secularism and democracy have been increasingly internalized by Muslims. This is not only visible in the growing strength of civil societies in Muslim nations, but also in the courageous attempts of Muslims to hold their autocratic rulers to account through appeal to international human rights law. This even includes the court cases brought against Turkey at the European Court of Human Rights by pious Muslim women, who are not allowed to wear headscarves at the universities and in the civil service. Today, oppressed Muslims all over the world appeal to 'democracy', 'freedom' and 'human rights' in order to be able to enjoy the same freedoms we rightfully cherish.

Fourthly, not every issue we confront is about Islam. The best example of this is the social cohesion issue in the UK. It is true that certain groups of Muslims struggle in adjusting to life in Britain. New Muslim immigrants, especially from less educated and rural origins, often retreat into the mentality of ghettos and safe-havens. On the other hand, significant portions of Muslims are able to integrate their faith, their home cultures and their values with their new British nationality, which suggests that the issue here might not be Islam itself.

This is also clear in the fact that cohesion problems are not unique to Muslims. The same problems apply to all immigrants around the world, including British families moving to Spain. Immigration and naturalization pose serious challenges and difficulties, both for the newcomer and the host, and it often takes generations for the immigrants to be fully integrated. Therefore, there is no 'eternal' reason why Muslim immigrants cannot live in harmony with the rest of British society.

These simple truths show that Islam is dynamic because it evolves and changes, and that the majority of Muslims are much closer to 'us' than we think. This should give us a strong hope that we can indeed work together to address and overcome the ills that are haunting both parties.

One must at the same time, however, also state a few other truths. There are certain areas of concern which demand urgent attention and reform by Muslims, and present a continuous challenge to us.

The treatment of apostates, those who leave Islam for another religion, remains a serious human rights issue both in Muslim-majority countries and here in the UK. The harsh reactions shown to Muslim-background Christians continue to be fuelled by traditional Islamic theology and jurisprudence. And the treatment of non-Muslim minorities across the Islamic world falls dramatically short of standards set by international human rights law.

A mixture of traditional theological views, supported or created by patriarchal social structures, continues to cause the denial of women's rights, to hinder equality and to block the public role of women. Similarly, a host of cultural values around the notions of shame and honour continue to result in honour killings and forced marriages.

Violence committed in the name of Islam continues to find an appeal in certain segments of the Islamic community and preachers of hate are not hard to find, even in Britain's mosques. Sinister and non-violent Islamist organizations continue to pursue their dreams of an Islamic world, and seek to promote Islam and the supremacy of Muslims in any way they can.

Even amidst these ongoing concerns, however, one sign of hope is the increasing number of courageous Muslim men and women of deep faith who are standing up for human rights, tolerance, peace and reconciliation. This does not make problems disappear overnight, but it gives us a strong reason to believe in the possibility of a shared future together.

Chapter 9

Part 1: Responding to Islamic Radicalism in Britain

Anthony McRoy and John Azumah

The watershed for the emergence of Islamic radicalism in the UK was the publication in 1988 of Salman Rushdie's *The Satanic Verses*, which was seen by many Muslims as an attack on the Prophet Muhammad. The Gulf War of 1990–91 accelerated the disenchantment felt by some UK Muslims as Western military forces invaded a Muslim country. Of particular concern was the presence of Western troops in Saudi Arabia, an act which was seen by many Muslims as a violation of the *Hadith* (narration of the Prophet) banning non-Muslims from Arabia.[1]

The sense of being a beleaguered community was exacerbated by the Bosnian crisis, beginning soon after the conclusion of the Gulf War. Prior to the outbreak of the Balkan conflict, most British Muslims were unaware of even the existence of the Bosnian Muslims. This in itself contributed to the shock experienced when the crisis began. The community suddenly discovered a nation of co-religionists native to Europe; but they received this revelation through TV pictures depicting forced deportations, burning houses, weeping women complaining of rape, and corpses, including dead children. The message they imbibed – and that Islamic activists promoted – was that Muslims in Europe were endangered.

In the British context, there was a link between the Rushdie and Bosnian crises. Every Muslim attempt at lobbying the British government to suggest a Kuwait-style UN military intervention to aid the Bosnians was dismissed. Suspicions arose in the community that the government was unwilling to help the Bosnian Muslims precisely because of their religion. The message British Muslims received was that they were endangered in Europe, simply because of their faith.

Islamic violence in the UK has taken several forms. Some young Muslims – especially students – support militant groups such as *Hizb ut-Tahrir* or *Al-Muhajiroun*. Others have taken an even more radical position by supporting or even joining al-Qaʿida, and the most obvious example of this was 7/7 – the 2005 London bombings. To this we should add another form of radicalism which is less political than that demonstrated by al-Qaʿida, but no less sinister – communal violence.

Examples of communal violence

In 2001, riots by Muslim youths erupted in Oldham, Burnley and Bradford. A police report on Oldham stated that 'The majority of violent racist incidents are perpetrated by Asians on whites, which is an ongoing trend involving primarily Pakistani and Bangladeshi teenagers.'[2] For example, one Muslim youth in Oldham's majority-Muslim Glodwick estate was reported by *The*

Guardian as referring to signs around the estate which stated 'Whites enter at your own risk'. This source felt it was a matter of revenge and that Muslims should give as good as they get from white youths.[3]

Significantly, Gerry Sutcliffe, Labour MP for Bradford South, recognized the reality of this problem: ' . . . there is a core of people who . . . want to create no-go areas.'[4] The police report into 'racial' attacks revealed that 'the issue of racist attacks on whites dates back to 1992 . . .'[5] The date is significant since it ties in with the Gulf and Bosnian crises.

In Burnley, Muslim youth violence was nakedly sectarian. In 2000, Muslims purchased some land behind Living Hope Christian Fellowship's chapel, and unsuccessfully approached the church to sell its property to allow construction of a mosque. In March, cars outside the chapel were vandalized, and leaflets attached to windscreens warning, 'Allah is the one true God. Leave now.' In April, the chapel doors were daubed with the word 'ALLAH', and once again the same leaflets were found. Two weeks later, while the congregation were at Bible study, the chapel was petrol-bombed. In October, the car belonging to Dave Bullock, church pastor, was petrol-bombed while parked outside his house, with a leaflet attached 'Allah is the one true God. You must leave – it could be you next.'

Likewise in Bradford in 2002 churches were vandalized, and pastors and church officials physically attacked.[6] Revd. Paul Bilton of St Columba's and St Wilfrid's, Horton Grange, stated that they had received physical threats from Muslim youths, and also had his church threatened with arson. Sexual threats were made against his wife. In his area, Muslim youths also harassed other whites and Hindus. Similarly, Revd. Paul Hackwood of St Margaret's Thornberry faced intimidation from Muslim youths, and threats were made against his family. St Phillip's Church, Girlington, was attacked by about fifty Muslim youths who dumped rubbish into the church and set it on fire.[7] They also smashed a stained-glass window dating back to 1860 and destroyed furniture. Its minister, Revd. Tony Tooby was chased with cries of 'Get the white b*******!', and had the back windscreen of his car smashed as he attempted to escape the gang.

This was the latest in a stream of assaults on the building that included the front door being vandalized a number of times and finally being attacked with a battering ram. At Easter the leader of the Brownies was chased by a Muslim mob shouting 'Christian bitch'.[8] The BBC programme reported the priest at St Cuthbert's RC church as stating that Muslims from the neighbouring mosque had urged him to close the building, and when he refused, Muslim youths began to threaten him, 'We'll get it [*the church*] one day!' This intimidation climaxed with the hanging of the caretaker's dog. Another church, St Clement's, was the victim of arson in October and again in November, causing tens of thousands of pounds of damage. This followed an unsuccessful approach by the neighbouring mosque to purchase the building.

A black majority Pentecostal church, Victor Road Church of God of Prophecy, was also attacked over a period of several years.[9] A spokesman reported that virtually all the building's top windows had been stoned, and protective mesh cut. At various times Muslim youths stormed in and overturned the chairs, shouting that the Christians should get out and sell the church to be turned into a mosque. Just before Bonfire Night, some Muslims threw fireworks into the church and then smashed the pastor's car window. Some Muslims – including even children – frequently abused worshippers outside the building. An Asian family who joined the church were the object of particular harassment, and Muslims often stormed in demanding to speak to them.

Attacks on ministers and churches continue to occur across Britain. In March 2008, Canon Michael Ainsworth was assaulted by Muslim youths in the grounds of his church, St George-in-the-East at Tower Hamlets, east London.[10] The police described this attack as a hate crime, although the judge at the subsequent trial accepted a defence plea rejecting this. However, in May, another vicar in the same borough, Revd. Kevin Scully, of St Matthew's Church, Bethnal Green, was also assaulted by Muslim youths in an apparent hate crime.[11] In February 2009, Zion Baptist Church in Rochdale and its pastor, Revd. Dennis Rigg suffered sectarian attacks by Muslim youths.[12] In March, an Asian Minister, Revd. Noble Samuel, was viciously assaulted by three Muslim men outside the Venus TV station in west London.[13] The geographical spread of such sectarian attacks and their increasing number, together with an apparent lack of zeal by the authorities in addressing them, suggests that the future does not bode well for communal peace in Britain.

Jihadi violence

Prior to 9/11, Osama bin Laden had already emerged as the hero of some young British Muslims, with his writings and tapes enjoying increasing circulation, as observed by Fuad Nahdi on the BBC1 programme *The Koran and the Kalashnikov*.[14] *Q-News*, reviewing the programme, noted that it ended with how British Muslims are responding: 'The increasing frustrations of seeing their fellow Muslims as the enemy is provoking many young men to seek combat training and voice their anger against Western power in more controversial ways.'[15]

The Sunday Times noted that, according to Muslim sources in the UK, it is thought that as many as 2,000 young Muslims travel abroad annually for training.[16] A Birmingham Muslim, Bilal Ahmed, 24, who was fighting for an Islamist group called Jaish-e-Mohammed, was allegedly killed in a suicide bombing in Kashmir, in which his action also killed six Indian soldiers.[17] Another Birmingham Muslim, this time a convert, was apparently killed when America bombed the al-Qaʿida base.[18] Another important indication of radicalization was the action of the British 'martyrs' Omar Khan Sharif and Asif Mohammed Hanif who sacrificed their lives in Tel Aviv in 2003, killing three people. A further case was the 'shoe bomber', Richard Reid, who tried to blow up an American plane in 2001.

Another watershed in 2005 was the attack against London on 7 July with bombings on the underground in Aldgate, Edgeware Road, Russell Square and on a bus in Tavistock Road. Britain had faced terrorist outrages before, notably by the IRA, but this time there were two essential differences: three of the four bombers were from mainland Britain, and the attacks were all 'martyrdom operations'. Over fifty people were killed in the attacks.

Some conclusions

It can be seen that Islamic radicalism is multifaceted, in terms of expression, group origins and aims. In some cases it is aimed against the Saudis, while in others its goal is to change UK government policy by tactical electoral strategy. Its most ambitious goal is the conversion of Britain, both in terms of popular faith identity, and political and constitutional considerations. Demands for the incorporation of *shariᶜa* law into the British legal system, whether at personal or even territorial level, is an indication of what the future holds. Of pressing urgency is the increasing sectarian violence in the UK. Whilst the authorities are naturally concerned about the terrorist threat manifested on 7/7, there has been a tendency to downplay or even ignore communal violence, most notably when it is expressed in assaults upon churches and pastors. The last-mentioned is of particular concern for evangelical Christians, and the evidence suggests that this problem is likely to increase in incidence and ferocity.

Part 2: An Interview with John Azumah

Interviewer: Is Islam intrinsically violent?

When people ask me this question I always respond in the same way: it depends on where you're looking from. The assumption behind the question is that Islam's sources, especially the Qurᶜan, are intrinsically violent. If the Qurᶜan is intrinsically violent it means that every Muslim who reads or recites it would go out and commit violence. There are 1.5 billion Muslims in the world. So if we say that Islam is intrinsically violent, it means that every single one of them is a terrorist. Obviously that is not the case.

What we have to remember is that people are responsible for their own actions. There are violent texts in the Qurʿan, of course, but Muslims would say exactly the same thing about the Bible. Or look at Hollywood films – how many of them are sexually explicit or violent? Yet not everyone who goes out to watch an American film is going to act in the same way. Humans are responsible for the choices they make in life; it is simplistic to blame religious texts for what believers do. So when Muslims commit violent acts they themselves are responsible for what they do; blaming a faceless and nameless 'Islam' stops people being held accountable for their actions.

The overwhelming majority of Muslims around the world live peacefully with their neighbours, yet the logical conclusion we should draw, if people really believe that Islam is intrinsically violent, is that Islam should be banned. Surely no sensible person would suggest such a thing. So what we need to do is find other ways of talking about this issue.

I believe that Islam has seeds of violence within its history, traditions and texts, but that it is social and political and economic realities which provide the soil for these seeds to bear fruit. Young Muslims in Britain are often angry about our involvement in Iraq and Afghanistan, and some go back to the Qurʿan to find evidence which validates and justifies their anger. A Muslim in Ghana, on the other hand, would not react in the same way because there are no local conditions which encourage them to do the same. This issue is more complex than simply saying 'Muslim violence is all caused by political factors' or 'violence is all intrinsic to Islam'. It is not as black and white as that. The point is that if we should use the actions of a violent minority to make sweeping generalizations that Islam is intrinsically violent, then by the same logic, we can use the actions of the peaceful majority to argue that Islam is intrinsically peaceful.

Interviewer: How do you account for Islamist violence?

I have a Muslim friend who, in a fit of rage one evening, hit his wife. When I spoke to him about it later he said, 'I know what you Christians would say: you would tell me that I beat my wife because it is permitted in the Qur'an. But that is not the case. I simply got angry and lost control.' The point he was making was this: although we might want to go back to religious texts to explain why people do things, we have to allow for the fact that humans are broken, sinful people. That fact causes much more violence than any religious text or tradition. Because we are fallen and sinful there is always a mess wherever we go. In fact I would say that there is always evil wherever we go, because we are prone to do evil things.

We Christians are often too quick to judge. Do we also go back to the Bible to account for the evil things that Christians do? How about secular people? I think that our human weakness is much more responsible for the things we do than the religious texts we read. Humans will latch onto any excuse to do evil things. I have met wonderful, gracious Muslims and horribly evil Christians, so how do we account for that? By blaming the religious texts that they read? I don't think so. Humans are not robots. We ourselves are responsible for our actions and we need to be held accountable for them. That means that we certainly need to condemn acts of Islamist violence when they occur, but we also need to recognize that not all Muslims behave in the same way.

Interviewer: Does Islam have to be in a position of political power?

Historically Islam progressed from the situation in Mecca, where it was relatively weak, to the situation in Medina, where Muhammad founded a community. When this happened he had to find ways of running and organizing that community, and a political unit therefore emerged. Since then Islamic religious practice has always been worked out in that kind of context – not necessarily a context of numerical majority, but definitely a context of political power and dominance. Muhammad needed Medina to actualize the things that he preached in Mecca. In that sense, Islam is intrinsically territorial.

However, Islam has not always felt the need to be in charge. In sub-Saharan Africa, Islam has been in the minority for centuries. Muslims in places like Ghana, where I am from, have lived alongside other believers for centuries. There was even a strong Islamic tradition in some parts of western Africa known as the Jakhanke, which asserted that religion and politics should not be mixed, as some Muslims felt that political power would corrupt their religion. In the nineteenth century, there was a militant revolution in parts of West Africa which brought in a new logic which stated that the religious affiliation of a territory depended upon the religious affiliation of its leader. Land ruled by a non-Muslim was therefore not *dar al-Islam* and was a legitimate target for *jihad*. This changed the situation. From now on the religious affiliation of a territory depended upon its ruler, not its inhabitants. For Muslims, political power was important because it enabled them to introduce *shari'a* law. For many Muslims today, *shari'a* law determines whether a territory is Islamic or not, and the issue is therefore of massive importance.

The issue of territoriality highlights a clear difference between Islam and Christianity. Territory is not important to Christians. People in the Bible are called and sent. If land were important we would be called to stay where we are! We are on the move all the time, believing that God dwells in us, not in the land we inhabit, whereas Islam calls people to stay and take control and rule. This core difference has huge implications for the ways in which the two faiths relate to each other.

One of the most important elements of the debate over territory is where non-Muslims fit into the Islamic scheme. Historically non-Muslims have been seen as second-class citizens in some Muslim countries. They were referred to as *dhimmis* and were historically obliged to pay a tax to their Muslim overlords. Even today, some parts of the Islamic world are off-limits to non-Muslims – for example, no non-Muslim is permitted to enter the holy city of Mecca. One of the main reasons for Muslim hostility towards the West in the 1990s was the presence of US soldiers in Saudi Arabia. This was considered a huge insult, as they are seen as non-believers trespassing on holy land. It is important to recognize that, in Muslim territory, non-Muslims are not seen as equals. In a multi-faith context, this raises a lot of issues. So it's important that we continue to discuss this topic with our Muslim friends and with the authorities.

Interviewer: How about 'no-go areas'?

There are two ways of looking at the issue of 'no-go areas': either as a concession of land or as a land grab. As I see it, when Muslims came to the UK from Pakistan or Bangladesh or wherever, they obviously came without land; so they moved to a place where they could afford to buy a house and they stayed there. It is a human tendency for people of the same ethnicity to cluster together. Immigrants have always done this, whether they are Jewish, Muslim, Christian, or anything else. So when more Muslims arrived in the UK, they instinctively moved to the same areas. Since the indigenous people had the same desire to live with people of their own ethnicity, they started to move out as their community changed. So within ten years the community changed completely. Can you blame Muslims for wanting to live alongside people who speak their language, who look similar to them, who understand their cultural and religious traditions? I see this as more of a concession of land by the indigenous people rather than as a land grab by the Muslims. However, when the Muslim community becomes numerous enough and begins to dominate a particular area, they can start to grab because they are more powerful.

It's important to remember that Britain has always received immigrants from around the world, and that it is much more diverse and complicated than we might think. After all, Scotland and Wales are part of our country yet they have their own legal systems and their own parliaments. Muslims are just one more group entering this complex mixture. So far we're actually doing well at managing this situation humbly and effectively.

Part of the problem is that there are two things about British culture which Muslims have yet to learn: self-criticism and the British sense of humour. Muslim culture is about honour and saving face, and the ability of the British to criticize themselves and openly question every aspect of their culture is foreign to them. So when the media criticizes Islam, it comes across as an attack on their faith, which is something they are not used to. This makes community cohesion more difficult. The second thing is the British sense of humour. British people are very gifted at making jokes and at making fun of serious issues; nothing is sacred. The British make jokes about politicians, about the Royal Family, about religion and about everything. That is not part of Islam. You certainly cannot poke fun at Islam or Muhammad at all, as we saw with the Danish cartoon controversy. This represents a serious clash of values which makes it hard for the different communities to understand each other.

Interviewer: How should we respond?

Archbishop Desmond Tutu said something very powerful when he was speaking once to black Christians in South Africa. He said: 'Be nice to the whites. They need you to help them rediscover their humanity.' That speaks a lot about how to respond to Islamic violence. Should we respond in kind? Or should we respond by seeking to help Islamic extremists rediscover their own humanity? There is no doubt that we have seen some horrific instances of violence committed by Islamic extremists. But the question I want to ask is this: what does our Lord require us to do in these situations? Should we compromise our Christian witness by responding in kind, or should we retain our witness in the face of this violence?

Our Christian witness should be three-fold: to seek justice, to love mercy, and to walk humbly with the Lord, as it says in the book of Micah. This means that when we're talking about the persecution of Christians in Muslim countries, which we must, we should not be seen to be undermining genuine Muslim grievances in the UK. We need to be consistent in how we seek justice. We should not allow the issue of Muslim persecution of

Christians to cause us to demonize Islam or to respond in kind. By demonizing Muslims we're not helping them to rediscover their own humanity!

We need to remember the constant need for love and grace. 'Grace' has become rather a dirty word in some evangelical circles when we are discussing Islam. It is as if Muslims don't deserve it. But should we really abandon these core Christian values because some Muslims are attacking us? Should we stop talking about love and grace and forgiveness? That scares me! We use the teaching on love and grace in Christianity as a polemic against Islam, but when anyone suggests that Christians should demonstrate love and grace to Muslims, they are accused of 'going soft' on Islam. The only way to turn this situation around is to demonstrate love and grace to Muslims, even violent Muslims, in order to help them redeem their own humanity.

The final issue is reconciliation. That, for me, is the core of the gospel. We have a ministry of reconciliation. We should therefore always ask ourselves: how do our actions and words help to bring about reconciliation? I don't just mean peacemaking, I mean God reconciling the world to himself through Christ. We can choose to be bridge builders or bridge blowers. And to me, the choice is obvious, if we are true to our own Christian values.

Chapter 10

Issues Related to Education

John Ray OBE

People involved in education in most British cities continually meet Muslims as teachers, children, parents or school governors. It is thus more natural and useful to think of 'Muslims' – who may be *Sufi* or *Salafi*, feminist, radical, communist or none of the above – than of 'Islam'. They may be British Bengali, Somali, Pakistani or Yemeni, and each is influenced by their individual culture. Many are nightly hooked on *EastEnders*!

The context is all-important. In many inner Birmingham schools nearly 100 per cent of the students are listed as 'ethnic minority', in the language of OFSTED. The context is also the secular frame of education, which provides both the freedom to ask questions and the opportunity, in a good school, to consider values in terms of faith. Besides the great pressures that impinge on all our young, Muslim young people struggle with multiple identity and, as they venture into the wider world, with varied levels of prejudice.

Education involves institutions and their control involves a power equation. The defence of personal freedoms becomes an issue whenever an unduly pre-scriptive group, religious or secular, dominates schools.

The pressures of our times, and in particular the politicization of faith, do indeed make it necessary to have a truer understanding of 'Islam'. What is more important than our perception of that faith, however, is our calling as Christians to build relationships, and God's word to us may be his last word to Jonah '. . . should I not be concerned about [Nineveh] that great city?' (Jonah 4:11, NIV). For those of us who have friends who are Muslims, personal relationship and trust are not to be endangered by writing heartless truth.

I write as someone with a lifetime in schools. After ini-tially teaching in Britain and then at Lawrence College, Pakistan, I was for twenty-five years Principal of the Tyndale Biscoe School in Srinagar, Kashmir. This is a diocesan high school with a difference, where my wife and I were intimately bound in with many local people. We witnessed at street level the baneful effects on a mainly Muslim local community of an increasingly politicized and ideological version of Islam alien to the genius of the Kashmiri people. In Birmingham since 1987 I have been a governor in several inner city schools and a trustee of various charities serving the local com-munity. In this chapter, I reflect mainly on my experience as a school governor in Birmingham.

Common values: What makes a good school?

People of all faiths or of none seek common values for their children's schooling. Teachers in particular can smell a good school from the moment they enter. Does the place feel like a genuine community of pupils, teach-ers and non-teaching staff? Is there a brisk friendliness about the place? Is there a sense that, while we all want the best 'results', the school is really about much more than that? Is the school genuinely preparing children for living life to the full?

Though under assault from hugely interfering politicians and bureaucracy, there remains a sturdy liberal tradition in British education. Teachers and teachers' unions are often the best guarantors of this. Christian and Muslim parents resist the permissive tide. For instance, both resist the notion that pre-marital sex is in order when the two persons are 'ready for it'. Teachers in inner city schools, themselves now a deeply cross-cultural body, will respect this. Both Muslim and Christian parents will want to see more respect for authority and age than is commonly accorded today. Both often have high aspirations for their children. As always it is the quality of the head teacher and senior staff which has the greatest impact, and there are very many Christian teachers and head teachers who are salt and light in all the day-to-day pressures.

Christians and Muslims both stand against the dogmatic secularist ideology which is prominent in national and intellectual leadership. Their expectations of the native English include a kind of 'default atheism', while at the same time they sometimes show an uncomprehending deference to a particular expression of Islam from fear of extremism. The extreme political correctness thus engendered fools nobody. Britain urgently needs leaders who are themselves committed Christians and who understand their commitment in terms of justice and service. It also needs all who value the common good to learn more about Muslim people, to grow in friendship and to hold ghettoization at bay. Fear and racism thrive on separation and ignorance. That way lies danger.

Muslims in Britain protest mainly not against Christianity, but against the godlessness which dominates the media and infiltrates our schools. They are mystified that Christians are so reticent about their faith. Many churches still support mission in Africa or Asia while ignoring areas of spiritual need on their doorstep such as the inner cities or the sixties' council estates. Perhaps because of the heritage of the past, Britain is also a mission field of great complexity. There is much to learn and much to encourage for those ready to cooperate with God's surprising initiatives. Schools are where the rubber hits the road.

Faith schools, assemblies and religious education

The phrase 'faith schools' usually refers to Church of England, Roman Catholic or Jewish schools. This may conjure up the village or suburban school, its governors chaired by the vicar, its classes filled by children whose parents may or may not have an intention of Christian commitment, but who know a good school when they see one. Unlike the C of E, the RC's have held on to their secondary schools, which in Birmingham and elsewhere have been a major factor in the uplift of the Irish community and its integration into wider society. Everyone knows that these Christian schools are so valued that no political change would disturb them. Over recent years, partly fuelled by the increasing trend of permissive materialism in mainstream society, a demand for Muslim schools on a parallel 'voluntary aided' basis has been accepted. There is great demand for such schools from a section of the Muslim community, though their performance as measured by OFSTED has been very patchy. Many church schools are multicultural with a

Christian ethos, building cohesion, while Muslim schools are often mono-cultural with an Islamic ethos, tending to isolation.

Since the 1988 Education Act and the mass of regulations that have followed, we have a complex set of approaches which seek to meet the cultural and spiritual needs of all our diverse children. One area where the law is commonly ignored or breached is the requirement for an act of daily collective worship which is to be 'broadly and mainly Christian' unless local needs suggest otherwise. In such cases there is detailed provision for teachers, parents and governors to be consulted when an application is made, for example, for some or all of the children to have some other form of worship. It is here that difficulties can easily arise. *The Times Educational Supplement* in December 1985 estimated that only 6 per cent of maintained schools came close to obeying the 1944 Act's requirement that each day begin with collective worship involving all pupils. The proportion today would hardly be greater. We should be real!

If most schools do not have worship, however, they do have assemblies. Church schools will have approaches to worship which vary greatly in content and tone. Schools in areas where children of varied faith backgrounds are present will usually make successful efforts to stress common values and to be truly inclusive in all that they do and are.

They also provide for, and indeed require, the teaching in most secondary schools of at least two faiths – which are often Christianity and Islam. Birmingham, like other authorities, has a Standing Advisory Council for Religious Education (SACRE), and their Agreed Syllabus for Religious Education (2007) is a model of its kind. A careful reading of this document shows how the essentials of the Christian faith are included in the statutory teaching of RE. In Religious Education the deepest values of human life are shared and discussed. Teachers – Muslim, Christian, of another faith or of none – have both the freedom and the duty to teach the basics of faith to the large number of children who choose this popular subject in GCSE.

The abuse of power

It is important in this context to be aware of abuses which subvert the best intentions of legislation and which, if unchecked, will undermine the basic freedoms of British people. A clear case in point is recorded in *The Times Educational Supplement* of 26 March 2010. In its judgement on the failure of Surrey County Council to protect a Woking head teacher who had been unfairly accused of Islamophobia, the Court of Appeal overturned an attempt to prevent payout of almost £408,000 to Mrs Connor. She had been brought to a point of breakdown by vituperative complaints against her by governors. Lord Justice Sedley spoke of 'a local education authority which had allowed itself to be intimidated by an aggressively conducted campaign to subvert the school's legal status'. Lord Justice Laws said that 'the root of Mrs Connor's breakdown was 'the Council's lamentable capitulation to aggression'.

Where vulnerable individuals face intimidation and aggression it may not be possible to name sources. Mrs Connor is not the only head to have been brought to a point of breakdown. It is a matter of public record that one such – a strong and committed Birmingham primary school head teacher, who had moved to a disadvantaged area to help children – took early retirement in

1993 following a breakdown. The then chair of governors and the small group supporting him disregarded proper procedure and overlooked several strong candidates for headship in order to appointed a lady of Pakistani origin. It later transpired that the latter had not completed her probationary year, had made false statements about overseas qualifications, and had questions of fraud hanging over her. She was subsequently dismissed.

Head teachers do not lightly complain, but in 1994 I took the detailed concerns of five of them to Lady Blatch, the Education Minister. It was not, of course, only head teachers who suffered; Muslim parents who opposed the disruptive activity of those who were always a minority also faced manipulation and intimidation. In an inner city community where everyone knows everyone else's business and probably come from the same village in the Mirpur district of Pakistan, it takes a lot of courage – and is sometimes impossible – to take an independent stand. It is all too easy for white middle-class decision-makers, understanding little of the realities, to listen to the loudest voices and mistake them for the true will and best interests of the community, and especially the needs of the less-educated women and school-age children.

Frank Field, back in the seventies, had won a notable battle with Militant, the extremist socialist group led by Derek Hatton that for a while dominated Liverpool City Council. As I described the Birmingham school scene – as I saw it – about this time, Field commented that the tactics of Militant were identical, using democracy to overturn democracy.

While a more sophisticated replay of a similar scenario has continued in some places, the important difference recently has been that there is now an effective

presence within the British Pakistani community of
voices which prefer assemblies stressing common values to any form of religious collective worship. As one
parent governor said to me, 'I could have sent my children to a religious school but chose not to.' She
certainly did not want to see a Local Education
Authority school moving in that direction. Unfortunately local and national government still tends, as in
the case of the Woking head teacher, to capitulate to
aggression – and also to deception. Whistle-blowers are
rarely popular.

The cause of 'collective worship' is the ideal can-
opener for Islamists. It is difficult to oppose because of
the 1988 Act, and it seems very reasonable. But in practise it can easily become the entrée to a parallel society
for the rising generation of Muslims. Most British Pakistani children and their parents, in my experience, are
loyal to their culture with all its pluses and minuses, but
do not want to be corralled into a ghetto dominated by
a theocracy. The younger generation is very averse to
local *biraderi* power politics and is breaking free of
them. It would be a tragic irony if the British establishment, by its naivety, collusion or cowardice, were to turn
the clock back by giving in to some of these pressures.
Positively it is important that able Christians, among
others, give priority to sharing in school governance,
thus serving to support cohesion and promote the common good.

Islamism – NO! Muslims – YES!

Islamism, which is not a faith but an ideology, is no less
dangerous than al-Qaʿida. It works more subtly, and in
the UK a key part of its frontline is the maintained

schools of our cities. It may operate through mosques or organizations, many of whose members simply desire the best for their children and assume 'Islam' (undefined) is the way forward. A rare degree of discernment is needed for people of all faiths or of none who, at different levels, are responsible for what happens in school. Christians have a particular responsibility.

God's call to Christians in this situation is, on the one hand, to be 'wise as serpents and harmless as doves' (Matt. 10:16, NKJV), and on the other simply to love Muslims. Love involves action and discovery, and the more we discover about our Muslim neighbours and their children in school, the more we will empathize with them.

Like us, they are strangers in our world gone crazy. Like us, they are caught up in world situations they did not choose (Israel-Palestine, Iraq, Afghanistan). Their family support systems can easily become prisons, but at least they are often spared the loneliness and breakdown which mark British life so much today. At their best, Muslims hold to a less fragmented vision of society and their diaspora cultures may be nearer the New Testament pattern than today's degraded Western culture. Subject, like us, to the pressures of globalized capitalism and media, they seek for a better world for their children, and for peace of heart and mind.

Among the pluses of the Muslim presence in Britain has been the return of the faith agenda on the national scene. Christians in the cities, often challenged by Muslim assertiveness, are recovering from the privatization of their faith without seeking to return to a Christendom that is long past. Rather they seek to serve in Christ's name. Those who are teachers or head teachers have, as always, the huge privilege of closeness to children and young people in order to befriend and inspire them.

Beyond teaching there is a fast-growing variety of Christian work, well attuned to today's realities, in urban schools and among young families. Charities such as Youth Encounter and The Feast and pace-setting initiatives such as The Springfield Project in Birmingham[1] all make for a degree of cohesion that government would love to see. There are many open doors in the world of education for Christians to show their love and support for Muslim people.

On a national level the Christian Muslim Forum seeks the good of society as a whole, not just of the two faith communities. Its 2008 conference, which had as its theme 'Belief and Being in School', involved the Association of Christian Teachers and the Muslim Teachers' Association, and addressed the question: 'Is belief relevant to teaching in secular schools and how can faith contribute positively?' One of the valuable aspects of this conference was that teachers and assistants working in secular settings clearly enjoyed each other's company as people of faith. They found much in common with each other and relief from the usual societal position of 'default atheism' which assumes that children and young people in mainstream schools are without faith. Among the list of the many positive benefits of the conference were the following: 'meeting others in a similar professional role from a different faith tradition' and 'the privilege of meeting and sharing with people from various backgrounds including committed Christians and Muslims and an atheist, i.e. sharing our beliefs and journeys'. There is clearly a striking chemistry when members of the Forum meet together. As believers in two very different faiths, they enjoy each other's company and work hard on the patient building of trust.

Conclusion

How do we balance the essential caution dictated by certain negative experiences with some Muslims in education with the very positive input from many others?

John Gray, the secular philosopher, wrote in 1984:

> A stable liberal society cannot be radically multicultural, but depends for its successful renewal across the generations on an under-girding culture that is held in common. This common culture need not encompass a shared religion, but it does demand certain norms and conventions of behaviour . . . in the British case vague but still powerful notions of give and take, of the necessity of compromise and of not imposing private convictions on others, are elements of what is left of the common culture, and they are essential if a liberal civil society is to survive in Britain . . . central are freedom of expression and its precondition, the rule of law.[2]

Today, society *is* 'radically multicultural'. Fortunately, however, many Muslim fellow citizens share the 'norms and conventions of behaviour' described by Gray. And Christians should follow St Paul's advice to pray for our rulers and those in authority so that we may live in peace. Head teachers have reason to be thankful for the Appeal Court judges in the Woking case.

We must also take seriously the warning of Hannah Shah in her book *The Imam's Daughter*: 'Freedom to believe as the individual sees fit – or not to believe for that matter – is a defining feature of civilization. If we no longer have the willingness or strength to defend people's freedom of choice in religion, then we have lost the very foundations of our civilisation. And that way, intolerance and totalitarianism lies.'[3]

Schools provide a really important opening for relationships with our Muslim neighbours. Ed Hussein's *The Islamist* shows clearly that the teachers in his Tower Hamlets primary school, who were strong and supportive in the face of racism, played a vital role in his return from his later active involvement in Islamism. Long-term friendship is a key to bringing even radical Islamists in from the cold desert of extreme frustration with all things Western.

In the multicultural cities of Britain today, especially among the young, the church is very much alive in loving service to all.[4] There are countless young people in our schools – of all faiths and of none – needing inspirational and loving teaching and support. For a Christian teacher, every child matters to God.

Chapter 11

Issues Related to Women

Emma Dipper

When I lived in an Islamic country, I expected to see women wearing some type of *hijab* – the colourful head-scarf worn around the head and shoulders, which leaves the face visible. Alternatively I might expect to see them wear a *burqa* – the dark garment that covers the wearer from head to foot, with netting covering a slit for the woman to see through; or else they might wear the *niqab* – a plain dark garment covering the head and half of the body, including the face, but leaving the eyes visible. I would wear the *chada* (sometimes spelt *'chador'*) – a full-length sheet-like gown in a dark fabric, which covers the entire body; a woman holds up the corner to cover her face, when necessary.

As women scuttled past me, heads facing downwards towards their feet, and their hand holding tightly to the garment below their chin, the following thoughts crossed my mind: 'Underneath that *burqa* there is a woman. But she has no eyes to see and no voice as she shuffles past me. I have no means of identifying her against other women in the street because they are all dressed the same. How can I relate? How can I make any connection at all?'

Over the weeks and months that followed I learnt to stop in the street when a woman passed by, greet her in her language and look into the place where I assumed her eyes would be. Within six months I could look across a group of women working in my project – all of whom were fully veiled and wearing the *burqa* – and recognize each one of them. Inanimate shapes had become people whom I could relate to and share everyday experiences.

Today, in British cities, I find myself in a similar position. Few women wear the *niqab* but many are veiled, in keeping with their Islamic tradition. It appears to have grown into a barrier to relationships and understanding, and has become a symbol of not just marginalization but segregation. Following a request made by Rt Hon Jack Straw MP in October 2006 that women in his constituency should remove their *niqab* to help community relations,[1] the response of many Muslims was summed up in these words: 'Veiled women are considered to be ungrateful subjects who have failed to assimilate and are deemed to threaten the "British" way of life.'[2]

The controversy that was stirred up by Straw's comments illustrates how issues related to women can lead to many misunderstandings.

What therefore are some of the issues that Muslim women face in the UK? How should the church respond, and how might individual Christians engage with Muslim women as they understand their issues more fully?

Some preliminary issues faced by Muslim women

Firstly, we must acknowledge the wide diversity among Muslim women in the UK because of differences in socio-economic, generational and cultural factors, according to their particular place of origin and status at birth. Whilst some will be limited by language and have a belief system based upon Folk Islam, which is common among women in rural Islamic communities, others are from the upper classes and are trained to bring significant contributions to the fields of medicine, academia and law. Increasingly, white British women are converting to Islam, many of whom have studied the Qur'an in depth and have fully embraced the religion.

Secondly, it is vital to understand the power of 'honour' and 'shame' in Islamic culture. One community worker described it in this way:

> Shame and dishonour are the biggest issues within the family and community. As a woman, you can never do anything in which your family loses face. You may object to how you are treated and even speak to older women about it but they simply tell the younger women to cope with it.[3]

Thirdly we need to be careful about the way we use language to refer to 'submission' and 'oppression'. While women in many traditional societies are thought of as being subject to the authority of men, many Muslims in the West speak of how Islam liberates women. 'The Qur'an provides clear-cut evidence that a woman is completely equated with man in the sight of God in terms of her rights and responsibilities.'[4]

Eman Penny, a white British convert to Islam, expresses her sense of empowerment because she is able to live and dress as a Muslim woman. Instead of speaking about being told what to wear and how to behave, she emphasises her willingness to worship God through a circumspect lifestyle. She understands the reactions of non-Muslims, however, and adds: 'You feel like you have to smile at other people just in case they think you are oppressed!'

Some obvious issues

Honour-based abuse

According to the Centre for Social Cohesion Report in 2010, honour-based crimes have increased within the UK. On average twelve to thirteen women are killed in the UK every year as honour punishments.[5] Although this is a relatively small yet disturbing figure, it is likely to be higher as some deaths are carefully described as suicide.

Honour-based abuse is not simply between husband and wife, but violations against the woman, in which the wider family are the perpetrators – including the woman's sons, brothers and sisters, as well as the extended family and in-laws.

How are we to account for this concept of dishonouring the name of the family? Unlike the Judeo-Christian view of marriage, which suggests the idea that a man and woman leave their own family to join together to make another family, for Muslims the parental authority and control continue throughout their lives. Dishonour occurs if the 'children' publicly defy their parent in a way that results in their losing status in the community.[6] They can defy their family by wearing Western clothes, copying Western attitudes or behaviour such as socializing with the opposite sex, using drugs or alcohol or by provoking gossip that brings the name of the family into disrepute, even if the reports are neither accurate nor true.

In his analysis of why honour-based crimes are so prevalent in Western societies, H. Bradby suggests that when a community is taken out of its original rural setting it is not able to operate in the same way in the new urban culture and context where 'Less [social standing] is gained from maintaining honour and reputation when one resides in an urban setting such as Glasgow.' Urban life in Britain brings opportunities to girls and women which are very different from those they enjoyed as wives and mothers in traditional Islamic societies, and the need for parental control expresses itself in honour-based abuse of different kinds.[7]

Female circumcision

In traditional cultures, a girl's honour rests on her virginity and fidelity and any potential risk of her losing her virginity results in the highest level of shame. This is one of the reasons why girls are subjected to circumcision or 'female genital mutilation' (FGM), the practice of removing or cutting a girl's external genitalia. This results not only in intense pain, but also in emotional trauma and other health problems.

Statistics reveal that 75,000 women in the UK have undergone FGM and 20,000 are at risk of FGM annually.[8] Almost all Muslim communities in the UK have practised or continue to practise FGM but it is most common in Somalian, Eritrean, Sudanese and Ethiopian communities. I can confirm this from my own experience as a community midwife in south London, where I would refer at least one woman a week to the FGM clinic for advice and to arrange corrective surgery following the delivery of their baby.

It is estimated that 2,000 girls are being circumcized inside the UK each year, and a new trend has developed of practitioners being brought from the 'home country' to perform the procedure in the UK with the cost being shared between families.[9] The FGM Act 2003 protects British nationals and UK residents against FGM, which is legally recognized as a form of child abuse.[10]

Beating of wives

While not all Muslim men abuse their wives or female relatives, the beating of women is very common, even if not officially reported. In a book called *How to Make Your Wife Happy*, the following instruction is given to men on how to treat their wives: 'The last solution is (when allowable) lightly hitting her . . . He should do it only in extreme cases of disobedience, for example refusing intercourse without cause frequently, constantly not praying on time, leaving the house for long periods of time without permission nor refusing to tell him where she had been . . .'[11]

Forced marriage

It is a common practice for marriages to be arranged across the Muslim community. This can be done with both partners being involved in the process of decision-making and can lead to lifelong marriages. This, however, is different from forced marriage, which is defined by the Muslim Council of Great Britain as 'a marriage without consent' and is described as 'unacceptable in both UK and Islamic law where mutual consent is prerequisite of any marriage'. According to the Forced Marriage Unit (FMU), 1,680 cases were reported in 2009.[12]

A community worker reported to me that she observes forced marriage going on and sees many cross-cultural and other difficulties when a bride is brought into the UK to marry a man who has been raised in Britain. One young bride spoke of the fact that her marriage was still not consummated after two years of marriage. The British government now offers awareness training for young people about 'forced marriage' and how to use the Forced Marriage Act 2008 to apply injunctions if there are plans being made to take a child or young person out of the country to marry against their wishes.[13]

Some less obvious issues

Isolation

One community worker in a Muslim community feels that the greatest issue for Muslim women in the UK is 'isolation'. Professionals working with these women follow a needs-based approach to help them in these situations. But one of the main reasons for isolation is that Muslim women are often unable to speak English and therefore cannot socialize – or do not wish to socialize – with the wider society. Jenny Taylor referred to the work of Werner Menski, who describes the withdrawal of the Muslim community as being an 'inward migration' which results in the preference to withdraw from mainstream society for the comfort of remaining inside the Muslim community.[14]

One outcome of this separation is increased aggression towards Muslim women whose clothing makes them stand out in public. Eman Penny (a British convert to Islam) told me, 'Before 9/11 people assumed you were a simple woman from a village; you were seen as stupid but harmless. After 9/11 that all changed; 12 Sept 2001 was the first time I got shouted at in the street for wearing my *hijab*.'

Verbal abuse

Penny reports regular verbal abuse when walking in the street. She has also been spat at and has stopped going out in the evening in an attempt to avoid provocation. She says no other Muslim woman she knows would go out to the shops in late afternoon, and the whole community stays indoors when England is playing football to avoid unnecessarily aggravating supporters. This is confirmed by Jenny Taylor, who describes veiling as promoting segregation and that it is 'culturally demeaning [to Western sensibilities] and therefore acts as a provocation.'

Political issues

In recent years, political issues have sometimes made verbal abuse more intense. After 9/11, another woman says, 'How can I have a rational discussion or give a defence to someone shouting at me in front of my children, "It's you what bombed the towers!"?'

Whatever the reasons, Muslim women who are isolated do not have access to the services that they or their family might need. They can therefore appear ignorant and are treated as such. Sian Nicholas explains how Afghan women in west London did not understand why their children needed to apply for a secondary school because they thought that the primary school they attended was good enough – especially compared to the education back in their home country.[15]

Literacy

In a project in South Lambeth for 'new arrivals', or families emigrating to the UK, a system was set up to have letters to parents from the school translated by children in the playground to ensure that mothers understood what was happening in their child's school.

A Christian response to the issues Muslim women face

Biblical starting points

We need to remind ourselves that the Old Testament reflects a culture of honour and shame much more than our own guilt-based culture. It also contains many examples of shameful behaviour, including especially the abuse of women. There is, for example, the story of the rape of Dinah in Genesis 34, which leads to an honour killing in the slaughter of the family of Shechem.

Throughout Scripture we are called to take care of the alien and the poor. Can we therefore find ways to care for those who migrate into our cities and communities? Can we represent their voices if they have none? Are we able to proclaim the truth in response to the lie that unjust behaviour 'is cultural and therefore acceptable'? As Christians, we do not need to accept the unacceptable in terms of our biblical ethics. We can speak with gentleness and respect and be ready to give an answer to all. 'It is better, if it is God's will, to suffer for doing good than for doing evil' (1 Pet. 3:17, NIV).

It must also be highly significant for us in this context that the Gospels record so many examples of Jesus relating to women. The Samaritan woman had led a shameful

life before she met Jesus at the well, and her life was transformed (John 4). The Syro-Phoenician woman demonstrated her wit and her persistence when she asked for
her daughter to be healed (Mark 7:24–30). The woman
who had suffered from haemorrhaging for twelve years
was healed of her distressing condition and released from
her uncleanness (Mark 5:25–34).

Pastoral responses

Women need to reach out and respond to women. In
order to encourage this, special training is needed to
help Christian women to understand the lives of Muslim
women which are often so strongly influenced by Folk
Islam. When one examines the training on Islam that is
available to Christians – including residential courses,
papers, DVDs and books – one clearly sees how mascu-
line much of the content is. But Muslim women do not
debate in the market-place as men do. Muslim women
require women who can accompany them on their journey through life. This does not deny the need for dialogue and a good knowledge of Islam; but the starting
place always has to be relational and without a hidden
agenda.

A community worker who has been working with
Muslim women in the south of England for over twelve
years, speaks of the need for long-term relationships in
which trust can be built – for this is the key. English,
Citizenship and IT classes run by trained, competent
Christians are also a genuine service to a Muslim community and an opportunity for relationship-building.

Women can easily and naturally pray together. This is
generally well received by Muslim women when trust
has been built and they are sharing their personal
concerns and challenges. If we ask if we can pray in the

name of Jesus, this is often quite acceptable and can lead to deeper discussions about what we believe as Christians.

We need be willing to become learners – for example, by asking about rites of passage such as the ceremonies of the naming of a baby, coming of age or funerals. We should be willing to receive their gift of hospitality, but not to abuse it. In many Islamic cultures you should refuse an invitation for a meal about three times before you accept it. Then you know the offer is genuine and they are not asking you out of duty! This learning and sharing is for both mutual benefit and correcting misconceptions about one another's culture and behaviour. This in turn can build a clearer picture of the Christian faith and what it is to be a follower of Jesus.

If we suspect that a woman is suffering abuse or violence of some kind, or if she confides about the violence she is facing at home, the greatest gift we can offer is to listen. The following are some practical suggestions:

a) Meeting them outside their community setting where other Muslims would not be present.
b) Arrange a time that links to the pattern in the day where the woman might already be outside, such as school times.
c) Be willing to sit and listen over a three to four week period – often just being silent.
d) Do not take their phone number unless in extreme circumstances, and don't phone them at any time as you may put them at risk. Pray instead. If they do take your phone number, record it as something neutral like 'clinic'.
e) If a woman does not attend a meeting, do not contact *her*. Try to find out through a third party.

f) Maintain a high level of confidentiality and *do* not report anything unless the woman requests help.

The following is a true story which, while ending in conversion, nevertheless summarizes several of the issues involved in a broader response, as raised in this chapter.

A Christian community worker was introduced to a young Muslim woman who was pregnant. She had heard about a centre that was linked to a church, and she was desperate for help. Her husband had threatened that if the ultrasound scan revealed a baby girl he would kill the woman with the unborn child. With no places available in any women's refuge, the young woman stayed in the offices for three days until it was safe to move to a refuge. She had left her home without any of the necessary documents and needed to attend dozens of meetings with social services and solicitors and then with the embassy of her home country as she did not have British citizenship at that time, nor did she have 'leave to remain'. This was obtained because of the high risk of becoming a victim of an honour-crime. The community worker attended all the meetings with her, translating and sharing in her frustrations and caring for her by simply being alongside. They became so close that the community worker attended the birth of her baby daughter. In the months that followed, the young woman decided to become a follower of Jesus and the community worker had the privilege of dedicating the baby to the Lord in church a few months later.

Chapter 12

Islamic Courts in the English Legal System

Julian Rivers

In February 2008, the Archbishop of Canterbury called for a reconsideration of the place of Islamic courts in the English legal system.[1] He offered this suggestion as part of a programme of 'transformative accommodation' of Islam in the United Kingdom. He left popular commentators outraged and lawyers bemused. For the general limits he set to the possible place of Islamic courts were precisely those which already exist. As a result it is arguable that 'transformative accommodation' is actually rather a good description of what English law already does to Islam. Of course, questions remain about whether the law should be more or less accommodating, or whether the transformation that is effected is wholly positive. But as an idea – that Islamic law is neither embraced in one of its many classical expressions nor wholly prevented from affecting the lives of its adherents, and that the inevitable reshaping of Islamic law that English law effects is to be positively evaluated –

transformative accommodation would seem to be legal orthodoxy. However, the point Rowan Williams was making was neither crazy nor obvious. There is a genuine problem to which he was proposing a possible solution. And even if ultimately one remains unpersuaded, an adjustment in the current legal status of religious courts is worth considering.

1. The significance of Islamic personal law

The debate about whether Islamic law should be given a formal status within English law stretches as far back as 1976, when the Union of Muslim Organisations issued a public call for Islamic personal law to be applied in this country. In order to understand that call, it is necessary to bear in mind both the experience of colonial rule, above all in British India, and the process of legal modernization in Islamic majority countries. In general terms, Islamic law is best understood not as a single system of law, but as a legal tradition or culture, existing in parallel to other great legal traditions of the world such as the Anglo-American, the continental European, Jewish, Hindu or Chinese.[2] The early centuries of Islam were a time of great legal creativity in which Islamic law was developed by scholars through a process of *ijtihad* (constructive interpretation). While sharing common roots in the Qu'ran, *Sunna* and *Hadith*, it quickly developed into four classical schools of interpretation, although there are also many other 'heterodox' versions as well. In practice, it existed for centuries as bodies of customary law in the Middle East, the Indian subcontinent and North Africa, all sharing a certain family resemblance.[3]

Under the British Raj, different communities were allowed a degree of autonomy in internal affairs. Since

the communities were significantly shaped by their religion, this led to the development of a body of 'Anglo-
Muhammadan' law, alongside 'Anglo-Hindu' and
'Anglo-Sikh' law.[4] Choice of law depended on the com-
munity-identity of the parties (or the defendant in the
case of cross-community litigation). The area in which
this law was most distinctive was 'personal law', or law
relating to matters such as marriage, dower, dissolution,
parentage, legitimacy, guardianship, maintenance, gifts,
foundations (*waqf*), pre-emption, wills, estates and
inheritance. In short, it applied to matters of family law
and family property law.

Apart from the colonial experience, the process of
internal legal modernization in the Islamic world can
be dated to the adoption of continental European codes
of commercial, penal and procedural law in the
Ottoman Empire from the 1850s onwards. Then, in
1869–76, the process of codification became domesti-
cated with the creation of the *Majalla* – a uniform
Islamic code of civil obligations based on a composite
of the four main schools of Islamic law. Early in the
twentieth century, some Islamic states started to reform
their family law as well, and this became a key point of
controversy between reformers and traditionalists.
How far can one depart from classical Islamic law
without betraying the tradition? Are the gates of *ijtihad*
open or closed?

Many first generation Muslim immigrants to the
United Kingdom carried with them the expectation that
their personal law would continue to apply.[5] It was an
important marker of community identity, and all the
more as the second generation started to find ways of
accommodating themselves to the surrounding dominant culture. At the same time, the substance of Islamic
personal law represents a key point of contention

between liberal and reforming movements on one hand
and radical traditionalists on the other.

2. Forms of accommodation

English law accommodates Islam in a wide variety of
ways. Given that English courts first came into contact
with significant numbers of Muslims as immigrants and
resident aliens, the first form of accommodation was
through private international law. This in itself indir-
ectly recognizes Islamic law. In any modern legal system, some questions of personal status and capacity are
determined not by reference to the law of the place in
which the litigation takes place, but by reference to the
law of the country with which the individual has the
closest connection. Under English law, the concept used
is that of 'domicile'. Thus, for example, if a question
arises in an English court as to whether a 17-year-old
had the capacity to enter into a marriage abroad in a
country which in general allowed such a marriage, the
answer would depend on the age of marriage under the
law of the person's domicile. The substantive English
law rules do not necessarily apply. The logic behind this
rule is the international law principle of 'comity of
nations', or respect for the cultural and legal conventions of other countries. Where another nation-state has
a legal system based on Islamic law, it is entirely possible that certain legal questions arising in English courts
fail to be resolved according to Islamic law as mediated
through that legal system on account of an individual's
domicile in that state.

However, comity has its limits. Some rules of foreign
law are sufficiently obnoxious to English judges to be contrary to public policy. A good example of the interplay

between these principles is provided by the distinction drawn by English courts between the 'bare *talaq*' and the 'procedural *talaq*'. Suppose a question arises whether a man or woman currently in England has the capacity to remarry on account of a previous divorce according to Islamic law in a country in which forms of Islamic divorce are legally valid and in which the individual was at the time domiciled. The courts draw a distinction between the informal divorce by simple declaration by the husband before witnesses (bare *talaq*) and forms involving court or administrative registration and regulation (procedural *talaq*). The former is not valid, since it is contrary to public policy; it contains insufficient protection for the wife. The latter is valid on account of the comity of nations. Not surprisingly, the law and the courts have sometimes changed in their assessment of the balance between these values: even the marriage of a single man and a single woman under a system which permitted polygamy (the 'potentially polygamous marriage') used to be void according to English private international law.

Unlike the equivalent rules of many other European states, the English law of domicile is relatively flexible. Immigrant residents are likely to gain domicile in England quite quickly. Once this happens, English law applies to its full extent.

The second form of accommodation is a rising level of social and legal acceptance of Islam as a matter of personal belief and behaviour.[6] Within contexts such as schools, the police and prisons, provision is increasingly made for prayer rooms and time for prayers, for traditional forms of Islamic dress and for *halal* food. The recognition of Islam has been more recently reflected in the law creating obligations of non-discrimination on grounds of religion in employment, occupation and education and in the supply of goods and services. It can also be seen in the way the incitement to racial hatred law has been expanded to cover incitement to religious hatred as well. Islam sits here on the race/religion divide, and it has been a long-standing grievance on the part of Muslims that although Sikhs and Jews were quickly accepted as ethnic groups within the protection of race discrimination laws, Muslims were racially too diverse. In fact, English law vacillates between accommodation of individuals on grounds of religion or conscience generally, and accommodation of members of specific religions. Many of the exceptions for Sikh dress are for Sikhs as such, not for 'religion'. The recent extension of the general law to cover Islam should not blind us to the fact that Islam is here being constructed as a matter of individual belief and behaviour, which while privileged as compared to matters of mere taste or hobby, may well have to give way to the uniform requirements of the secular state or employer.

Closely allied to this is the increasing acceptance of conventional forms of collective religious expression in the founding of mosques and cemeteries. There is a new diversity of architecture in the inner cities, but that diversity is not deep: prayer and teaching are familiar forms of religious expression, and a mosque is a voluntary religious body with a charitable purpose like any other non-established church. Just as it is possible to get married in a church, so it is possible to get married in a mosque, so long as the form of marriage is that sanctioned by the law.

The importance of this point cannot be underestimated. Religious freedom and equality has developed in this country by increasing toleration of Christian and eventually non-Christian religious doctrine and liturgical practices, but the social significance which religion is allowed to have in individual and collective life has been much slower to change. In that sense, the diversity is superficial. For example, when a court has to consider whether a boy is Muslim to determine whether it will permit circumcision against the wishes of one parent, it looks not at Islamic law's definition of when a child is Muslim, but at the home environment and upbringing of the child. One can bring up a child as a Muslim – to that extent there is freedom – but one cannot insist on an Islamic understanding of when a child is a Muslim. It is in this context that we should locate the debate about faith schools. Parents have long had the right under international law to secure the education of their children in accordance with their religious and philosophical beliefs. The recent movement towards state funding has been as much about bringing independent Islamic schools under closer state control as it has been about fairness for different religions. This has occurred both through the articulation of new legal standards for independent schools to secure civic participation and integration as through financial inducements to bring independent schools within the state system. In all this, the model for the proper place of any religion in school is arguably the genteel religiosity of the typical church school.

Thirdly, Islam is having a certain moral impact on the law. Within the context of schools one notes a slightly higher degree of sensitivity around issues of gender differentiation, decency and personal privacy, but the most striking example is the development of 'Islamic banking'.[7] The Financial Services Authority is clear that it operates a policy of 'no obstacles, no special favours'. The most important expression of that policy is that newly authorized products are defined in neutral terms. Thus an 'Islamic mortgage' is an arrangement whereby the lender buys the freehold and charges a rent for occupancy as well as periodic repayments until such time as the loan is repaid and the owner can exercise his right of pre-emption to buy the house outright. This avoids the charging of interest, and required the adjustment of stamp duty law to ensure that duty was not paid twice – as it would have been under previous arrangements, since there are two sales rather than one. Here we see an obstacle being removed, and a product authorized for the consumer market. But any bank or building society can offer such an arrangement to any customer. Many high street names now provide such services to appeal to Muslim customers. There is nothing intrinsically Islamic about the product, except the moral inspiration. In fact, until the protestant Reformation, the Christian church also worried about the charging of interest.

The strongest form of accommodation is that provided by plural laws. Different bodies of law apply to different communities of people by virtue of their membership of that community. This must be clearly distinguished from membership in a voluntary association, which is a matter of personal choice, at least from a legal perspective. Examples of plural laws are very hard to find in English law. When Mennasseh ben Israel petitioned for the readmission of the Jews in 1655, he asked for a separate court system under the oversight of the royal courts. He was unsuccessful, and the subsequent history of British Jewry is in part a history of the adoption of Protestant non-conformist (Board of Deputies) and Anglican (United Synagogues and Chief Rabbi) structures. The obvious example of plural laws is that of ritual slaughter, in which separate regulations apply to slaughter according to kosher methods. Jewish institutions are also given a regulatory role over the qualification of slaughter men. Of course, it is still a matter of choice whether one chooses to adopt those methods and to buy the finished product.

This self-regulatory role also applies in the case of shops' opening hours, where Jews have long been able to open on a Sunday on condition that they closed on a Saturday, laws which have been policed by the Board of Deputies. Formalities concerning the marriage of Jews have largely been excepted from state regulation, as they are for Quakers. It is also arguable that the Divorce (Religious Marriages) Act 2002 just sneaks into the category of plural law. Under this act, a court can deny a decree absolute to a Jewish man who refuses to release his wife by obtaining a *get* (religious divorce). While the former wife would be free to remarry under English law, social and religious convention might prevent this, and the court can thus create pressure on the man to free her in both respects. The power to do this may be extended to other religions, but as yet has not been.

Several fundamental principles of English law constrain the wider adoption of plural laws. The Rule of Law is usually taken to require 'equality before the law', which is itself understood to mean that all people are governed by the same law.[8] More precisely, it is taken to mean that each person's rights and obligations should in principle be identical, except to the extent that they have themselves chosen to alter them. And this is particularly the case in respect of religious obligations, for there is to be no compulsion in matters of religion. Apart from the period of childhood, being born into a religious community is not a legitimate basis for the exercise by a religious court of coercive – i.e. non-consensual – jurisdiction.

3. Religious courts in secular systems

The principle of non-coercive religious jurisdiction is not breached if the parties choose to enter into a formal

arbitration contract. This is the basis on which the
London Beth Din and other Jewish courts operate. The
Arbitration Act 1996 expressly allows parties to choose
a non-state system of law as the basis for their arbitration, or even to require a resolution of their dispute
according to general principles of justice and fairness.
Once the arbitrator gives his or her decision, it is binding on the parties on account of the contract they have
entered into. As with private international law, courts of
law will not enforce an arbitration agreement contrary
to public policy, and very occasionally this causes tensions, as with different approaches to the effect of ille-
gality on contracts in Jewish and English law. More
significant are the limits of arbitrability. One can only
arbitrate matters of private right such as property and
contract; one cannot arbitrate cases involving the public
interest (e.g. welfare of children) or personal status
(paternity, legitimacy, marriage, divorce etc.). For practical purposes this means that inheritance disputes can,
if all the parties wish, be determined by a religious
court in a legally binding fashion, but most family disputes cannot be.

However, there is a less formal way in which religious
courts can have an effect on a family law dispute. As a
broad general principle, it is the case that family law is
highly dependent on the cooperation of the parties, and
that whatever the law might prefer, domestic living
arrangements are largely designed by the individuals
concerned responding to the various social and economic pressures upon them. This is patently the case in
arrangements made after separation and divorce, in
which the court has jurisdiction over the welfare of the
children and the family's economic arrangements, but in
practice encourages the parties to settle their dispute
and then approves their agreement. There is nothing to

stop the parties seeking informal mediation and bringing the mediator's solution to the court as their own. So long as it is not patently unreasonable, the court is likely to 'rubber stamp' it. Islamic mediation is no different. It is in this context that we can locate the vast majority of the work of the Islamic *Shariʿa* Council. This was founded in 1982 and has considered over seven thousand cases to date, most of them involving marriage breakdown.

Nor should we ignore the possibility of the completely informal use of religious courts. As the example of rural Turkey under Kemalist rule shows most graphically, Islamic law continued for decades as a form of social law much stronger than the 'official' Swiss civil code of family law. Ihsan Yilmaz has recently argued that Muslims in the United Kingdom are developing an indigenous form of anglicized *shariʿa (angrezi shariat)*.[9] He gives examples such as 'assisted arranged marriage', which modifies traditional arrangements in the direction of a parental dating agency, various blends of *nikah* (religious marriage) and civil registration, and perhaps most intriguingly of all, instances in which men – apparently with the connivance of all parties – go through civil, but not religious, divorce, in order to re-marry and thus in practice to enter into a polygamous relationship.

The truth is, we do not yet have a clear picture of the role of Islamic religious courts in the lived reality of British Muslims. We do know that they exist, and that there is a gap between their legitimacy in the community, the social experience of the extent to which recourse to them is 'obligatory' and the formal legal position. There are widespread concerns about oppressive behaviour towards women and children in the domain of personal and family relations, which operates on the edge of the radar of state law. This is the context in which the comments of Archbishop Rowan must be placed. It is a pragmatic question which we can put as follows: given the role of personal law in the identity of British Muslims, given that it is a key point of contention in the battle for the heart of Islam, given the lived reality of Muslims, which includes the use of more or less informal religious courts, would we do better to let matters lie as they are, or to enhance their formal status, and thus bring them under the closer oversight of secular courts? Since a coercive community jurisdiction is off the agenda, the question, in short, is this: should more matters of family law be arbitrable? That is a question well worth asking.

The fullest official consideration of this problem in recent times took place in Canada. The government of Ontario set up a commission chaired by Marion Boyd which concluded in December 2004 that an extension of the arbitration-based system was advisable.[10] The precise scope of the matters which could be subject to arbitration should be clarified, and the form that arbitration agreements needed to take in order to be legally binding should be set out. In particular, parties would need to be told that they were under no compulsion to enter into arbitration, that they would have to reconfirm any early agreement in writing at the time of the dispute, and that the decision could be challenged before the ordinary courts if it infringed the human rights of the parties or was in other ways unconscionable. A decision could always be set aside if not in the best interests of the children. The principal argument of the Commission was that this would facilitate the creation of a body of civil-religious law which more closely reflected fundamental legal values and protected the parties concerned. It was an argument about the cost – above all to women – of backstreet adjudications.

The reaction to the Boyd Report was rather similar to

that given to the Archbishop of Canterbury. Many groups were hostile and mounted a successful campaign to get the Ontario government to drop the proposals. There are genuine concerns: if one passes Islamic family law through a modern human rights filter, perhaps not many distinctively Islamic principles survive.[11] If we enhance the legitimacy of religious courts, that might act to the detriment of vulnerable people, particularly women, in spite of increased state oversight.[12] Yet it is hard not to see many of the responses as ideological, in the sense that they are driven by a concern to preserve the 'purity' of the law's egalitarian values, rather than grapple with the practical problems at stake. This is particularly the case for family lawyers, who are often committed to the development of their subject in terms of the overthrow of patriarchy in the name of gender equality and child welfare. There is a striking similarity with earlier debates about 'morals' laws in which conservatives would defend the law's disengagement with social problems in the name of its moral rectitude. The content of public morality has now shifted, but the unwillingness to let the law do its practical, messy, work of preserving freedom and resisting oppression in all its forms has stayed the same.

4. Conclusion

By way of conclusion, it is possible to state four theses:

(1) In general terms, English law requires Islam to be reworked into the institutional forms of a secularized Christianity. The principal features of this reworking are a narrowing of the boundaries of the 'religious' around

a core of worship and teaching, a re-presentation of Islamic law as a matter of personal belief and behaviour, and an insistence that collective identity be treated as a matter of individual choice. Of course, there is a complex relationship between law and social reality; so this reworking is only partially experienced and partially internalized on the part of British Muslims – and to differing degrees. But in principle we should affirm this transformation: it makes it possible to live with religious diversity.

(2) In matters of property and contract, there is nothing to stop parties seeking binding arbitration, and nothing to stop Islamic courts developing an arbitration service on the Jewish model. However, the real point of tension around 'Islamic courts' lies in matters of family law. The reasons for this are partly historical: the colonial experience together with twentieth-century legal reform in Islamic countries has left family law as a significant marker of personal and community identity. By contrast, post-Christian secularism treats domestic relations as a matter of personal choice within a single set of fairly minimal public normative constraints, backed by protective remedies. Concern about the nature of childhood, sexual promiscuity and family breakdown in a culture of increasingly radical pluralism makes this Western model seem increasingly inadequate.

(3) Plural laws might seem an obvious solution to social pluralism in the ethics of family life. But adopting a 'religious community law' on a colonial model, for example in Muslim-majority inner city districts, runs counter to some of our deepest political and legal convictions. There should be no compulsion in matters of faith,

religious identity is not automatically inherited, and it is not territorially bounded. Our understanding of 'equality before the law' rightly presupposes a certain constrained and optional place for religion in the law. Formal provision for polygamy is extremely unlikely in the foreseeable future, and provision for specifically Muslim polygamy even less so.

(4) We are left with the Archbishop of Canterbury's proposal: resolution of some family law disputes by courts whose jurisdiction is consensual, not coercive, or in other words the shift of certain disputes from mediation to arbitration under the oversight of the civil courts. The only basis on which this would be acceptable is if the law allowed all individuals a greater ability to fashion legally binding family relations. To some extent this is already happening with the rise of pre-nuptial contracts. While we should defend a legal policy which prevents the signing away of certain rights in advance, particularly in respect of future children, there may still be scope for undertaking additional obligations. For example, Christians could enter into 'covenant marriages' in which the grounds of divorce for both parties would be restricted; Muslims could enter into agreements that divorce would only be sought with the agreement of an Islamic court selected by both parties. The oversight of the civil courts would continue to ensure that, for example, inadequate financial provision for a divorced wife in accordance with *shariʿa* law would not be lawful.

However, even if we accept that family law should be more a matter of contractual design by the parties than fixed in advance by the state, the scope for that design is probably not very large. The real question would seem to be whether we want to support a shift in authority within Muslim communities away from individuals to religious leaders and courts. If this is really what is at stake, one might conclude that the archbishop's cure is worse than the disease.

Part III:
Models of Positive
Relationships

Part III
Profile of Positive Relationships

Chapter 13

Holistic Responses in Multicultural Birmingham

Richard J. Sudworth

As I walked into the café, I looked for my friend Mounir amongst the crowd of young men. Unusually, they were all in rapt attention by the television screen. The MTV rap videos or Lebanese singers this time were replaced by an image of two towers smoking over a strap line 'America under attack'. I took a coffee from the bar, still unversed in the North African practice of nursing this tiny, bittersweet dram over what could be thirty minutes or more. I eventually spotted Mounir and we hugged and greeted each other, my rudimentary Arabic flattered by the comfort of the customary greetings.

All the men were agitated and keen to deliver their version of events unfolding on the big screen: 'Someone is attacking the White House', 'It's war!' The CNN images transfixed us all with their horror. When the first tower collapsed, the sense of unreality that I've since heard from so many others was palpable. Was this a Hollywood movie, prime-time entertainment, or brutal terror? As the dust rose, amidst the posters of European football teams and American pop starlets, a great cheer erupted from the men around me.

Here I was: a British man working for a Christian development organization in North Africa. These were my friends: Muslim men who had opened their homes and their families to me. I had experienced generosity from my Muslim neighbours that I had never encountered anywhere else. There was such warmth and a confidence about faith issues that my own Christian beliefs were regularly a part of conversation – as were their Muslim beliefs and practices. Yet as those symbols of Western might and wealth toppled, they cheered.

I deliberately take you on a journey from North Africa to Birmingham to talk about holistic mission and Islam because we cannot address this issue without recourse to our global context. And for me, personally, it was in that formative experience of 9/11 that I truly asked myself: how do we make Jesus known to Muslims today? I had asked that question in an abstract way by studying holistic mission. I had even applied the theory to some of my practice. What took root in me in 2001, though, was a deeper sense of how Muslims themselves might feel about that question. I didn't cease to be friends with Mounir after 9/11; our relationship wasn't affected by that event, and he continued to be generous and warm to the clumsy guest in his country that I was. What I had come to realize, though, was the strength of the accumulated baggage of Christian-Muslim relations that we were negotiating.

The inescapable truth of Christian mission amongst Muslims is that we do not start with a blank sheet of paper. There are numerous skeletons in our respective cupboards, whispered truths and half-truths that can hobble our relationships. The café scenario I described contains echoes of our respective histories that take in the colonial past, global inequalities, Israel-Palestine, and consumerism affecting even our very attitudes to faith. I never ceased to be surprised at the number of times the Crusades were mentioned to me in conversation in North Africa. Events going back over seven hundred years were a folk-memory that seemed to define the 'Christian West' and the Islamic Middle East and North Africa. And whether or not we like the designation 'Christian West', for most Muslims that is but one 'half-truth' that is part of the background noise of our interactions.

The emphasis on our history is made in order to stress the urgency of holistic or integral mission. When there is 'baggage', our words can seem empty at best – sometimes even provocative and confrontational. This was epitomized in the pronouncement by President George Bush Jr about a 'crusade' against terror. What he was saying was heard very differently by Muslims across the world! As with global politics, so it is with local relations between Christians and Muslims. We might think we are announcing that Jesus is the Son of God; Muslims are probably hearing a blasphemy about sexual relations between God and Mary. We might believe we are inviting Muslim children to a holiday Bible club; Muslims might perceive that we are trying to corrupt their young and erase their culture and family values. This is not to say that any of these activities is inherently wrong, but rather to point out the need for embedded relationships of understanding – to see mission in its breadth.

I will prefer to choose the term 'integral mission' over 'holistic mission' for the purposes of this chapter. This is part of a description of integral mission used by the Micah Network:

> In integral mission our proclamation has social consequences as we call people to love and repentance in all areas

of life. And our social involvement has evangelistic consequences as we bear witness to the transforming grace of
Jesus Christ. If we ignore the world we betray the word of
God which sends us out to serve the world. If we ignore the
word of God we have nothing to bring to the world. Justice
and justification by faith, worship and political action, the
spiritual and the material, personal change and structural
change belong together. As in the life of Jesus, being, doing
and saying are at the heart of our integral task.[1]

What I like about this description is the attention to the
world, and the realities of relationship, social structures
and our own personal brokenness. It is suggestive of a
whole range of transformations that requires action,
speech, prayer and political involvement. The urgency
of this task amongst Muslims is that we have inherited a
legacy as Christians that demands we prove something
of the gospel. A vision of what God wants to do in our
contemporary context that is too small is an irrelevance
to Muslims. In many ways – and this reflects something
of my own story – the encounter with Islam pushes us
back onto what it really means to be a disciple. Muslims
are essentially saying, 'show me'. The church, too often,
like a hapless Brit on holiday in France, is merely turning the volume up. Rather, a demonstration of what the
good news looks like is demanded. This is not about
technique and strategy, ultimately, but how we as
Christians are obedient and faithful as agents in the
implementation of the kingdom of God.

To Birmingham: Another Muslim context

After working in North Africa, as a family we were asked
to join a church community in the Springfield area of

Birmingham, another context where the majority population are Muslim and where the key interface between the Christian and Muslim communities is a social project. St Christopher's Springfield is an evangelical congregation in a Mirpuri-Pakistani background-dominated area of Birmingham's inner city. The church building sits directly opposite a large mosque that has been converted from two terraced houses. The very geography of the parish church makes plain the cheek-by-jowl presence of the Christian and Muslim communities. The congregation itself draws from the wider multicultural mix of the parish, bringing together Afro-Caribbean, white middle class and working class, Asian and refugee background Christians.

Over fifteen years ago, the church experienced something of a renewal in its worship, drawing a number of new members in commitment to this local presence. Several women became convinced that the renewal in worship they were experiencing had little value if it remained confined within the walls of the church. The work of the Holy Spirit in the lives of the church members would surely push them outward in service to the wider community. Like so many churches across the country, a natural step forward was to provide a 'stay-and-play' facility for other mothers, sharing their lives in the common struggle of bringing up young children. This took place in one of the church members' home and for over a year, this 'stay-and-play', now named Seedlings, consisted of just three families.

During a pivotal summer holiday break, the women prayed about the future of this fragile group, deciding to continue but prepared to terminate the provision should numbers fail to grow. When the new term began, several more families arrived and the venue had to be switched from a home to the church hall. What had happened was that local families were beginning to grow in confidence with what the church members were providing; trust was growing and word was getting out as local parents, including Muslims, were recommending Seedlings to their wider family and friends.

Today, the Edwardian church hall has been replaced by a large children's centre, the largest children's centre in Birmingham and home to The Springfield Project, the church's charitable company working in partnership with Birmingham City Council in delivering services to young families in our locale. The vision birthed in that small group of women continues, and has helped frame the mission of the church to this date. The Seedlings stay-and-play is now hosted in the main body of the church (there are thankfully no pews!). So, for three mornings a week around forty parents and children, many of them mothers in *hijab*, belie all preconceptions and enjoy shared space with a growing corpus of volunteers. In a congregation of around one hundred and thirty, we estimate that about forty church members either work for The Springfield Project or serve as volunteers at some point during an average week. Latterly, Christians from a suburban church near to Birmingham have been feeling called to serve us in Springfield too.

As Seedlings grew, funding was obtained for a feasibility study to research what the local community actually needed. This confirmed the desperate need for support for young families in matters of health, hygiene, coping with budgets and the challenges of domestic burdens often in isolation. What began as a stay-and-play group enlarged to encompass a professional nursery, family support, employment and health advice, after-schools clubs and fathers' work.

It is an exhilarating context to work in. I share an office with Christians, Muslims and Sikhs and am privileged to be in a building that is inextricably intertwined with church yet so trusted as to be a safe space for all faiths and none. The journey to this point has not been smooth, and church members that predate my arrival would talk of the challenges presented by this path – challenges even to our very conception of what 'mission' is. Here are just some of the lessons as I see them from The Springfield Project.

Doing God

Alastair Campbell famously said of Tony Blair that he 'does not do God' and it would seem that events have largely overtaken the government and media in terms of having to be able to 'do God'. Evangelicals have for many years been engaging in community transformation. We need only be reminded of the likes of William Wilberforce, the Clapham Sect that initiated the Church Missionary Society, and William Booth. The Lausanne Covenant of 1974 famously articulated an evangelical commitment to social action under the aegis of John Stott.[2] Today, organizations such as Interserve, Tearfund and Faithworks are at the vanguard of Christian mission for community transformation. Churches with a clear commitment to the personal claims of Christ, a gospel of conversion, are also seriously engaged in the lived issues of some of the poorest communities across the world.

It is sometimes less clear, though, how the faith claims of Christians are apparent in the services provided by specific projects. There are sobering reminders of initiatives growing and becoming uncoupled from the source church, as if the spirituality undergirding the community work were in fact an embarrassment. For The

Springfield Project, the numerical commitment of Christians involved in the work has helped to give confidence in a very public ownership of the faith roots of the provision. This has often been translated into an openness to pray for people. Indeed, the Islamic context has helped in owning prayer as a practice within the project. We really would seek to 'do God', and for many of our Muslim neighbours that is very welcome, because they 'do God' too.

As I found in North Africa, conversations about faith, prayer and our sacred texts are often very natural, and when Christians are seen as serious about their faith, there is actual respect from Muslims. Going back to the 'baggage' that clutters Christian-Muslim relations, when the Christian faith is seen as more than a nominal, cultural label for a Sunday rite but as an all-encompassing radical alternative to the givens of Western society, we will find Muslims prepared to listen.

The Springfield Project therefore provides an anonymous prayer box to respond to the written requests of everyone coming into the building. During special events and celebrations, we endeavour to offer creative opportunities for prayer. Seasonal festivals such as Christmas and Easter are acknowledged, the stories told, and the Christian understanding of these events shared. For staff and volunteer days away, we aim to reaffirm to everyone the Christian foundations to the work and how they connect with values, behaviour and objectives. Those that are not Christians should be able to affirm these; but we own the story that supports them from within the church. The very public nature of the church's engagement with the community and unashamed connection with the Christian faith has, we believe, freed up many Muslims to be comfortable being in a church, entrusting their children to our care. Rather than being threatened by us, it is our transparent spirituality that gives comfort to many Muslims with a deep yearning for a life lived for God.

Doing justly

Coupled with a transparency about the spirituality of The Springfield Project is a concern for appropriate ethical practice. Part of a commitment to integral mission, of demonstrating the kingdom of God, must be an attention to being who we say we are. IT experts talk of software systems that are WYSIWYG (pronounced as 'Wizzywig') – an acronym for 'What You See Is What You Get'. If we are providing a nursery or family support service, then that is what we should do, and to the best of our ability. Christians should not be in the business of 'twist and sell' – offering one thing and manipulating those we are with, only to slip them something else.

This is a delicate balance because in the realities of relationship, what started out on one track can change to another. I may have come to the stay-and-play session looking for company, but find myself sharing with another parent and admitting a need for help at home managing the children. Life does not come in neat compartments. What this lesson refers to, though, is as much about 'attitude' and 'agenda'. What is our real reason for serving? Are we seeing Muslims for who they are, in all their fullness, or as recipients for what we want to do for them? Once again, the baggage of history will make many Muslims keenly aware of colonizing approaches.

The lesson of ethics, of doing justly for those we serve, is actually about love. I like to talk of 'cruciform ethics': practice that is informed by the self-giving love seen on the cross. Jesus gave and gave, and continues to give whether we receive that grace or not. Though an encounter with Christ is deeply transformative, Jesus embraces us as we are. Tom Wright explains this eloquently when he says: 'The lover affirms the reality and the otherness of the beloved. Love does not seek to collapse the beloved in terms of self.'[3] Mission as the embodiment in the church of God's love will not impose on people things we think they need, and will value each person regardless of their responsiveness to the deeper truths we may have to offer. Miroslav Volf describes this process as 'double vision'. It is about 'allowing them to help us see them, as well as ourselves, from their perspective, and if needed, readjust our perspectives as we take into account their perspectives'.[4] In other words, we need to make efforts to stand in their shoes and interpret how our actions may actually be perceived.

For The Springfield Project, this means that treating our largely Muslim constituency as a captive audience to disseminate tracts or to preach evangelistically when there is a celebratory event is shunned. Added to the ethics of not manipulating 'opportunities' to proclaim when we are providing another service entirely, we have an ethical responsibility to people who are frequently very vulnerable not to exploit them for our own ends. The distinction is not always clear-cut, though. 'Doing God' as I described earlier includes its own proclamation. When I talk of owning our story and serving ethically, we are actually embarking on a journey that is as much about the questions we ask ourselves as it is about the answers we have to give.

For St Christopher's, the journey has been transformative for us and perhaps that is one great proof of the character of the services. Genuine relationships cannot be packaged and strategized, and they bring mutual change and discovery through risk and vulnerability. Often it has been very unclear where we have been heading and what might be the outcomes. At crucial milestones in our history, the church has been prepared to halt progress and withdraw, making very clear to secular funders that there is an evangelical faith at the heart of the project. We have been explicit about our beliefs to the city council and voiced our determination that those beliefs had to continue to shape the project's ethos if the church were to endorse the expansion into a children's centre. At every stage, that risk has been honoured and The Springfield Project remains a very clearly Christian hub available to the whole of the surrounding community.

A longstanding member of our church who volunteers for Seedlings, preparing refreshments and setting out activities for the children, was asked what had changed for her in the years she had been a member of St Christopher's. Her reply was telling: 'I used to pray for my Muslim neighbours as enemies; I now pray for them as friends.'

Pray for the good of the city

An important biblical motif for St Christopher's has been Jeremiah 29. In the context of the exile of the Jews in Babylon, Jeremiah prophesies that God's people are to 'seek the peace and prosperity of the city to which I have carried you into exile. Pray to the LORD for it, because if it prospers, you too will prosper' (v. 7). Remembering that the Jews are in an alien land with alien gods and belief systems, God is tying the fortunes of his people to those around them. It is an injunction that prefigures

Jesus weeping over the city of Jerusalem in Matthew 23:37–39 and Luke 13:31–35, and then being crucified outside the walls of the city. At Pentecost in Acts 2 the Holy Spirit comes in power in the heart of the city, tangibly present and impacting the maelstrom of cultures gathered there, and inaugurating a movement outwards through the Roman Empire. The kingdom of God makes a difference in public. The city in all its structures, cultures and civic practice is a ground for the redemptive work of Christ.

This understanding not only underpins the work of The Springfield Project as I have described it, but also opens up the breadth of the church's calling to the area. In a climate charged with fear about religious violence, one aspect of our 'mission' has involved intentional acts of peacemaking and collaboration with our neighbouring mosque. There are regular meetings between the respective church and mosque leadership, and the church has been instrumental in bringing together public statements that demonstrate the ability of Christians and Muslims to work together for the common good, against extremism and for the improvement of the city. Mosque members are invited to special events in the church and project, and in return we are invited to significant Islamic festivals.

Restating the thrust of Jeremiah 29, as a church we see our presence as something that local Muslims can feel has enhanced their lives whether they eventually come to faith in Jesus or not. Archbishop William Temple is reputed to have said that 'church is the only society on earth which exists for the benefit of non-members'. It means that a vision of integral mission will sometimes result in partnerships – partnerships that are necessarily awkward and uncomfortable, but are another aspect of the unfolding of self-giving love in the world. I have already mentioned the partnership with the city council. But for The Springfield Project this also includes seeing our local mosque as a partner in shared concerns, such as provision for young families and youth, or the place of faith in the public life of the city.

Interestingly, this process of partnership becomes a two-way street because mission then is not all about 'what we do to them' but how we may receive in turn. During discussions about the planned building of the new children's centre, The Springfield Project faced some political opposition from someone opposed to a church becoming the base of a major statutory-supported provision in a predominantly Muslim area. Our neighbouring mosque intervened on our behalf, making clear that the church was acting in the interests of the community and could be trusted as an honourable and professional custodian for local families. We also are beginning to receive! Are we able to see our Muslim neighbours not as objects of our charity, but created in the image of God and thus able to be bearers of gifts to us also? The 'double vision' I referred to earlier will push us into places where we become open to receive and even to learn from others.

Interestingly, we are very conscious that the discomfort the church community has sometimes felt about its partnerships – occasionally feeling swamped and wondering how close we should actually be to our neighbours, has also been manifest in the mosque. One of the joys of being an evangelical congregation in a Muslim-majority community is that our neighbours are often very evangelical Muslims. They, too, are keen to proclaim their faith to us, consciously redrawing boundaries at times, praying for us (sometimes in our presence!), and making sometimes very direct appeals to us as individuals about the claims of Islam. It makes for a robust honesty that does not pretend to gloss key differences or search for some common core to Islam and Christianity. Instead, through our differences, we aim to bless and be blessed. As Christians, to serve in the name of Jesus, finding grace in the most surprising of places and welcoming it when we do.

A community of worship

Integral mission amongst Muslims, as I have described it, demands risk and vulnerability and has pushed us out as a church community into a deeper understanding of what God is doing in our locality.[5] The formative missionary prayer of 'your kingdom come' underlines for me the context of worship that frames such an engagement. The story of The Springfield Project begins with the renewal of worship of a local church community. A thoroughgoing engagement with Islam drives us constantly back to the source and inspiration of our Christian roots. Only in the repeated recourse to the Bible, to prayer and to the church at worship will we find ourselves able to continue to be resourced to be 'the difference that makes a difference' in a Muslim context. The Catholic Islamicist Louis Massignon famously talked of Islam being a 'foil' to the church. Islam offers a profound challenge to the Christian faith and its credibility in public life. As the church takes this challenge seriously, integral mission becomes more than a mere optional device for church growth, but a response in worship to the lordship of Christ where the church begins to actually find its true self. This true self will be an echo and anticipation of Jesus – an embodied witness where Muslims can discover in tangible ways what the kingdom of God is like.

Chapter 14

Working with Muslim and Christian Young People

Andrew Smith

'What would you like to say to Gordon Brown?'

This was the question a youth pulled out of the hat at a recent Christian-Muslim lads' event. We were camping together and it was a dark, very cold night. We'd been sitting round at the end of an exhausting day's canoeing and I'd prepared one of the simplest activities imaginable. It was nothing more than an envelope with slips of paper with a question on each one. We passed the envelope round and took it in turns to answer the questions. That evening the lads got totally absorbed in the activity and then one Muslim youth pulled out that question. He paused and said, 'I'd say thank you for all you are doing to help the poor in Iraq, and thank you for what you are doing in Afghanistan because somebody needs to sort out the terrorists.'

Working with teenagers often produces both the unexpected and the profound. Listening to two girls share their testimonies at a recent event was very moving, as

one girl spoke of how her life had been changed during
a meeting at Soul Survivor – a national youth event – and
another spoke of the transformation in her life during the
Umrah pilgrimage to Mecca. The other teenagers present
listened to both testimonies of experiences that were new
to them and of people's beliefs and experiences that
affirmed or challenged the views with which they
arrived. We then split the group into twos and threes to
share our experiences of God touching our lives.
Stopping the conversations was the really hard part.

Both of these stories come from events that have taken
place during the months just prior to writing this as part
of a programme called Youth Encounter, which has been
facilitating Christian-Muslim dialogue with teenagers
since 2000. The programme has produced many encouraging stories like these, but also many frustrations and
difficulties. Let me tell you a much older story from way
back in the last millennium (about 1997).

Beginnings

I was a schools worker for Scripture Union in a secondary school where all the pupils were Muslims. I'd been
teaching in RE lessons and was starting to get into some
good discussions with lads at lunch time. They wanted
to tell me about Islam and why I should convert, and I
was keen to share with them the good news of Jesus
Christ. However, our discussions kept ending in frustration and without any real progress. The trouble was that
whenever I shared anything, they just threw back at me,
'The Bible's been corrupted – you're stupid to believe it.'
Now this was nothing new and I'd swatted up on the
answers, but they just rejected my answers out of hand
as further lies by Christians. They then came up with

other (rehearsed) criticisms to which I then rehearsed the answers. It all felt rather unsatisfactory and unfruitful. Added to that it was obvious that whilst they were happy to quiz me about my faith, they were uneasy being quizzed about Islam.

As a youth worker I had to think carefully about the power dynamics at play: it would have been easy to spend much more time dismissing their arguments, but that would have left them upset and frustrated. So one day I suggested that we change the rules as we were getting nowhere. I suggested that for five minutes I would not doubt the truth of the Qur'an but would allow them to tell my why it's so good being a Muslim. We would then reverse the roles: they would not doubt the truth of the Bible and would allow me five minutes to tell them why it's so good being a Christian. We could then ask questions about what we believe rather than whether it was true or not. Watching those lads think carefully about their faith (some I suspect for the first time) was a privilege. Then at last being able to talk to them of God's grace and mercy and the significance of Jesus' death and resurrection was very special. It's conversations like these that we now seek to nurture through the Youth Encounter project (www.youthencounter.org.uk). Our aim is to give young people the tools to explain their faith to someone of another faith.

The bigger picture

Every day in schools up and down the country young people of different faiths are living side by side. Sometimes this leads to constructive friendships; at other times it leads to tension and conflict. I recently undertook some research and asked several groups of

Christian teenagers to tell me about the Muslims they meet at school and how they get on. In talking to Christians some significant themes emerged.

Overall Christian young people are very relaxed about having Muslim friends. They didn't see the faith of someone as a significant issue in determining whether they could be friends with them or not. This was true of Christians who did have Muslim friends and with Christians who had never met any Muslims. Both groups thought that meeting Muslims was a good idea and could see that it provided opportunities for friendship and understanding. Both groups also thought it was a good opportunity for Christians to witness to Muslims about their faith. I also asked them whether such meetings were a good opportunity for Muslims to witness about their faith to Christians. There was much more hesitation about this, but those who had Muslim friends were more likely to affirm the place of Muslim witness in friendship. What emerged was a picture of young people very relaxed about having Muslim friends, able both to share their faith and to give space to their Muslim friends to talk about theirs.

Some young people talked very clearly about the positive influence their Muslim friends could be. The experience of many of the young Christians I spoke to was that they live in a world where peer pressure is a significant pull away from their faith. In this context, Muslim friends were perceived, by some, to be a positive influence through their example of prayer and commitment. Some Christians were inspired to pray more and to give more through the example of Muslim friends. What also came out was that those who were convinced that only people who believed in Jesus as their Lord and Saviour would get to heaven were the same young people who felt that they had something to learn from their Muslim friends. While some Christian leaders question whether young people should be mixing with Muslims, where it is happening naturally, it has the potential to be a positive influence on the Christians and create opportunities for them to share their faith with Muslim friends.

The picture, of course, is varied, and other Christians I spoke to talked of negative and confrontational meetings with Muslims. Some had invited them to church, only to have the service ridiculed. Others found that Muslims they knew were very dismissive of the Christian faith and continually questioned and challenged it, often in confrontational ways. These encounters often left the Christians feeling marginalized at school and excluded from some activities or friendship groups.

It's important to note, however, that not all the negativity was to do with faith; some of it was to do with culture, and some of the negative experiences described to me exposed some deeply negative attitudes towards Muslims from the Christians. One further interesting thing emerged from the discussions I had: the Christians were far more wary about Muslims they'd never met than ones they knew. The experience of meeting Muslims was almost always far less intimidating than the young people imagined it might be. Their perceptions of Muslims in general bore little relation to the perceptions they had of their friends. Fortunately the negative images and stories they hear don't seem to have much impact on their friendships. Sadly, however, their friendships don't seem to challenge more general views they might have about Muslims.

That research which looked at encounters young people were having as they went about their lives also sheds light on what is happening day by day and equips us to look at how we can facilitate and encourage more structured and purposeful encounters between Christian and Muslim young people.

Getting involved

There is a great deal of hesitation amongst adults about letting Christian young people mix with Muslims. This comes from a variety of reasons: they might be concerned that the young people will be asked or told things that confuse them; they might be worried that they might become interested in Islam to the point of conversion; or they might be worried about the spiritual influence of mixing with Muslims and what this might mean for their young people. Others just don't see the point of meeting unless it has a clear evangelistic agenda, or just think that life is busy enough as it is without worrying about getting involved in Christian-Muslim dialogue. Others, sadly, express negative attitudes about Muslims that border on being Islamophobic or racist. While some young people share some of these (and other) concerns, my experience is that on the whole they are more relaxed about meeting Muslims than their parents or faith leaders are.

Jesus' disciples were a group of young men who were involved in business in one form or other. Jesus was taking them on a significant spiritual journey over the three years he was with them. He would teach them and live with them, preparing them to take his message once he had returned to heaven. We might think that, given all they would need to learn and understand, Jesus would do all he could to protect them from influences which could cause them to fall away. Yet in Matthew, Mark and Luke we read of Jesus sitting with his disciples in the company of 'tax collectors and "sinners"' (Matt. 9:9–13,

NIV), and very early on, sending them out on their own to proclaim the kingdom of God, heal the sick and raise the dead (Matt. 10:7,8). Discipleship was lived out in situations where it would be tested and amongst people who could potentially lead them astray. This isn't the only picture of course. Jesus also spent time alone with the disciples, teaching away from these distractions. But his model of discipleship included both engagement and withdrawal. We need to look at our model of discipleship in this light. We are often good at the withdrawal; at discipleship in safe situations. But if we are to follow Jesus' model, then discipleship needs to be lived in the real world and young people need to be equipped from the outset to be disciples wherever they live and amongst all people – including their Muslim peers.

Fear of conversion is something I run up against from both Christian and Muslim parents when we talk of running events for teenagers. As a parent I understand that we want our children to grow up secure in the Christian faith. But as I highlighted above, Christian young people are growing up meeting and hearing about Muslims. If we are keen to do evangelism but don't want others to evangelize us, we have to ask whether this kind of attitude is ethical or practical in today's society.

Sadly, many young people grow up within the Christian faith but drift away during their teenage years. The vast majority of these do not convert to another religion but just get caught up in the prevailing secular, consumerist society we live in. Whilst many leaders or parents are all too aware of the negative peer pressure from society, they are often happier for their young people to mix with secular young people than with Muslims. This is despite all the evidence which suggests that mixing with secular friends is far more likely to have a negative impact on their faith than mixing with Muslims. In fact, as I pointed out earlier, Christian young people often find their faith strengthened when they build friendships with Muslims.

Encouraging participation

'What have you done to show your Muslim neighbours that you really love them?' When Jesus was asked which were the two most important commandments he famously replied that all the law and the prophets could be summed up with the commands to 'love the Lord your God and love your neighbour as yourself'. Holding these two commands in tension is crucial to the work we do in bringing Christian and Muslim teenagers together. Learning to love our Muslim neighbours is a vital task for Christian young people in Britain today. But the fact that Jesus put these two commands together is important. Love for our neighbour does not compromise our love for God, but is rather inspired and driven by our love for God. We do not need to become a Muslim to love our Muslim neighbours with a genuine self-giving love. We somehow have to learn to live in God's love and express that love to those around us.

Saying we love Muslims is an easy task (for most people!); but expressing that love in practical ways is often harder. Sometimes this is just because we haven't had an opportunity to or we're not sure how to. Many Christian young people in Britain hear about Muslims or see them in town or at school but often don't have an opportunity to get to know them. Even if they live in an area where there are Muslims, the two communities often don't naturally mix. Consequently, demonstrating love to Muslim neighbours can feel quite difficult.

Creating an environment where Christian and Muslim young people meet as equals creates a great opportunity for Christians to learn to love their Muslim neighbours. Just the simple act of spending time with them and getting to know them can give opportunities for acts of loving kindness to take place. If we look at 1 Corinthians 13 as a blueprint of Christian love, we can see that patience, kindness and humility are all attributes of Christian love and are all things which can be practised amongst the Muslim young people they meet.

In the Beatitudes, one of the groups Jesus calls 'blessed' are the peacemakers. Sadly many communities in the UK are not at peace with one another. While many young people who come to events we run are not at war with one another, the peace they have is born out of complete lack of contact. This peace is little more than an absence of violence, and it isn't peace as a positive force for good. This often means that the young people arrive nervous and anxious about who they might meet and what might happen. I'm sure we are all peace-supporters, but the challenge of Jesus' words is that we should become peace*makers*. Building a peace that moves from suspicion and avoidance to positive engagement can be relatively easily and quickly achieved with many groups of young people. Engaging them as young people, through ice breaker games, lively activities and relevant discussion topics, results in friendships forming very quickly. Working with groups of around ten Muslims and ten Christians can mean that by the end of a day together they are enjoying one another's company, and arranging to keep in touch online or to meet up in town on another date.

This kind of work has also led to more specific peace-making. Discussions between some young people who all lived in the same area resulted in comments about where people felt safe or frightened in the area. When one white Christian youth told everyone that he would never get on the bus at a certain bus stop because he would get beaten up by Asian youths, there was genuine shock amongst the Asian, Muslim lads in the group. They resolved to look out for him and tell the other guys to leave him alone in future. This event, along with some other antagonisms between Christian and Muslim lads, was raised when we held a meeting in a local mosque. The mosque leaders were also shocked and said to the whole group that if any of them were facing trouble, they should report it to the mosque as they wanted to help everyone in the area to live in peace – not just the Muslims.

One of the concerns about dialogue is that it leads to a watering down of one's faith; or that we have to deny those things that we hold most dear – such as our faith in Jesus Christ as our Lord and Saviour. Bringing together teenagers, especially those with a deep passion for their faith, can become a place for them to explain their faith, to 'give the reason for the hope that [they] have [within them]' (1 Pet. 3:15, NIV). One of the ways we structure the discussions is to ask the young people to explain to one another what is the best thing about being a Christian or Muslim. Starting the discussion this way encourages the young people to speak about their faith without criticizing the faith of the others they are meeting. Just as with the lads I talked to when I started this work, this way of engagement leads to positive discussions with the chance for truths to be proclaimed.

In addition to the positive and deep exchanges that can come from this simple question, young people are helped to reflect on their faith in a new way. Many of them have never been asked to reflect on the best things in their faith. Some (both Christian and Muslim) struggle, realizing that they have never owned their faith but are only going through the motions. Others jump at the chance to share enthusiastically about the joys and comforts their faiths bring. When we have feedback from these discussions, the response is often surprise at the similarities the young people have found in their answers. They discover that they are all talking about the comfort they find from knowing that God is with them, or being forgiven, or having a clear purpose in life or certainty of life after death. While these similarities are highlighted, it gives a great opportunity to discuss positively the clear differences that also exist even within things that sound similar.

By creating the right atmosphere through discussions and games young people often open up to each other with remarkable ease. Many of them are keen to talk about their own faith, interested in the views and beliefs of others and happy to make new friends. Another piece of research I did explored the reasons why Christian and Muslim young people got involved in dialogue. By far the most popular reasons were to make friends and understand one another better. The chance to witness was important for some, but engaging with global or historical issues was off the agenda for most. The very few who mentioned Christian-Muslim conflict did so in order to learn from the mistakes of others and to avoid them happening again. None saw any need for apportioning blame or seeking apologies from young people they might meet here. This willingness to meet without bringing lots of 'baggage' can create a very positive, lively atmosphere where the young people discuss issues they are concerned about rather than ones that others (especially adults) think are important.

One activity we regularly do is to have small pieces of paper available during the event. The young people are encouraged to write down any question they want to ask a Christian or a Muslim. This could be something they've wondered about before the day or something that crops up during conversation. We then take the questions and read them out, inviting one young person to give a short, personal answer. This is not a time for sermons or for reciting a chapter from a book. The questions range from the curious, such as, 'How do Christians worship in church?' and 'How does your headscarf stay on?' to the profound, such as 'What do you think happens to people when they die?' or even 'How do you believe God forgives sin?' Some will probably only crop up at a youth event – such as 'Which is best, Starbucks or Costa?'

Often these spontaneous, quick-fire questions and answers are one of the highlights of the day, as the young people give personal responses to questions often in ways that include humour that has everyone laughing. But they are anything but trivial or flippant. Recently a Muslim asked the Christians what they thought happened when people die. A girl answered confidently, but aware of the sensitivity of what she was saying, that the Bible teaches that those who believe in Jesus as Lord and Saviour will go to heaven. The Muslims were then asked the same question and one girl said that those who believed in Allah and that Muhammad was his Prophet and followed the example of the Prophet would go to heaven. This was a point where things could have got tense, but by setting the tone first, and by leading the discussion in a careful way, truth claims were spoken and deeply held beliefs were listened to. There was even some laughter when we thought about the surprises that might be in store for us when we get to heaven and find out who is (or isn't) there!

Even with these three reasons for getting involved – loving, peacemaking and proclaiming – there are still many adults nervous about letting their young people engage in these kinds of activities. As the make-up of society in the UK changes we can find ourselves bringing up young people in a very different society to that which we experienced (back in the 'good old days'). We need to make sure we don't project our fears or prejudices onto our young people.

Difficulties and challenges

So far, I've looked at how we can create opportunities for positive encounters between Christian and Muslim young people. But what if this doesn't happen? How do we help young people who are finding it difficult to live as Christians amongst Muslims? Firstly we need to find out where this is happening. This might mean creating the space where they can share about difficulties they are having at school. This is never easy and requires good relationships between youth leaders or parents and young people before they will feel safe to share issues like this. It also means that we need to make sure that parents and youth leaders are aware of these issues and equipped to help young people through these difficult situations.

One of the things we have to help young people wrestle with is the balance between a Christ-like response to suffering (which as outlined in Luke 6 is deeply challenging and requires us to pray for and bless those persecuting us) and standing up for justice. This is especially true in a school context where it is quite appropriate to see this as a bullying issue and talk to the school in those terms. At the same time we should not be seeking revenge, but wrestling with the challenge of forgiveness and 'turning the other cheek'. None of this is easy but is arguably where the deepest and most profound opportunity for witness comes in.

The challenge of Jesus to take up our cross and follow him (Mark 8:34) is surely the challenge to be weak and at the mercy of others, not as a self-righteous martyr, nor as a self-pitying victim, but rather by living in the truth that when we are weak, then we are strong (2 Cor. 12:10). This way of seeing weakness and strength, I believe, lies at the heart not only of how we respond to attacks, but also of how we approach the whole area of dialogue. In evangelical churches we are quite good at being in con-trol – and I write this as a self-confessed control freak. We are good at running events where we set the agenda, control the mike and invite the approved speakers. While this can result in some very good events, it can also create the idea that it is our strength in organizing or speaking that is powerful. The challenge of dialogue or facing attacks and harassment is that some of that control is ceded to the other people. The Muslims in the room have equal, or greater, control or strength.

A few years ago I ran a residential event which some of the Christian participants found difficult at the start. One young woman particularly struggled with sharing a bedroom with a Muslim, as the Muslim prayed at 5 a.m. It wasn't so much being woken up (although that didn't help), but rather her feeling of uncertainty as to what was going on and how she should respond. This, for her, was real vulnerability. After chatting it through with me, she decided that the next morning she'd ask her roommate why she was getting up at 5 a.m. to pray. When I caught up with them at breakfast, they were both chatting animatedly. And when I got a chance to ask the Christian woman how the morning had gone, she excitedly explained that she had asked her room-mate about prayer and that they had been talking about prayer ever since. 'I talked about the Holy Spirit and Jesus being with us,' she said, 'and I've never shared so deeply about prayer before.' It was in that moment that I realized that sharing our faith from a position of vulnerability and weakness is something profound, and requires us to lean on God's strength in ever deeper ways. It is this reliance on God when sharing from a position of vulnerability that so often draws young people into a meaningful and profound dialogue with their Muslim neighbours.

Chapter 15

Taqiyya (Dissimulation) and Integrity

Toby Howarth

'Can we trust Muslims when they are allowed and even encouraged by the Islamic doctrine of *taqiyya* to lie?' That is a question that I have heard from Christians over the last couple of years as I have been speaking at churches in my work as the Bishop of Birmingham's Inter Faith Adviser. This is not a question that I would have expected when I was doing research into *taqiyya* twelve years ago in India as part of my doctoral studies. *Taqiyya* is a relatively obscure concept mainly confined to *Shiʿite* Islam. It allows a Muslim to conceal his or her belief, or to avoid practising aspects of the Islamic faith when their life, property or honour would otherwise be in danger.[1]

The origin and development of *taqiyya*

The doctrine of *taqiyya* was particularly developed by *Shiʿite* Muslims because they have at various times in their history been persecuted by *Sunni* Muslims. As a result, both in scholarly and also in popular Muslim discourse, *taqiyya* has become a point of contention between them, with *Shiʿites* arguing from the Qurʾan that it was a religious duty under certain circumstances to hide their faith, while *Sunnis* accused *Shiʿites* of using *taqiyya* to justify hypocrisy.[2]

I suspect the doctrine would largely have remained in these sectarian backwaters had not Islam become perceived as a growing threat to the West – in particular since the collapse of communism and the events of 9/11. The debate around the (*Shiʿite*) government of Iran's true intentions with regard to the development of nuclear weapons has featured in arguments, both at a scholarly and a more popular level, about the Iranian use of *taqiyya*. So for example, Mamoun Fandy writing in *The Christian Science Monitor* has suggested that *taqiyya* means that President Ahmadinejad and his regime are able to persuade themselves that Islam obliges them not to tell the truth.[3]

On the internet the word has now become common parlance in debates within 'neo con' circles in the United States about the threat of Islam. It has been used particularly during Barack Obama's campaign to become US President, and indeed after his election, in arguments that in spite of his claims to be a Christian, Obama is really a Muslim who is using the doctrine of *taqiyya* to lie about his true religious and political allegiances.[4]

Interwoven with these political debates, the doctrine of *taqiyya* has also become a feature of semi-popular evangelical Christian discourse about Islam particularly in the US, Australia and the UK. In this context, as in its more overt political use, the word has taken on new and much wider 'freight'. From the earlier technical usage concerning dissimulation of one's religious identity in a time of persecution, the term has become the focus for a wider suspicion that certain Muslims are lying about their true agendas. So, for example, *taqiyya* was defined by a Christian relief agency, the Barnabas Fund, in 2007 as, 'the long standing Islamic practice of deception in favour of Islam and its goals'.[5]

This doctrine is used, it is asserted, not only by political groups such as Hamas, but also much more broadly within Islamic circles. So, for example, Dr Ataullah Siddiqui of the Islamic Foundation in Leicester, one of the most respected Islamic research institutes in Britain, was said to be practising *taqiyya* when he denied formal links between his organization and the Pakistani political party, the *Jama^cat-i-Islami*.[6] Similarly, the 138 Muslim scholars, clerics and intellectuals from across the world who signed the 'A Common Word' which claims, 'for the first time since the days of the Prophet to declare the common ground between Christianity and Islam' are said to be practising *taqiyya*. The friendly words are, it is claimed, not representative of what these scholars really believe.[7]

Two recent books by the International director of the Barnabas Fund, Dr Patrick Sookhdeo, include a discussion of *taqiyya* and are important in this context: *Islam: The Challenge to the Church*, and *Global Jihad: the Future in the Face of Militant Islam*.[8] The first of these books was sent free and unsolicited to a large number of British clergy. A review of the second book, by Ben White, was posted on the Fulcrum website and critically addresses the discussion of *taqiyya* in some detail. A subsequent detailed defence of the book's treatment of *taqiyya* from the Barnabas Fund is also posted on the Fulcrum website.[9]

Can Christians and Muslims trust each other?

The charges outlined above concerning *taqiyya* are serious and threaten to undermine trust between Christians
and Muslims. I saw an example of the effect that they
can have when I was invited to speak to a church about
how Christians can develop good relationships with
people of different faiths. In the course of my talk I
spoke about the good relationships that the local church
of which I am a pastor has with the mosque across the
road. During the discussion afterwards someone asked,
'How do you know that you can trust those Muslims?
When they are being friendly, they may be just practising *taqiyya*.' The implication of the argument presented
there, and which I have come across in my work more
frequently, is that if Islam permits lying, not only
Western politicians but also Christians at a local level
should be wary of engagement with Muslims, especially if they appear to be friendly.

The distrust of Christians about Muslim agendas is
unfortunately mirrored by many Muslims about the
agenda of Christians. Again, this lack of trust often
begins with international politics. Many Muslims
(among others) for example, have suspected that Tony
Blair and George W. Bush, who both profess a strong
Christian faith, were dishonest in their claims about the
dangers of weapons of mass destruction in Iraq as they
prepared for the Gulf War. This distrust is fuelled by stories of missionaries using the economic and political
power of the West to convert Muslims to Christianity. I
have also been at local meetings where Muslims have
been openly suspicious that Christians who claim to be
acting in the name of friendship or humanitarian aid are
in fact using these tactics as 'cover' for an attempt to
proselytize.

The invitation to write this chapter gave me the opportunity for a fascinating journey. This was a journey not only into a deeper understanding of Muslim and Christian teachings about truth and lying, but a journey of building trust and therefore the possibility of increased truthfulness personally with the Muslims and Christians with whom I discussed these issues. As well as having the opportunity to speak about honesty and trust in Muslim-Christian relations with two groups of Christians, one as part of a lecture and discussion hosted by a group of Christians in the West Midlands, and one as part of another lecture and discussion at an evangelical theological college, I also talked about the subject with Muslims. Among other conversations, I spent a couple of hours with a friend who is an imam going through some of the texts and talking about how these relate to the situation of Muslims in Britain today. On another occasion, I was invited to lead a seminar on the topic of *taqiyya* will a group of students and faculty at a British *Shiʿite* Muslim seminary.

Is it always wrong to lie?

Before looking in detail at the Islamic sources which speak about truth and deception, it is good to remind ourselves that in many faith traditions there is a concept that might be called the honourable lie. Such a concept simply recognizes that people are sometimes faced with situations in which speaking the truth can be dangerous for themselves and others. The classic example is the ethical dilemma faced by someone hiding a Jewish person when the Gestapo come knocking at the door. A Christian or Jew defending the use of a lie in that situation could appeal to the biblical story of the Exodus in which the Hebrew midwives lied to Pharaoh when he ordered them to kill the baby boys they were helping to deliver, and were said to be rewarded by God for their actions.[10] Similarly, although in a more complex ethical situation in the book of Joshua, when Rahab hid the Hebrew spies in Jericho and lied to the city rulers about them, her life and the life of her family was spared and she was granted a place in Israel.[11]

Teaching about the 'honourable lie' in both Islam and Christianity needs to be understood against the background of a general stress on the importance of telling the truth. Muhammad is reported to have said:

> It is obligatory for you to tell the truth, for truth leads to virtue and virtue leads to Paradise, and the man who continues to speak the truth and endeavours to tell the truth is eventually recorded as truthful with Allah; and beware of telling of a lie for telling of a lie leads to obscenity and obscenity leads to Hell Fire, and the person who keeps telling lies and endeavours to tell a lie is recorded as a liar with Allah.[12]

The point here is that telling the truth or lying is about more than isolated acts; it is about a process of developing one's character before God.

Similarly, the Christian tradition affirms the seventh of the Ten Commandments, 'You shall not bear false witness' (Exod. 20:16, NKJV) as a general prohibition of lying, and Christians are instructed in the New Testament to grow up into Christ, 'speaking the truth in love' (Eph. 4:16, NKJV).

Permitted deception in Islam[13]

It would need much more than the space available here to look in depth at the subject of permitted deception in

Islam in the contemporary world, and I hope that such a study can be made. But from the study and conversations that I have had, the Islamic teaching relating to whether Christians can trust Muslims in this specific way can be divided into two areas. The first is related to the permissibility of hiding one's religious identity under threat (*taqiyya*), and while there is some positive teaching from *Sunni* commentaries on two particular qur'anic texts, the scholarly and popular discussion of this concept is overwhelmingly either *Shi'ite* or directed polemically at the *Shi'ite* tradition. The second area of teaching relates to the permissibility in certain situations of lying. This teaching relies generally on different sources, does not use the term *taqiyya* and does not have such a sectarian flavour.

Taqiyya

The word *taqiyya* derives from an Arabic root meaning 'fear' or 'prudence' and is known both within Islamic studies generally and in popular usage as a *Shi'ite* concept.[14] The word *taqiyya* itself does not occur in the Qur'an, but two particular passages are taken by scholars to relate to the concept covered by it.

The first is Qur'an 16:106

> Anyone who, after accepting faith in God utters unbelief
> – except under compulsion, his heart remaining firm in
> faith – but such as open their breast to unbelief – on them
> is wrath from God and theirs will be a dreadful penalty.[15]

The overt meaning of the text is a warning against turning away from Islam having once embraced the faith. This passage, however, is said to refer to the case of a young man who turned from Islam having been forced to do so by enemies of Islam who had captured him. Later, when he returned to the Muslim community, he reaffirmed his faith in Islam and was accepted by the Prophet Muhammad.

Shi'ite Muslims are generally clear that this passage gives divine sanction to a Muslim who under persecution pretends outwardly to believe one thing, but in their heart actually believes something else. One of the major early *Sunni* historians and commentators on the Qur'an, Al-Tabari (d. 923) agrees, writing on this passage, 'God takes his servants as their hearts believe.'[16] Similarly, the Qur'an, while stressing the importance of dietary laws, seems to allow Muslims to eat non-*halal* food if it is done 'under compulsion' (Sura 6:119).

While the first qur'anic passage and its commentary is fairly straightforward, the second passage (Sura 3:28) is more difficult for Christians:

> Let not the believers take for friends or helpers unbelievers rather than believers; if any do that, in nothing will there be any help from God: except by way of precaution, that ye may guard yourselves from them . . .

Believers here are Muslims, and the word translated 'friends' or 'helpers', can also mean 'protectors' or 'benefactors'. The words related to *taqiyya* are the ones translated here as 'precaution' and 'guard', and refer to a situation in which the Muslim feels threatened by non-Muslims. The great *Sunni* theologian and philosopher of religion Al-Razi (d. 1209) wrote in his commentary on this passage:

> A man is allowed to practise *taqiyya* if he lives among rejecters of faith whom he fears for his life and property

> ... He is even allowed to speak misleading words of love
> and loyalty provided that he conceals in his heart the
> opposite of what he manifests.

For Al-Razi this use of *taqiyya* is 'absolutely forbidden' if
it results in harm to others, such as 'killing, adultery, the
usurpation of wealth, giving false witness, killing chaste
women or informing the rejecters of faith of the faults of
the people of faith.'[17]

Muslim and Christian responses to the texts

I have found the Qur'an 3:28 passage difficult as it does
seem to discourage Muslims from entering into friendships with non-Muslims. Further, depending on the
level of threat which a Muslim feels, Al-Razi and other
commentators seem also to allow a false show of friendship. I put these concerns to Muslims who I know and
who in various ways I would count as colleagues and
friends. Their responses did sometimes reveal a degree
of discomfort, but they focused on readings of the text
that allowed them to be friends with me as a Christian.

Firstly there was the clause ' . . . rather than believers'.
This, Muslims pointed out to me, was not a blanket prohibition of non-Muslim friendships but rather an
encouragement for Muslims to develop their primary
friendships within their own religious community. A
couple of people mentioned the term 'unbeliever' (*kafir*)
as not applying to Christians anyway (though some
Muslims do apply it to Christians). Then, in relation to
al-Razi's allowance of ' . . . misleading words of love and
loyalty', the response was that Muslims in Britain don't
fear for their life and property. Such teaching might have
applied, for example, in Bosnia when there was real

danger to Muslims from Christians, but it doesn't apply here now.

The imam with whom I spoke was frank with me that there was a clear distinction in his mind as a Muslim between himself and his community and me and my community. We Christians were among those who had not taken up the 'trust' or relationship with God that Muslims had taken up, and Muslims should relate to us differently, keeping more of a distance. I thought of online guidance I had seen on Muslim websites discouraging Muslims from becoming close friends with Christians, and how the language there reminded me of advice sometimes given to Christian young people to keep a distance in their friendships with non-Christians. I also reflected on the experience of teenagers in our church fellowship who have found friendships with Muslims, Sikhs or Hindus from religious families vitally important precisely because with them there was not the same pressure to drink, take drugs and engage in casual sex as with many of their other friends at school or college.

When Muslims are allowed to lie

The second area of teaching is derived from various Traditions related from the Prophet Muhammad about when a lie would be permissible. The most commonly cited of these Traditions, considered reliable, well known among religiously educated Muslims and featuring in websites where ordinary Muslims ask for guidance on religious matters, allows Muslims to 'speak falsehood'

> . . . in battle, for bringing reconciliation amongst persons, and the narration of the words of the husband to his

wife, and the narration of the words of a wife to her husband (in a twisted form in order to bring reconciliation
between them).[18]

Another Tradition relates an incident in which
Muhammad allowed his companions to lie to one of his
enemies, Ka'b bin Al-Ashraf, in order to kill him.[19]

In his discussion of sincerity and truthfulness, Al-
Ghazali (d. 1111), one of the greatest *Sunni* Muslim religious authorities, draws on Muhammad's teaching and
example concerning lying 'in order to do good'. He
writes that sometimes circumstances create a context in
which the truth is served best by a lie. These include

> . . . avoiding evil and fighting enemies and guarding
> against their scrutiny of state secrets. Whoever is
> required by one of these things, then telling the truth
> about it consists in speaking for God concerning what
> the truth commands him about it and religion demands.
> If he speaks about it, he is truthful, even if his speech is
> understood in a different way to how things really are,
> because truthfulness is not an end in itself but is a point-
> er to the truth and an invitation to it. So one does not pay
> attention to its outer form but to its meaning.[20]

Again, in another place, Al-Ghazali writes:

> Know that a lie is not wrong in itself, but only because of
> the evil conclusions to which it leads the hearer, making
> him believe something that is not really the case.
> Ignorance sometimes is an advantage, and if a lie causes
> this kind of ignorance it may be allowed. It is sometimes
> a duty to lie . . . if lying and truth both lead to a good
> result, you must tell the truth, for a lie is forbidden in
> this case. If a lie is the only way to reach a good result, it

is allowable. A lie is useful when it is the only path to duty . . . We must lie when truth leads to unpleasant results, but tell the truth when it leads to good results.[21]

The key here in Al Ghazali's thinking is that 'speech', as he says, 'is a means to an end'. Whether words serve the truth or falsehood depends both on the 'context' in which they are spoken, and the 'intention' of the speaker. If we go back to the Gestapo officers at the door, telling them that there is no one else in the house would be for Al-Ghazali the 'outer form which would look like a lie', but would point to the greater truth that a human life is worth defending in this way from a murderer.

There are a number of difficulties in interpreting and responding to these texts today in Britain that became clear in my conversations with Muslims about them. The difficulties arise partly because the texts themselves seem to permit lying in quite a wide range of situations, and partly because the issues around both context and intention are so complex today.

In terms of context, for example, clearly at a formal level within Britain, Muslims and Christians are not at war but rather live peacefully together as neighbours and co-citizens. However there are some Muslims and others, including some Christians, who see the relationship differently, engaging in activities and using language which assumes that some kind of state of war does exist. But, as has been pointed out in terms of the so-called war on terror, this is a different kind of war, where old definitions and therefore ethical categories no longer apply in the same way.

In terms of intention within Islam, the permitting of a lie in order, for example, to 'bring reconciliation' raises important cultural issues about the relative values of truth, honour and shame. In a couple of conversations

that I had with Muslims about these texts, I sensed conflicting allegiances: how does the authoritative teaching
of someone like Al-Ghazali, from such a different time
and place, apply to Britain in the twenty-first century?
One of the strong Muslims with whom I discussed Al-
Ghazali's teaching, for example, spoke passionately of
her desire as a mother to bring up her children as honest
people. She understood and respected Al-Ghazali and
the Traditions of the Prophet that he quoted, but was not
prepared to apply them in her own context to allow
'white lies'.

Another more serious issue raised by Al-Ghazali concerns the permitted use of a lie in order to 'cover over
sins'. He writes, reflecting a wider concern within Islam
about modesty, that 'the revealing of a scandalous act is
another scandalous act'.[22] Until fairly recently, such an
attitude would have been widely shared within Britain.
But issues particularly of child protection have forced a
change in the way that our society understands the
value of honesty and openness relative to the value of
the honour of a family, institution or community. This
change, however, has not always been easy for church or
mosque to embrace. Thankfully attitudes are shifting
and institutions are coming to understand that truth and
openness are paramount both in protecting vulnerable
people and in bringing justice to them when they have
suffered abuse.[23]

Is it right to use *taqiyya* to refer to all kinds of permissible lying in Islam?

It was striking to me how distinct *taqiyya* and permitted
lying were in Islamic scholarship and also in the minds of
the Muslims with whom I spoke, both *Sunni* and *Shiʿite*.

Although the Muslims were happy to have a lively discussion and to disagree strongly with me and each other about whether, when and why it might be acceptable to lie, most of the time, and especially with *Sunnis*, we were not talking about *taqiyya*.

While *taqiyya* may have been written about and allowed by *Sunni* commentators, these texts are hugely overshadowed among *Sunnis* by the *Sunni-Shi^cite* polemic in which *taqiyya* is seen as a *Shi^cite* 'problem' and argued against. Given the overwhelming *Sunni* majority within the Islamic world and the Muslim community in Britain, I believe that Christians need to be very careful about labelling a debate about deception in Islam as necessarily a debate about *taqiyya*.[24]

Bringing the two areas of teaching together can be misleading not only in confusing two separate categories of Islamic scholarship, but also in giving the impression that there is a doctrine, clearly defined and labelled, that goes back to the Qu'ran for its authority and that is largely unquestioned and widely practised. A more helpful approach, I would argue, is to look at the 'honourable lie' as an issue debatable within Islam, within Christianity, between Christians and Muslims and more widely in our contemporary society.

The 'honourable lie' in Christianity

I write that the 'honourable lie' is an issue debatable within Christianity because conversations about lying within Islam of course raised this issue within my own faith. As well as looking at the issue for myself, Muslims asked me about it, simply assuming that any religious tradition worth its salt would have the ethical resources to be able to cope with an ethical dilemma such as the one with the Gestapo officer that I have already cited.

It was interesting that the current debate between Christians and Muslims over lying and trust mirror an old intra-church debate between Anglicans and Roman Catholics in the mid nineteenth century as to whether Anglicans could trust Catholics if Catholics taught that lying was not always a sin. The Cambridge Anglican clergyman and professor Charles Kingsley wrote against the famous convert to Catholicism, John Henry Newman:

> Truth, for its own sake, had never been a virtue with the Roman clergy. Father Newman informs us that it need not, and on the whole ought not to be; that cunning is the weapon which Heaven has given to the saints wherewith to withstand the brute male force of the wicked world . . .[25]

In his defence, Newman draws an analogy between lying and murder. Just as the act of killing someone becomes murder in a particular context and with a particular intention, while in other contexts (such as war or self-defence) it is not generally regarded as such, so in certain contexts and with certain intentions a lie can also be acceptable. The difference for Newman is that while the distinction between morally acceptable killing and murder is clearly defined by society, the distinction between acceptable and unacceptable lying is not so clearly articulated. As he writes,

> I would oblige society, that is its great men, its lawyers, its divines, its literature, publicly to acknowledge as such those instances of untruth which are not lies, as for instance, untruths in war.

The relevance of that nineteenth-century debate and Newman's call for clearer teaching about when it is right to lie came home to me when a friend of mine told me how he had been invited to a leaving party for a couple going to work as evangelistic missionaries in a Muslim country. The couple would almost certainly have been denied visas if they had told the consulate the full truth about what they intended to do; so they applied to go in another capacity. At the Christian theological college at which I spoke, I related this and asked the students whether that act which included an element of deception was justified. Most thought it was the right thing to do given that government's hostility to Christianity.

But the story continued. My friend found that the leaving party he had been invited to had been thrown not by Christians, but Muslim immigrants living in Britain, happy that the couple were going to serve their home country. These Muslims had even collected money towards the couple's air fare. As my friend entered the party, one of the missionaries asked him to be careful not to tell people there the real reason why they were going. I asked again at the theological college whether this deception was justified. The students were more uncomfortable this time, but many still thought the couple's action was justifiable.

The debate between Kingsley and Newman was part of a much bigger debate within the Christian ethical tradition regarding lying. Some great thinkers such as Augustine of Hippo and Emmanuel Kant forbade lying, as they defined it, under any circumstances. Others, such as Newman, above, or the German protestant Dietrich Bonhoeffer, thought differently.

Concluding reflections from Dietrich Bonhoeffer

Bonhoeffer (1906–45) was a pastor in Nazi Germany hanged by the Gestapo for his part in the attempt to kill

Hitler. The last chapter of his unfinished book, *Ethics*, is entitled, 'What Is Meant by "Telling the Truth?"' The words were written at a time of moral crisis in which Bonhoeffer refused to run away, but felt called to become deeply involved, even though he would inevitably become compromised in doing so. As he writes from prison:

> We have been silent witnesses of evil deeds; we have been drenched by many storms; we have learnt the arts of equivocation and pretence; experience has made us suspicious of others and kept us from being truthful and open; intolerable conflicts have worn us down and even made us cynical. Are we still of any use?[26]

Bonhoeffer may have despaired, but his very commitment to deep engagement in the compromised reality of life gave him, I believe, insights that are important for our context too. His contention is that truth is not, finally, contained in particular things we say, but in the relationship that lies behind the words. My task as a Christian is to find truthful words appropriate to the relationship. This, claims Bonhoeffer, is not the same as a 'situational ethic' so that 'truth' is different in different situations. But it does mean that I need to work hard at understanding any relationship in which I find myself, and finding an appropriate way of speaking so that my words are true.

A consequence of Bonhoeffer's focus on the relationship behind the words is that, as he writes, truth is something which must be learnt.[27] It takes time and effort to become truthful people because only with hard work and experience can we figure out the truth appropriate to the relationship and how it is to be expressed. Bonhoeffer gives the example of a child confronted by his teacher in front of the whole class who asks, 'Does your father come home drunk?' The boy says 'No,' even though he knows that his father does indeed come home drunk. Bonhoeffer argues that the important thing in this situation is not the actual lie told by the boy, but the fact that the boy has not yet learnt how to respond appropriately to an improper question from his teacher.

It seems to me that Christians and Muslims are engaged in relationships in which we are constantly learning what it means, in our complex realities, to be truthful. I wonder if the pickle that the missionary couple found themselves in at their leaving party was more a consequence of not having learnt how to tell the truth in their calling and context than a moral failure. I understand the conversations between our local church and mosque, sometimes over tea (including the conversations that we have had about the 'honourable lie'); sometimes we even share in the car park, where small steps are also taken towards a more truthful relationship. On a different level, I hope that 'A Common Word', written by Muslim scholars, can be read and responded to as part of a similar process, robustly and yet with the intention of opening up and deepening a relationship rather than closing it down.

In these different relationships, and even when there seems to be little or no progress in trust, Bonhoeffer's words remind us that the 'truth' is not simply the responsibility of one or other party. When a journalist asks a British Muslim organization whether it is affiliated to an international Islamist movement, the journalist and the wider society legitimately expect a truthful answer. But the journalist also has some responsibility in being willing to take the time and effort necessary to hear a truth that may be complex and nuanced. Can we learn to both tell and hear the truth about a complex issue like that, or are we simply aiming to score points?[28]

Bonhoeffer roots his ethical struggles deeply in his theology and spirituality. For him as a Christian, truth is essentially Jesus Christ, the embodiment of God's costly engagement with the reality of our human world. The purpose of our words is to 'express the real as it exists in God'.[29] The reality that we encounter both in the world and in ourselves is disrupted and contradictory and in need of healing and reconciliation. But it is not a Christian option to withdraw either because of our own weakness and failings, or because of the weakness and failings of others. It is our privilege and calling to reach out in love.

Chapter 16

The Case for Polemics

Jay Smith

Since the events of 11 September 2001 (and for those in the UK, 7 July 2005), there has been a dilemma in missionary circles concerning correct missiological methods to use with the more radical fringe groups whose violent acts have brought death and destruction to so many innocent people. Radical Muslims like these are new to the missiological task, forcing an evaluation of adequate responses to them.

New emergency and new need

Inter-faith dialogue, while proven adequate in bringing about mutual understanding between Christians and Muslims, can no longer cope with today's more aggressive and growing radical element within Islam. Those who take this view believe that the roots of radical Muslim anger against the West is not an aberration, nor a recent phenomenon, nor is it due necessarily to nineteenth-century colonialism, or American imperialism, or even to recent geo-political flare-ups. They believe that, 'Islam, throughout its history, has contained within itself a channel of violence, legitimized by certain passages of the Qur'an, and exemplified by their prophet Muhammad himself.'[1]

This group therefore sees the need to incorporate new approaches to deal with such a paradigm, including apologetics and polemics, which not only defend the foundations of our faith, but also confront the foundations of the more radical elements within the Muslim community, particularly those theological and historical foundations rooted in Islamic scriptures and Islamic Traditions, to which most radicals look for authority in substantiating the actions they carry out. We now live with a newly invigorated and increasingly militant Islam which is no longer distant, but has brought their 'battle' to the West in an attempt to seduce young and impressionable minds to their way of understanding Islamic scriptures and traditions.

The rise of radical Islam

Many pundits in the West seek to dismiss these militant elements as irrelevant extremists, representing only a small minority of the Muslim community. Recent research shows, however, that they are rapidly growing in numbers and importance, and are prepared to die, as well as kill, for what they believe.

In the United Kingdom, the mood among resident Muslims is becoming ever more antagonistic towards the West, particularly against the governments of the United States and Great Britain. According to a BBC Gallup and *Q-News* poll, taken in 2001, soon after the 9/11 incident, radical Muslims constituted roughly 15 per cent of the Islamic community within the United Kingdom. By 2002, however, the radicals had gained up to 25 per cent of the UK Muslim population.[2] According to more recent polls taken in February 2006, over 40 per cent of Muslims now want Islamic *shari'a* law to be introduced to Britain, while 20 per cent of those polled supported the 7 July 2005 London suicide bombers.[3] There are some who believe these percentages may be due to the recent Iraqi and Afghani conflicts; yet they are nonetheless troubling as they are taken within a strong Western environment, situated outside the traditional world of Islam, and therefore away from their traditional vehicles of influence.

If one were to look to the more traditional Islamic societies where people are fed anti-Western views regularly with little recourse to alternative opinions, the statistics are even more startling. According to a recent poll of four mainly Muslim nations taken in 18 March 2004 by the Pew Global Attitudes Project of the Pew Research Center, around 31 per cent of Turks now support the radical movement of Osama bin Laden, while in Morocco it is 45 per cent, and in Jordan it is 55 per cent. Of particular concern, according to this poll, support for Osama bin Laden in Pakistan, the second largest Muslim country, has risen to 65 per cent of the population, or roughly 80 to 90 million people.[4]

Fortunately, some Christians are willing and equipped to work among these more radical Muslims. Yet they are few, ill-trained and ill-equipped to meet the growing challenge, and this is indeed troubling. Within the church there are few facilities dedicated to training professionals or the laity in Islamic apologetics (i.e. answering the questions posed by the Muslims). What is worse, there is no training place to my knowledge anywhere in the world willing to venture into Islamic

polemics (confronting the foundations of Islam publicly).

This is indeed disturbing, since the radical Muslims
are confronting the foundations of our Christian faith
more vociferously and more comprehensively than ever.
A recent survey of videos on *YouTube* discovered more
than forty-three thousand videos attacking the foundations of Christianity, almost all by Muslims, and all in
the English language. Conversely, the surveyors could
only find between ten to fifteen videos challenging
Islam's foundations, and almost all of them filmed by
individuals with little or no formal training. Muslim
daᶜwa material in the form of books, tracts, tapes, videos
and the internet, is filled with vociferous material attacking Christianity, focusing in particular on our foundation, the Bible, as well as the person of Jesus Christ.
Their passion, though misguided, is indeed amazing –
even impressive.   Somehow our weak and feeble
response suggests we either have no solutions or simply
lack their passion, or both.

How then, might such radical Muslims be confronted? Is there any way not only to grab their attention, but
to address the issue of their deep anger and to keep it
from spreading to other sectors of the Muslim community?

A solution for radical Islam

Many politicians and a growing number of Christians in
the West believe that the only way to deal with this
growing radical threat is to either ignore it, or even
worse, to eradicate it through repressive laws, or the
'barrel of a gun'. There is little evidence that a philosophy or a belief which is perceived by its adherents to

have its source in divine revelation can be removed by the use of repressive laws or violence. History has in fact shown that movements such as Christianity and Islam have thrived and even expanded when repressed or attacked violently from without.

A better solution, I believe, is the 'tough love' practised by Jesus, his disciples, and the early church in the first century. This solution is one which employs a verbal and public defence (apologetics) as well as a verbal and public offence (polemics) against those who choose to challenge our foundation (the Lord Jesus Christ) and our revelation (the Scriptures) – not with the use of a sword, but with one's mouth, mind, and volition.

In order to do this today, we need to begin by confronting the very foundations of Islam – namely, their paradigm, the Prophet Muhammad, and the revelations, the Qur'an and Traditions, which speak about him.

New Testament precedents

It might be wise here to ask whether it is possible to find a case for a confrontational or apologetic/polemical model of evangelism in the New Testament. Some Christians make reference to the classic text in 1 Peter 3:15,16 which stipulates that Christians should be prepared to defend their faith 'with gentleness and respect' (NIV).

Yet, defence, or *apologia*, against an accuser should not come as a surprise as it is mentioned five times in the New Testament: Acts 22:1; 25:16; 1 Corinthians 9:3; 2 Corinthians 7:11; and 2 Timothy 4:16. Twice Christians are asked to defend the gospel (Phil. 1:7,16; and 1 Pet. 3:15). A strong defence of our beliefs is thus not foreign to New Testament teaching as it was practised by the early church.

Jesus' example

Jesus was a Jew from the Mediterranean world, an environment similar to that which birthed Islam. When approached by those who came to listen and to learn, he treated them in kind, listening courteously and engaging them in friendly dialogue. Nicodemus, a Pharisee who came to Jesus at night (John 3:1–21) is a fine example of such an approach. We too are asked to follow the example of our Lord, and respond to the Nicodemuses of our world, answering their questions and sharing with them the truths of the gospel in a spirit of 'gentleness and respect'.

However, when approached by those whose sole purpose was to confront, Jesus met them with a mode of conversation they understood. Take for example Jesus' exchange with the rich young ruler (Matt. 19:16-22), or his confrontation with the Pharisees and Herodians (Mark 12:13–17), or his rebuke to his Pharisee host at a dinner party (Luke 7:36–50).

Perhaps the best example of a confrontational response is found in Matthew 23:13–33, where Jesus referred to the Pharisees who came to challenge him as 'hypocrites', 'blind fools', 'whitewashed tombs', and as 'snakes' and 'vipers'. He was equally confrontational with the money-changers at the temple (Matt. 21:12,13; Luke 19:45,46) by overturning their tables.

We do not have the authority of Jesus and it would be ill-advised to literally 'upset the tables' of those who stand in opposition to the church. Jesus' example and resolve, however, should be a model for us as we seek resolutely to confront opponents to the kingdom of God in our day.

Paul's example

But let's not stop with Jesus, for Paul is another prime example of a person who used confrontational apologetics and polemics in his ministry. Like Jesus, Paul was multifaceted in his methodology. At times he contextualized his message, such as when he met dispersed Jews on their territory across the Mediterranean world and read the Scriptures with them (Acts 13:13,15); or when he borrowed ideas from Greek philosophy when formulating a response to the thinkers of his day at the Areopagus in Athens (Acts 17:22–31).

Paul was not averse, however, to confrontation, and was in fact remarkably proactive in his apologetics and polemics, venturing into the synagogues and the market-places to reason with some, and to speak boldly, refute, debate, and argue with others (Acts 13:46; 17:17; 18:28; 19:8,9; 2 Cor. 5:11; 10:5). He received rough treatment from both Jews and Romans in the form of flogging, riots, imprisonment and stoning.

Paul's resolute and uncompromising stance can be traced throughout his ministry in the book of Acts. There were times when he went outside his Jewish community to the Greeks in their territory, reasoning with them from within their traditions (Acts 17:1,2,17). In the pagan city of Ephesus, he began first by 'arguing persuasively' in the Jewish synagogue for three months (Acts 19:8, NIV). When forced to leave, he went on to the lecture hall of Tyrannus, a secular institution, where he continued his discussions with both Jews and Greeks for two more years (Acts 19:9,10). Later, in Rome, Paul pursued his ministry in his rented apartment, from morning till night, for another two years, where he boldly 'tried to convince' those who came to talk to him about Jesus (Acts 28:23-31, NIV).

Through it all, Paul preached the gospel unremittingly (Rom. 1:16; 15:20; 1 Cor. 1:23). Uppermost in his mind was the need to persuade people of the truth of Christ's gospel. As he himself wrote, he sought to 'demolish arguments and every pretension that sets itself up against the knowledge of God, and we take captive every thought to make it obedient to Christ' (2 Cor. 10:5, NIV). As a consequence, Paul obtained results using both eirenics (Acts 13:13–15; 17:22–31) and a more confrontational, even argumentative, approach (Acts 13:46; 17:17; 18:28; 19:8,9; 28:23–31; 2 Cor. 5:11; 10:5).

Other apostles also employed confrontational approaches. Stephen, for example, when challenged by members of the Synagogue of the Freedmen (i.e. the Jews of Cyrene, Alexandria, Cilicia and Asia), held his ground and returned their arguments – so much so, that 'they could not stand up against his wisdom' (Acts 6:9,10, NIV), and finally decided to execute him (Acts 7:57 – 8:1). One does not get executed for merely 'agreeing to disagree'.

Confront only co-religionists?

A popular assumption is that the early church challenged only those within their own community of faith – the implication being that we likewise should refrain from challenging those who are not 'of our kind', such as Muslims. Yet some of those suggesting this also suggest that Muslims are co-religionists with us, contending that we share the same 'god', and trace our lineage back to Abraham. One cannot have it both ways. What is more, the example of Paul given above, who was often speaking to Gentiles living outside the Jewish community, provides a more than adequate model for those of us wishing to employ a similar paradigm with Muslims.

Philip was likewise comfortable when engaging the Ethiopian (Acts 8:26–40). Why then do we consider this proactive and resolute form of witness, often addressed to people outside of the Christian community, detrimental to the gospel, when it was this very model that was used so often by the earliest believers who gave us the gospel?

Sauls becoming Pauls

In my work I often use a confrontational approach, employing both apologetics and polemics, many times challenging the historicity of what Muslims claim concerning the Qur'an and the Prophet Muhammad. I have used both formal debates with Muslim scholars (around sixty to date), as well as more 'ad hoc' informal debates (i.e. confronting radical Muslims from a ladder at Speaker's Corner in Hyde Park).

We have seen results from both these kinds of debate, as well as from the material engendered by them. Recently, two Muslims with status, one a high-ranking doctor in a Middle Eastern country, and the other a champion martial arts fighter, have both given their lives to the Lord after reading polemical papers I wrote on the Prophet Muhammad, and then comparing him with the Lord Jesus Christ.

Another Muslim, a graduate with honours from Al-Azhar University in Cairo, having studied videos of me in order to attack my ideas and tactics, has now met the Lord in a remarkable, almost Pauline-fashion vision, and at times joins our team at Speaker's Corner. He believes it is one of the most effective arenas not only to train

Christians to define and defend their faith (something we are poor at), but to confront the foundations of Islam publicly as well. These are the men like Paul that we are looking for, men and women who had status to begin with, as Saul had, who then as 'Pauls' can go back into their own communities and make a greater impact on them than any of us from without. They are the 'Sauls' who become 'Pauls'.

While many of us have been at the forefront of dialogue with Islam, few have sought to confront its foundations polemically. This may be out of fear, or perhaps due to our methodological restraints. This is unfortunate because it is possible to become equipped to enter into such a challenge. This is not only because we refuse to resort to violence, but because, like radical Muslims, we start from a similar pre-suppositional framework and trust the efficacy of revelation as a source for all we believe and practice. We can and must debate the truth of these different claims to revelation. What's more we have by far the best material to defeat their authority and the only antidote, the gospel of Jesus Christ.

The situation post 9/11 and 7/7 has brought into focus a need to reassess whether there is room for some of us to return to the early church models of active engagement using both apologetics and polemics in order to confront radical Muslims, especially with regard to their theological and historical foundations. It is from these foundations that they derive their authority and substantiate their actions.

We need to learn from those who have been at the forefront of this debate, and ascertain whether we can benefit from the materials and methods that have been employed in this approach to the Muslims. Perhaps these, then, could be applied to a healthy ongoing public debate with our Muslim brothers and sisters who far too often see us as a threat to much of what they hold true and dear.

Both Muslims and Christians, when true to their faith, have a passionate commitment to truth, and both believe that ultimate truth can only be known through revelation. What Muslims and Christians hold dearest to their hearts is revealed truth. So we enter the debate not to destroy one another necessarily but rather to destroy falsehood, and uphold the truth.

Jesus and Paul gave us an example of this kind of confrontation in the first century which I believe is just as applicable today in the twenty-first century. Therefore, may we not also, like them, chosen to confront; and is there not a place for apologetics and polemics?

Chapter 17

The Case for Dialogue

Chawkat Moucarry

I was born into a Catholic home in Syria and was an altar boy in my early teens. I attended a Catholic primary school where I first had the opportunity to discuss religion with my Muslim peers. My first significant conversations about Christianity and Islam, however, started after I moved to a government secondary school where the majority of pupils were from working-class families, unlike the Catholic school. I was very surprised when I realized that many Muslim schoolmates were very interested to know more about Christianity and Christians. I too wanted to get a better understanding of Islam. A unique opportunity presented itself when the teacher of Islamic religion accepted my request and granted me permission to attend his class. I was the only Christian in the classroom. I remember he would regularly ask me to give my views as a Christian on certain topics. These discussions were often extended outside the classroom. As far as I know none of my Muslim peers became a Christian, but I am still moved when I think of the friendliness that marked our relationships.

In Paris, after I graduated in Christian theology, I felt a compelling need as an Arab Christian to relate my faith to Islam, which required studying this religion. This need was reinforced after I started working for the International Fellowship of Evangelical Students (IFES) amongst Arab and Muslim students. Sometimes they would ask me challenging questions which I had not seriously considered as a theological student. Hence it wasn't difficult for me to choose research topics for my Islamic Studies dissertations at the Sorbonne University. For my first degree in Islamics I looked into the Islamic charge against the reliability of the Bible, and in my PhD I examined Islamic and Christian teachings on forgiveness. Needless to say, studying Islam unavoidably implied re-examining Christian beliefs which I had often taken for granted. My work with the Christian Unions was very diverse, and included bookstalls on university campuses and Bible study groups, as well as public debates on Christianity and Islam in France and abroad. When invited to such debates I always recommended that a Muslim speaker be also invited. It was much fairer to have a Muslim rather than a Christian present an Islamic perspective on a given topic; the debate was much more engaging and sometimes more heated, when it took place between two people of different persuasions. Often debates such as these attracted a large number of Muslim and Christian students.

As a lecturer at All Nations Christian College in the UK I had fewer opportunities for public debates. For twelve years I ran the college Islamics course, and each year we had a Muslim lecturer among our guest speakers. Their talks were one of the high spots of this ten-day course, as they unmistakably provided an opportunity for a genuine and often animated interaction between students, the speaker and myself.

For four years now I have been working for a Christian aid organization, World Vision, which operates in twenty Muslim-majority countries. In all of them we have Muslims on the staff, and in some, the staff is predominantly Muslim (e.g. Afghan, Mauritanian, Somalian). Part of my work is to provide orientation on both Christianity and Islam to our staff. It has been a fascinating exercise to lead workshops in several countries. Christian and Muslim staff are given the opportunity to engage with faith issues, to learn about each other's faith and often about their own faith too. They learn to appreciate the common ground between the two faiths and how to use it to enhance their work in the community.

What is dialogue?

Many definitions have been suggested for dialogue. My own definition would be something like this: 'A deliberate effort to engage genuinely and respectfully with each other; a willingness to listen and understand; a readiness to learn and be challenged; it is also a desire to relate to, communicate with and be understood by one another.' In Christian-Muslim dialogue the focus is the Christian and Muslim faiths and their implications for individuals and communities in this life and the next.

For many centuries, Christians in the West have either ignored or confronted the Muslim world. Ignoring Muslims is hardly an option nowadays since Muslims and Christians no longer live apart. Some Christians seek to reach out to them in a rather confrontational way. They consider polemics as a perfectly legitimate way to approach Islam. Polemics, as the Greek word suggests, is about waging a war of words against Muslims by attacking their religion. Taking a confrontational approach to Islam generates more heat than light. It tends to be counterproductive as it usually provokes a defensive response, with Muslims becoming more radical in their beliefs, and often also an offensive reaction, with Muslims attacking Christianity even more vehemently. Such an approach is also incompatible with 'the gospel of peace' (Eph. 6:15). I believe, therefore, that a polemical engagement with Islam is misguided on all counts, particularly when it is adopted by Westerners who are perceived by many Muslims as Islam's traditional enemies.

Engaging in respectful dialogue with Muslims reflects the way God himself deals with humanity. He created human beings in his image with a view to having a close and loving relationship with us. He committed himself to humanity through a covenant relationship in which he became our Partner (without giving up his divine attributes and prerogatives). He revealed his word to us in human languages and, in Jesus Christ, became one of us. Throughout the Gospels, we see Jesus engaging with his people in a dialogue mode. Even when he addresses the crowd he speaks the good news into their own context (religious, cultural and personal). When he occasionally adopts a polemical mode it is always with the Jewish leaders who have deliberately rejected his message.

The disciples walked in the footsteps of their master when they preached the gospel. The book of Acts provides us with eloquent examples of dialogical preaching of the good news, such as Peter's sermon to the Jewish pilgrims gathered in Jerusalem for Pentecost (Acts 2:14–41) and Paul's speech at the Areopagus in Athens (Acts 17:16–34). Writing to Christians who were beginning to experience persecution, he encourages them to give a reasonable account of their faith but without attacking their opponents:

> In your hearts revere Christ as Lord. *Always be prepared to give an answer to everyone who asks you the reason for the hope that you have. But do this with gentleness and respect,* keeping a clear conscience, so that those who speak maliciously against your good behaviour in Christ may be ashamed of their slander. For it is better, if it is God's will, to suffer for doing good than for doing evil. (1 Pet. 3:15–17, NIV 2010; emphasis added)

The Greek word for 'to give an answer' in the above quotation is *apologia*, 'apology', which means 'a defence' and has nothing to do with 'apologizing'. As the immediate context clearly indicates, the only adequate response for Christians who are under pressure is not to retaliate but to witness which, in such circumstances, means spelling out boldly and peacefully why they believe what they believe. In other words, Christian dialogue may well take the form of a defence when the Christian faith comes under fire. Then dialogue naturally turns into apologetics. Even in a heated debate, the Christian apologist must refrain from polemics and always show respect for the audience.

Christian-Muslim dialogue often takes the form of apologetics for at least two reasons. First, Christianity and Islam make conflicting truth claims about God's revelation, which reached its climax for Christians with the coming of Jesus Christ, and for Muslims with the disclosure of the Qurᶜan. Second, Islam acknowledges Christianity (and Judaism) as a God-given religion; at the same time, the core of the Christian faith (the divinity of Christ, his crucifixion and resurrection) is rejected.

Dialogue is one of those words which divide Christians because of what they take it to mean. Some consider dialogue as the rightful and necessary alternative to mission. Christians, they say, are only to build bridges of understanding with people of other faiths without expecting them, let alone pressing them, to convert to Christianity. This is especially true of Muslims who believe in and worship the same God as Christians. Others believe that Christian mission is about preaching the gospel which should not be compromised through a demeaning dialogue with other religions. More than any other religion Islam is anti-Christian, they say, because of its denial of the tenets of the Christian faith (Trinity, Incarnation, Redemption). These antagonistic views do not do justice to two biblical truths, respectively the uniqueness of God's revelation in Christ, which is the yardstick for all religions (including Christianity), and the incarnation of God's revelation in Jesus Christ which compels us to engage seriously with everything human, including religions. Not only is dialogue compatible with mission, but the two are in fact inseparable.

The scope of dialogue

Dialogue is often understood in terms of verbal engagement, but this is an extremely narrow view. Dialogue is first of all about an open attitude towards others, a disposition that seeks to reach out and to welcome people, including those who are different. Dialogue is a way of life. Understood in these terms, Christian-Muslim dialogue is an encounter at three distinct and interrelated levels. Jesus' encounter with the Samaritan woman is paradigmatic in this regard (John 4:1–26).

Christians and Muslims are first of all human beings. They have the same physical and emotional needs, human and spiritual aspirations, joys and sorrows, hopes and struggles. They are part of the wider community and they face the same issues as anyone else (education,

health, employment, housing, etc.). They need to get personally involved, together with people of other faiths
and of none, to meet the challenges faced by society at
large. Our future depends on our commitment to the
common good of our community. Whoever we are, we
are brothers and sisters in humanity.

As monotheistic believers, Christians and Muslims
share many beliefs (e.g. creation, human stewardship,
divine guidance, sin, forgiveness, final judgement) and
ethical values (e.g. moral standards, the sacredness of
human life, sexual fidelity, commitment to the poor). It
is true that we do not understand our religious beliefs
the same way; but this is precisely what makes dialogue
possible and necessary. When differences are examined
openly, they contribute to mutual understanding and
enrichment. Dialogue in general is a learning experience
for all parties; for believers it is no exception, especially
when it is carried out with the expectation that God may
well use it to teach them, deepen and possibly purify
their faith of all things contaminated by sin.

Finally, Christians and Muslims claim to be *God's witnesses* on earth. Christianity and Islam are both missionary religions. There is nothing wrong with this. Each
community has the right, and from their perspective, the
duty and the privilege to carry out the mission they
believe was entrusted to them. They only need to use
legal, honest and peaceful means, and to show due
respect to people's freedom and conscience. Christians
and Muslims have huge misunderstandings about each
other's faith. Removing these misunderstandings is an
integral part of dialogue. Misunderstandings about
Christianity are theological ('the Trinity consists of God,
Mary and Jesus'), cultural ('Western culture reflects
Christian values'), and political ('Western nations are
Christian'). At the same time we need as Christians to

give Muslims the same opportunity to dispel misunderstandings about their community and religion. As we explain our respective faiths to one another, each community bears witness to the Creator according to its own understanding.

Too often dialogue is limited, when it happens, to the leadership and institutional levels. It is very important that Christian and Muslim leaders encourage their respective communities to do the same at grass roots level. Christian-Muslim dialogue is more likely to be fruitful when it is not limited to the verbal dimension and when it involves ordinary believers. The more people get to know each other, work together, socialize and have fun together, the more their dialogue will be useful.

Expected outcomes

A fruitful dialogue is measured by its outcomes. It is a dialogue that results in a better understanding of each other's faith and of one's own. It is likely that we will realize that there is a significant common ground to Christianity and Islam as well as many misunderstandings and some crucial differences. Our theological differences make it difficult for us to worship together without compromising the fundamental tenets of our respective faiths. If we cannot honestly consider ourselves as brothers and sisters in faith, we will nevertheless appreciate more and more our common humanity.

Hopefully dialogue will also lead to better relationships between the two communities and will strengthen their social commitment. This will provoke them to work together as members of the same society for the common good of the people. The moral and religious values we share will enhance our collaboration.

Dialogue is also an excellent school for tolerance. It helps us overcome our ignorance, our prejudice, our self-centredness, our fanaticism and our spiritual pride. We are made aware that people are as much committed to their faith (and perhaps even more) as we are to ours. Their faith does make a real difference in their lives. It does give them a sense a fulfilment and meet their spiritual needs. It has a powerful rational attraction and provides meaning, purpose and hope to their existence – all things we thought only our faith was capable of!

Is conversion a legitimate result of dialogue? Some believe that tolerance requires that Christians and Muslims refrain from seeking to convert each other. It is indeed unhelpful to see conversion as the primary goal for dialogue. Christianity and Islam teach that God alone is the one who converts people. Therefore Christians and Muslims should not by any means entice or force people to convert.

Having said this, it is perfectly legitimate for believers, who take seriously the exclusive claims of their religion, to try to persuade others of the truth they believe in. There is nothing wrong with hoping, and perhaps even with expecting, that some people, having carefully examined these claims, will make a life-changing decision as a result of a transparent and free dialogue. In other words, while conversion is not the only or even the main purpose for dialogue, it is to be seen as a possible outcome. Who are we to deny anyone their right to change their religion if this is really what they want to do? Unless we accept conversion as a possible outcome for dialogue our claim to be tolerant remains unproven. Only when conversion (to a faith other than our own) happens will we be able to demonstrate how tolerant we are. Conversion must not be seen as a victory by one side or a failure by the other side, but rather as the outcome of a personal journey of which only God knows the secret.

Dialogue today

The Qurʿan has numerous and ambivalent texts about Christians. On the one hand, they are described as people who are full of 'compassion and mercy' (Sura 57:27). They are humble and friendly towards Muslims (Sura 5:82). They are praised for their godliness (Sura 3:113–115) and they should have no fear with regard to the day of judgement (Sura 2:62). On the other hand, Muslims are told to take neither Jews nor Christians as allies (Sura 5:51). Christian and Jewish leaders are blamed for abusing their authority and for possessing unlawful wealth (Sura 9:31,34). Christians are accused of having invented monasticism (Sura 57:27). They are unbelievers because they worship Christ as the Son of God (Sura 9:30,31). Christians and Jews should be fought against until they submit to Islamic rule (Sura 9:29). However, as Jews received the Torah and Christians the Gospel from God, they form 'the People of the Book' they can live alongside the Muslim community without having to convert to Islam. Muslims have the duty to invite everyone to embrace Islam 'by way of wisdom and good exhortation' (Sura 16:125). This command about *daʿwa*, Islamic mission, applies to Jews and Christians too: 'Do not argue with the People of the Book but in the best possible way, except in the case of those among them who have been unjust' (Sura 29:46; cf. 3:64).

On 13 October 2007, 138 Muslim scholars and leaders published an open letter. The signatories represented virtually all Muslim denominations worldwide. The recipients were the Pope and the leaders of main Christian denominations. The title of the letter, 'A Common Word Between Us and You', derives from the following qur'anic text which invites Christians to join hands with Muslims on 'the most solid theological ground possible', namely the respective teachings of the Qur'an and the Bible:

> Say: O People of the Scripture! Come to a common word between us and you: that we shall worship none but God, and that we shall ascribe no partner unto Him, and that none of us shall take others for lords beside God. And if they turn away, then say: Bear witness that we are they who have surrendered (unto Him) (Sura 3:64).[1]

Two main characteristics of this document should be noted. The first is the judgement made by the signatories that Christians are indeed a monotheistic community. This is a huge step forward in terms of Christian-Muslim relationships. For centuries Muslim scholars considered the Christian doctrine about the Trinity (Father-Son-Holy Spirit) as a subtle form of polytheism, *shirk*. Christians were therefore seen as a kind of polytheistic people. Their Trinitarian faith not just undermined but practically nullified their belief in God's oneness.[2] The second noteworthy characteristic of this document is that it sums up Islamic teaching and practice in *The Commandments of Love*: loving God and our neighbour. Christians are familiar with this summary that was first made by Jesus Christ himself (Matt. 22:34–40). That Muslim scholars have formulated their faith in such terms is no coincidence. It shows that they have made a deliberate effort to reach out to the Christian community through identifying in their own tradition those elements that achieve a real rapprochement between the two communities. In fact, the document makes several quotations from the Bible. Clearly through this open letter, Muslim leaders have extended a hand of friendship to the Christian community and expressed a strong desire to engage in dialogue with them. Thankfully many Christians have responded positively to this initiative.[3]

Unlike Muslims, Christians do not find in their Scriptures clear guidelines on how to relate specifically to Islam. Christians are in fact divided over this matter and, like Muslims, they find in their Scriptures different texts to back up their different perspectives on Islam. This is not the place to review Christian approaches to Islam; we can only suggest a general framework for our relations with Muslims. We have in another summary of the law by Jesus a short and meaningful guiding statement: '. . . in everything, do to others what you would have them do to you, for this sums up the Law and the Prophets' (Matt. 7:12, NIV). How do we want Muslims to relate to us as Christians and to our faith? I would like here to highlight some implications of this golden rule for us Christians who engage with Islam and Muslims.

First of all, we must show respect to Muslims, their prophet, their religion, and their scriptures. This is a particularly important expression of loving our neighbours. Muslims revere all prophets including Abraham, Moses and Jesus. In fact every time they mention a prophet they say, *'alayhi as-salaam'* (i.e. peace be upon him). We must reciprocate their respectful attitude regardless of what we think of their faith. We need to adopt an attitude that is conducive to mutual understanding. This requires avoiding embarrassing questions, derogatory comments and inflammatory language. It is true that some Muslim polemicists and extremists do not comply with the qur'anic recommendation to argue with Jews and Christians 'in the best possible way'. This is no excuse for Christians to indulge in vitriolic criticisms of Islam. Jesus tells us to treat others the way we would like them to treat us, not the way they actually do.

This does not mean abstaining from any criticism of Islam. When we have critical comments to make we need to put them in the least offensive language and to ensure as far as we can that they are substantiated. Jesus enjoins his disciples not to be naïve and to look critically at self-proclaimed prophets (Matt. 7:15–20); he also commands them in the same breath to take a critical look at themselves (Matt. 7:1–5; 21–23). People who live in glass houses should not throw stones! Therefore we should abstain from a systematic, let alone polemical, criticism of Islam. Church history shows that Christians in general do not live up to their faith any more than Muslims do. As for our Scriptures, the fact that they are indeed the reliable Word of God does not make them beyond critical examination from outsiders, let alone from some Christian theologians. Muslim theologians in particular have developed their own theories about the so-called falsification, *tahrif*, of the Bible.

Secondly, we need to do our best to be fair. This means, for instance, when comparing Christianity and Islam, having the balance right between highlighting similarities and pointing out differences. Focusing on either of them will give a distorted image. However, in certain contexts (when peace-building is needed), it is useful to point out the similarities; in others (when political correctness is prevailing), showing the differences might be more helpful. Fairness also requires comparing like with like, for instance, not comparing moderate Christians with extremist Muslims, ideal Christianity with popular Islam, beautiful texts in the Bible with problematic passages in the Qur'an, and vice versa.

Some Christians are too often tempted to compare Islamic teaching with the New Testament, which is understandable from one point of view. However, Christians do not disown the Old Testament, and it would be unfair to ignore the Old Testament altogether when looking at issues such as holy war, polygamy, penal code, prophethood, and theocracy. Some Christians often challenge Muslims about the prophet's wives and his military career; yet, these same Christians have a great deal of admiration for Old Testament figures such as Joshua, Elijah, David and Solomon.

Finally, we cannot engage in Christian-Muslim dialogue without seriously studying Islam and befriending Muslims. It is legitimate, in fact unavoidable, for Christians to use Islamic material in their interaction with Islam, but it is critically important that we do it in an appropriate way. We should adopt a learning and humble attitude. We need to acknowledge that it is the Muslim community who are the custodians of their own tradition. Therefore they are the authoritative interpreters of their Scriptures, not us. While we can offer our own understanding of Islamic sources, we should not consider ourselves in a better position than Muslim scholars to interpret Islamic scriptures. Some Christian approaches tend to Christianize Islam, others to demonize it; neither does justice to Islamic teaching, which should be considered on its own merits.

A Christian perspective on Islam ought to be at the same time incarnational, sympathetic and critical. It should be concerned more with Muslim people than with Islam. Muslims are first and foremost human beings, made in God's image and loved by God as much as we are. As disciples of Jesus Christ we are under a double obligation, to love our Muslim neighbours as ourselves and to share the good news with them. Not only do the two commands go hand in hand, but the second is best carried out as an expression of the first. Dialogue is indeed the best way for 'speaking the truth in love' (Eph. 4:15) to Muslims, as well as to other religious communities.

Chapter 18

Promoting Other Voices?

Rt Revd Dr Bill Musk

Towards the end of 2008, my wife and I moved from Tulse Hill in London to Tunis in North Africa. In the process of moving and resettling, two issues came especially to occupy my mind. The first concerned my involvement as an Anglican minister in Christian relationships with – and attitudes towards – Muslims in the UK at local, regional and national levels over the past twenty years. The second issue concerned my re-immersion in the Islamic world and my perception of how Muslims view their relationship with Christians, and specifically with 'the Christian West'. In this chapter I would like to unpack these matters, and explain why they both encourage and worry me. They lead me to plead that, between us, we try to promote some other voices.

Here from there

Let me begin with my second issue, partly because it is most fresh in my mind and partly because it throws my first concern into sharper relief. I am thinking about how Muslims perceive their relationship with Christians, and with what they view as the Christian West.

On my way to my present post in Tunis, I attended the Eighth General Conference of the World Islamic Call Society (WICS). WICS is a society of Muslims concerned with *da'wa* – holistic, Islamic mission. The society was founded in 1972 in Libya, and has from its inception been generously funded and promoted by Libya's leader, Muammar Qaddafi. One motive for the establishing and sustaining of this society has been the desire to promote Islam throughout the world. WICS has representatives, or field-workers, in most countries. Another motive for creating WICS as a successful *da'wa* movement has been the desire to provide a coherent and attractive alternative to the kind of Islam exported over many decades from Saudi Arabia. The WICS mentality and spiritual genius abhors the Wahhabi perspective.

The Eighth General Conference (held in October 2008 in Tripoli, Libya) was the most recent in a series of such in-house conferences that are convened every four years. WICS representatives attended from around the globe (from Australia to Mauritania). The conference felt rather like an Islamic equivalent of a Lausanne conference. Prayer and worship were central, and public. The Qur'an was regularly quoted and sometimes chan-ted. There were plenaries and smaller workshops on specific issues. National representatives gave their feedback and appeals for the prayers and help of the wider Muslim community. Such representatives were involved in education, health, infrastructure-building, poverty alleviation, religious education and – as a central core of the society's ethos – inter-faith dialogue.

This last provided the reason for our invitation as Christians to be present. WICS has recently taken to dialoguing directly with various Christian constituents – including key evangelical mission and church leaders. After hesitations from the Vatican in responding to invitations from WICS for dialogue, WICS sought a direct and fairly high-profile link with the Archbishop of Canterbury and the Anglican Communion. That is why specifically Anglican Christians (myself included) were invited to be present at the Eighth General Conference. Although there has apparently been something of an in-house struggle to get the 'interfaith dialogue' aspect of their ethos accepted and practised throughout the WICS organization, that aspect continues to be promoted as part of the essence of what WICS is about – relating across the faiths. Such relating does not prevent their *da'wa* intention from including a dedicated, multimedia attempt to counter arguments of Christians against Islam and provide Muslims with knockdown proofs against Christianity! At the conference I attended, there was a wide range of views within WICS about what 'inter-faith relating' might mean, with some espousing polemics in the Ahmed Deedat mould and with others simply wanting their good works, performed in God's name, to speak for themselves.

I observed (as per Lausanne and other international forums?) a frustration that the whole event might be overly stage-managed by the staff of WICS with not enough time or space for input from 'field workers'. And there were the usual cross-cultural issues to be faced up to in a gathering organized by those from one particular host culture. As a German representative of WICS said to me in confidence in the lift one evening, after a day in which the programme got progressively delayed by flowery speeches: 'We don't do "conference" like this in Germany.' Women also (especially from Africa) requested that their gender be allowed a much higher profile.

The spirit of the whole conference was, nevertheless, very positive and warm. My small group of Christian attendees provided the only experience, in a non-plenary meeting, of some actual dialogue between two world faiths. We were well received. I was very moved after a rather sharp conversation with one South African (Muslim) delegate in the foyer of the hotel in which we were staying when, following our disputation, he jumped up to shake my hand, declaring, 'I would like to apologize for the mistreatment of Christians by Muslims.'

I hope the previous paragraphs manage to convey a little taste of the kind of Muslims (of the ilk of the late Shaikh Dr Zaki Badawi) who were attending this conference in late 2008. They were orthodox, committed, pious, (mostly) open-spirited, prayerful people. That encouraged me! Here is what worried me. Nearly every WICS delegate – from around the world – who took the platform to make their presentation, spoke as if they were convinced that the 'West' or the 'Christian West' was out to destroy Islam. The defensiveness and sense of being pointedly victimized was universal. The developing 'credit crunch' was hailed by many speakers as constituting God's action on Muslims' behalf to humble an aggressive, Western world that was dead set against Islam and Muslims.

Since moving to Tunis and coming to appreciate the slick, in-depth and emotive reportage being conveyed to most people of the Middle East by al-Jazeera TV, it is plain that the defensiveness expressed by WICS members is being daily sharpened by anger at current world politics. Graphic images of dead civilians, adults and children, in what was headlined as Israel's 'war on Gaza', expressed the bloody consequences of the military and political argument between the State of Israel and Hamas for the lives of ordinary people. America's long silence about that war was 'heard' as tacit approval of the state of Israel's actions. It confirmed to many Muslims that the 'Christian West' is seeking to destabilize, destroy, dehumanize Muslims – either by direct action or through proxy partners.

My observation of this attitude, shared widely across the Muslim world – even by the kind of open-minded Muslims gathered for the WICS conference – worries me considerably. It is an attitude that is being intensified and radicalized daily through the local media. Mutual understanding and healthy interaction between Muslims and Christians, between Middle Easterners and Westerners seems daily more difficult to realize. Current defensiveness in the face of the religious other consolidates views that are stuck in extreme mode. Such radicalization of the default Muslim perspective forms the background noise against which Christian groups in the West (like CRIB) fulfil their callings in relating to Muslims and Islam.

There from here

This brings me to my 'first' issue – first in importance, that is. My primary concern arises from my involvement as an Anglican minister in the area of Christian relationships with – and attitudes towards – Muslims in the UK at local, regional and national levels over the past twenty years. I believe that Christians in the UK, and specifically evangelical, mission-minded Christians, have moved a long way – in both positive and negative directions – in responding to the presence of Muslims within the British Isles.

What positive direction? Well, at least today, no serious Christian church or movement is unaware of the significance of Islam as a world faith, or unconvinced that 'relating to Muslims' has to be part of what it means to be an engaged Christian in many parts of the UK. There is a general recognition that, under God, Christians in the UK are called today to produce a faithful 'missional' response to the 'Muslim in our midst'.

The negative direction that worries me is the seeming attitude of spirit in some of those who, as informed church and mission leaders, advise the church in the UK in its response to the presence of Muslims among us. In the following paragraphs I would like to lay out some grounds for my pleasure and concern – at national, regional and local levels – out of my own experience. In doing so, I would like to remind us of a standard set by the apostle Paul: 'If it is possible, as far as it depends on you, live at peace with everyone' (Rom. 12:18, NIV).

National level

For several years I have been a member of the national task force within the Church of England called Presence and Engagement. This group is directed by one of the advisers to the Archbishop of Canterbury. Its aim has been to help Christians who belong to the Church of England to live alongside and relate positively to people of other faiths in local communities. It resources that offering of help via three centres of excellence: one in Bradford, one in Leicester and one in London. Through representatives in nearly all the dioceses of the Church of England, the expertise and experience of those who do enjoy positive relations with people of other faiths (including Muslims) are shared via conferences and consultancy visits. Many of the Anglicans serving on this task force are evangelicals with significant experience of involvement in Christian mission within Muslim countries around the world. The Church of England is committed to remaining present within inner city communities of Britain where people from a Christian background are by far in the minority. Models of positive relating and strategies for responsible and incisive mission are gradually being shared on a national basis. There is, of course, a lot of work still to be done (perhaps we are still very much in 'catch up' mode) but the Presence and Engagement movement within the Church of England is able to offer support at national, diocesan and parish level to leaders who aim at relating positively – beyond the stereotypes – to people of other faiths.

Through my involvement with the national task force, I was privileged to attend the inauguration (in January 2006) of the Christian Muslim Forum in Lambeth Palace, to which the then prime minister of the UK, Tony Blair, came and spoke on behalf of the British government. The inauguration was held in the very week that Shaikh Dr Zaki Badawi (of WICS fame) passed away. There was very much a sense that the establishment of the Christian Muslim Forum was a fitting testimony to his kind of approach to relating to people of faiths different from his own. Representatives of the Jewish faith community were included as guests at this Christian Muslim event. This kind of national, Anglican initiative encourages me.

Regional level

Whilst living in Tulse Hill, London, I became a member of the South London Interfaith Group (SLIFG), one of many regional networks that together make up the national Inter Faith Network within the UK. The SLIFG has worked hard at improving relationships between many faith groups living south of the river Thames. It has organized annual 'inter-faith walks', where groups of people from different faith backgrounds spend a day walking from one religious building/community to another to get to know each other better. Food and conversations are shared in a positive and natural way. Whilst it is true that I found myself one of few evangelical, mission-oriented Christians within the SLIFG, I believe it is still important that we (evangelicals) become involved in this type of group precisely because they are promoting good relationships between the various faith communities – and especially their leaders. Also, it has often been my experience that people from a non-Christian background really appreciate meeting a Christian who adheres to a distinctive and committed 'Christian' faith. That they can understand and relate to better than some universalistic, smorgasbord kind of Christian.

In my local borough I ended up as 'coordinator' of the Lambeth Multi-faith Action Group (LAMAG). LAMAG holds public meetings on issues of concern to people living in the borough: crime, policing, health, ageing, youth issues and so on. The steering committee of LAMAG is chaired by a Jew, with Muslim, Hindu, Buddhist and Christian representation. Involvement in such a regional group does not provide a platform for preaching, but it does provide an opportunity for undoing negative stereotypes of what a Christian is, and for building positive relationships that can lead to faith-sharing on a personal level.

I think that it is clear that it was the steady work over many years of regional groups like the SLIFG and LAMAG that largely prevented a backlash against Muslims in the Lambeth area of London after the bombings and attempted bombings on the London transportation system in the summer of 2005 (7/7). Members of those regional groups visited and stood by Muslim friends in solidarity, and their gestures were gratefully received.

Local level

For eleven years, I enjoyed being the minister of an Anglican church in inner city south London. That church has a Church of England primary school associated with it. Over several years, the school built very positive relationships with a nearby, state-funded Muslim primary school, such that there came to be regular exchanges of pupils and staff between the two schools. The experience has been much appreciated by the communities of both schools. As well as sharing educational sessions in the classroom, the children from both schools have been able, with parental permission, to observe worship in each other's context. This has undermined stereotypes and helped the children, staff and parents relate naturally and respectfully to one another as people of distinctive faiths. It was my privilege on more than one occasion to welcome classes of Muslim students, with their teachers, to my church. For most of them, it was their first experience of entering a Christian place of worship. Inside, after looking around and discovering some things that provoked their curiosity, I received on each occasion a broadside of provocative questions about Christianity. In a wonderful way, in a context not of hostility but of fun, built upon years of cross-relating between the two schools, I was able to witness to Jesus Christ before Muslims on a scale and in an atmosphere not normally possible. Who knows what might become of that?

'Them' and 'us' versus 'the rest'

The UK today is not what any of us would describe as a 'Christian' country, though its roots reach back to a strongly Christian heritage. Rather, it is secular humanism that provides the rationale for our education system, for our convictions in law-making, for our ideas about how people should live together in a modern context.

Confessing Christians, with real faith and trust in God and a concern for pleasing Jesus Christ in all aspects of living, find themselves part of a minority in today's UK. Committed Christians and committed Muslims have discovered each other as friends in seeking to bring to bear on some of the public structures of British society our convictions about the sanctity of life, the role of religious faith, the inappropriateness of lewdness and mockery in the media of important figures within various faiths, the need for generosity instead of greed, the importance of family structures and so on.

Government in Britain – at central, regional and local level – is certainly cognisant of the significant leadership and skill that people of real faith have to offer at all levels of society. Ministers tend to think in terms of promoting 'social welfare' or 'community cohesion'. But it is no secret that the various faith communities in the UK have produced a lot of goodwill on the ground and supplied a huge variety of voluntary service on behalf of needy individuals and communities throughout the country. The government, and society generally, appreciates the end result of the contributions of people of faith, even if they do not share, or understand, the religious motivation that inspires us as believers.

In many ways I am encouraged by some of the positive relating between and across the faiths that is going on – involving committed, mission-minded evangelicals – in Britain today.

Challenges

Now for my 'dismay'! The truth is, sadly, that positive relating does not always go on between Christians and Muslims at local, regional and national level. The truth is, also, that the words and actions of some minorities of Christians and Muslims serve only to make secular humanists, members of government and the public generally, distrust all the more those of us who profess to know God or to submit to his will. To a considerable degree God, and religion generally, have a bad press in the UK today, and for that we evangelicals are partly responsible.

Many British Muslims feel scapegoated as a community at the moment because of the process of guilt-by-association that occurred after the London bombings in 2005. Young Asian men are now being disproportionately stopped and searched by our police; they know the experience today that young men within the black community felt for many years at the end of the twentieth century. Muslims are not understood nor liked by many people in the UK, simply because they are assumed to be extremists, 'Muslim terrorists', or supportive of such kinds of people. Perhaps one of the unhealthy results of this kind of negative experience has been that various cities and towns with significant Muslim populations are in danger of becoming ghettoized. It is easy to understand why this might be the case.

There does, however, need to be an increasing willingness by Muslim leaders within the UK to encourage integration and to play a contributory role within a diverse ethnic and cultural context. It is really important that Muslims in Britain – British Muslims – look less to heritages from the Indian subcontinent and promote instead the selecting, training and employing of imams who are British by birth and educated in English within our nation. This is happening, but it needs to be more openly encouraged. After my experience at the WICS conference in Tripoli, Libya and the almost universal sense (by moderate Muslims) of being marginalized and victimized, I am not as surprised as I was by the oft-iterated sense of being misunderstood that British Muslims seem constantly to express. Who is going to be at the vanguard of encouraging a more open, positive, engaged attitude within British Islam? Who is going to help promote voices of moderation and peace and integrity within local, regional and national networks of Muslims? Isn't that something that we Christians who are present with such Muslims are now being called by God to do: promoting other voices?

Many strongly committed Christians in the UK are predisposed to a negative view of their Muslim neighbours because of the tendency of some theologies to focus uncritically on the role of Israel in eschatological events. In such a perspective, Muslims, or at least Arab nations, become 'the enemy' of the people of God. Some Christian leaders in the UK have insisted on promoting a monochrome and negative view of what Islam is and what Muslims intend for the UK. Their doomsday prophesying has tended to be underlined by the secular media's almost exclusive courting of non-moderate Muslims in the 1990s. Too often such men were given television time as they outlined their aim to turn the UK into an Islamic state. Those personalities and provocative declarations stick in the public mind. It doesn't take much these days to awaken in Christians in the UK an unhealthy image of 'the Islamic menace'. Sadly, some Christian spokespersons take delight in doing precisely that.

I am convinced that negative stereotyping and non-engagement between different communities needs to be replaced by something more positive at all levels of our society – national, regional and local. This is a task that engages all of us. For the British government following 9/11, and especially following 7/7, radical Islam or Islamism has mostly been viewed as a security issue. Perhaps these days there is an increasing willingness for government ministers and other national figures to listen to voices from within the Muslim community that speak coherently and differently for the majority of Muslims in the UK. Together we need to get those voices heard in the relevant quarters. The community associating going on at regional level needs to grow across the country so that good practice is less patchy than at present.

The most significant context for bringing positive change is that which occurs at local or neighbourhood level. At that ground level, Christian leaders such as those within the CRIB network have a lot of work to do convincing other committed Christians to get to know their Muslim neighbours as fellow citizens who are motivated by faith. One doesn't lose one's Christian identity in meeting with people of different faith, different *real* faith. One need not be any less fervent or faithful to one's own Christian convictions if one becomes involved in listening to and conversing with people from other faith backgrounds. My own trust in Jesus Christ has been hugely challenged and deepened through getting to perceive life and faith from the perspectives of those with religious allegiances differing from my own. We can truly be Christians of integrity, we can disagree with friends of other religious conviction, we can be 'missional', but we can also acknowledge our common humanity – all of us are 'made in the image of God', in biblical terminology. We don't need to demonize the religious 'Other'. Of course, at the local level there is much for Muslim leaders to be doing, especially today in a climate in which the temptation for the Muslim community is to withdraw and turn inwards.

For the most part, interfaith relationships at neighbourhood level are initiated by non-Muslims; Christians and others visit mosques at their own request to try to learn more about Islam and Muslims. It would be wonderful if, increasingly, equivalent initiatives could be taken by local Muslim leaders. Can we encourage some of our Muslim friends to be the first to make an approach to their local church? Can we suggest to them that they might ask whether a group from the mosque could observe Christian worship and listen to a presentation of the Christian faith from a Christian, or visit a synagogue to learn of the Jewish faith from a Jew?

'How much depends on us?' we ask the apostle Paul, or through him, the Lord himself. 'If it is possible, as far as it depends on you, live at peace with everyone' (Rom. 12:18, NIV) is his instruction. Perhaps the Lord has in mind a greater degree of possibility than our egocentric, ethnocentric, perhaps ecclesio-centric, selves can manage at the moment. Are we able to 'see' Muslims differently? Do we have the connections to be able to promote other voices from within the Muslim communities in our country so that our fellow citizens also get a chance to view Muslims with different eyes? Or are we instead finding ourselves increasingly trapped in a default mode that freezes in place hostility, suspicion and a tendency to demonize the religious Other, especially when that religious Other is Muslim?

Conclusion

Colin Chapman

A middle path between naivety and hostility?

Have we succeeded in charting a middle way? We've tried to address some of the main reasons why the general public – including many Christians – feel fearful of Islam and hostile towards Muslims. We have named, for example, the concerns about honour killings, female circumcision, forced marriages, the bullying tactics of some Muslim school governors, and the violence against Christians. But instead of using these practices to demonize Muslims and Islam, we have tried to understand them in their broader context. At the same time we have tried to avoid the other extreme of painting a sanitized picture of Islam and suggesting that there's absolutely nothing about Muslims and Islam that we need to worry about.

The approach that we have been commending, therefore, demands that we face up to all the difficult questions, try to put our fears and prejudices to one side and then analyze the issues as cooly and calmly as we can. We have all written as practitioners who are involved in long-term engagement with our Muslim neighbours in the British context, and have again and again stressed the importance of building genuine relationships. But we have also written as students who want to use every academic discipline at our disposal. So Martin Whittingham has reminded us of the importance of seeing Muslim-Christian relationships in Britain today in the context of 1,400 years of quite complicated relationships. Philip Lewis has demonstrated how a sociological approach can help us to understand the processes of change within Muslim communities in recent decades. And to deal with the complex and sensitive issue of *shari'a*, we have turned to a professor of law, Julian Rivers, who really understands both the theory and the practice of the English legal system.

Does this sound as if finding a middle path means sitting on the fence or 'going soft on Islam'? We look forward to hearing the verdict of readers! For our part we will at *some* stages and in *some* contexts want to engage in 'hard talk' with our Muslim friends – for example, about the political agendas of some British Muslims and the treatment of Christians and of converts who are regarded as apostates in Muslim-majority countries. But we will do so with full acknowledgement of the failings of our own society and the failings of Christians in particular, recognizing that 'people in glass houses shouldn't throw stones'. We will also be reminding ourselves that we are not dealing with abstract systems, religions or ideologies, but with *people* – people whom we want to love as our neighbours.

What's new?

I very much doubt if a book of this kind could have been written twenty or even ten years ago. This is not only because of changes within the Muslim community, but also because Christians in recent years have sharpened their thinking in a whole number of areas and branched out in new kinds of very active engagement with Muslims.

There's no recourse here to simple proof-texting, but a more serious attempt to engage with Scripture and relate it to the actual people and issues that we're dealing with. There's no written or unwritten 'party line' to which all evangelical Christians must adhere, but rather a frank recognition of a wide variety of responses to Islam. And instead of thinking of Muslims simply as people who need to be evangelized, there is a much more holistic approach which thinks in terms of the community as well as the individual, the body as well as the soul, and the political and social as well as the spiritual issues.

If Christians relating to Muslims have been involved for decades in social projects of different kinds – through visiting families, teaching English and running drop-in/advice centres – we have been introduced in these pages to a wide variety of fresh models of good practice. It is new to see Muslim and Christian young people being brought together in an organized way to share with each other at quite a deep level what their faith means to them. It is new to hear of a church cooperating with local and national government to build facilities to be used by the whole community, and thus demonstrating a more robust place given to Christian faith by statutory bodies. It is significant to hear that there may still be some contexts in which it is appropriate to bring people of the two faiths together in public meetings – whether they turn out to be more confrontational or more dialogical in nature. It is encouraging to find Christian leaders who have the knowledge, experience and confidence to engage in long-term relationships with Muslim leaders. And one can only wish that more local churches would take the step of turning themselves inside out to relate in meaningful and relevant ways to the Muslim communities around them.

Faced with so many different approaches, it would be only too easy for us to respond by saying, 'It couldn't work in my context!' But there must be models described here which could provide inspiration to *every* group of Christians that is serious about relating to their Muslim neighbours.

Where do we go from here?

We are very conscious that (largely because of the limitations of space) we have not covered all the ground that we had hoped to cover, and are therefore already thinking of issues which will need to be addressed in any further publications. We had wanted, for example, to trace the development of the concept of 'multiculturalism' and evaluate its strengths and weaknesses. And since 9/11 and 7/7 have marked such a signficant watershed, it will be important to analyze the policies of successive British governments towards the different faith communities in general and Muslims in particular. Another area that needs to be explored is the shape of the new multi-ethnic churches which are coming into being in different cities.

There's certainly more of a debate to be had on the subject of the growing number of Muslims, referred to by some as 'a demographic time bomb'. Is it possible to find a middle way between interpretations that amount to scaremongering and those which are naïve about the projected growth of Muslim communities? And if we've reflected with Tim Green on conversion *from Islam* to Christianity, we will need to reflect just as seriously on the reasons why people in our society convert *to Islam*.

Lesslie Newbigin reminded us in his contribution to *Faith and Power: Christianity and Islam in 'Secular' Britain*,[1] published in 1998, the year of his death, that the presence of Muslims in Britain was exposing the inability of the secular world to come to terms with the religion of Islam, and at the same time the timidity and weakness of the churches for whom Christianity had become a totally privatized religion. Christian-Muslim relations in Britain are therefore being played out in the context of an increasingly secularized society which wants to banish all religion to the sidelines. How does this secularized context affect the relationships and the dialogue between Christians and Muslims? And in this constantly changing situation, is the Establishment of the Church of England a relic of the past which needs to be swept away, or does it continue to have some real value – if only because it recognizes a certain role for religion in public life, and because both Christians and Muslims want God to be recognized in some way in the public sphere?

At some stage we will need to widen our horizons to address the bigger picture of Islam in Europe. Are we to listen to those who predict that by 2050 Muslims will outnumber Christians and that Europe will have been transformed into 'Eurabia'? Or should we be convinced by writers like Philip Jenkins who in his *God's Continent: Islam, Christianity and Europe's Religious Crisis*[3] describes a much less pessimistic scenario in which Europe becomes a fascinating laboratory of religious experimentation? How significant is the politicization of religion, the growing popularity of far right and anti-Islamic parties and the drives to ban veils, *burqas, niqabs* and minarets? Whether we like it or not, the UK is a part of Europe, and Islam in Britain cannot be treated in isolation from Islam in Europe. And will the continuing involvement of Britain, the EU and the USA in conflicts in several different parts of the Muslim world continue to have a profound effect on the feelings of British Muslims?

At the end of the day, in trying to understand 'the mind of Christ' in our relationships with Muslims, everything will depend on how faithfully we are following the teaching and example of Jesus in the complex situations in which we find ourselves today. At this particular time in history, when most of the old securities and boundaries of Christendom have gone and we are confused about how to come to terms with the secularization of public life and the growing numbers and influence of different faith communities, perhaps it is good for us to feel as powerless and vulnerable as Jesus was. And, as Ida Glaser has reminded us, following Jesus means not only taking up our cross, but also keeping the cross central in our understanding of who God is and in our testimony to what we believe he has done.

Appendix 1

Gracious Christian Responses to Muslims in Britain Today

Background and introduction

In July 2008, a group of people involved in ministry to Muslims in the UK met at All Nations Christian College (ANCC). The group was called by a few individuals to consider the training of evangelical Christians in Islamics. However, they quickly recognized that often Christians in the UK respond to the presence of Muslims out of fear, which stifled any effective Christian response.

A major outcome of the meeting was a desire to encourage Christians to learn more about Islam, to relate to Muslims with genuine respect and friendship, to recognize the many different kinds of Muslims and Islam in Britain today, and to wrestle with the complexities of the political and social issues raised by the presence of Muslim communities.

The following statement is not officially endorsed by any group, and while it reflects the views of those at the July meeting, it should not be assumed that everyone who attended will want to be associated with it. It is laid out as a set of Christian principles to help inform our relationships with Muslims, while recognizing that this is part of a wider debate as to how people of all faiths and none relate to each other in Britain today.

The Statement

'Let your speech always be gracious . . . so that you may know how you ought to answer everyone . . .' (Col. 4:6)[1]

1. Concern for Total Human Well-Being and for the Whole Community. *We see all human beings as created in the image of God, and are concerned for the well-being of the whole person and the whole community. We are committed to love our neighbours as ourselves, and see personal relationships with our Muslim neighbours as foundational to such a holistic vision.*

2. Hospitality, Inclusiveness, Listening, Understanding and Respect. *We want to welcome people of all kinds into the community and into our churches; we want to listen to one another with genuine respect, even when we don't agree. It is important to try to understand the faith and practice of others, and we are open to be challenged and learn.*

3. Awareness of History – Theirs and Ours. *We cannot deny our history – in Britain, Europe and the West – any more than Muslims can deny the history of Islamic countries. These histories contain not only examples to follow but also episodes to remind both faiths to be humble and penitent. We trust that Muslims in our society will recognize the significant contribution of Christianity to our history and culture.*

4. A Vision for Society. *While we no longer live in Christendom and do not seek to build a Christian state, we* *have a vision for a society in which the values of the kingdom of God are upheld and honoured. We believe that such a society will safeguard expression of faith in the public sphere without its imposition, the exercise of free speech without unreasonable giving or taking of offence, and the uniform rule of public law without this being unnecessarily intrusive on private conscience. In seeking the common good of the whole society, we work together with Muslims within these broad parameters, seeking justice and peaceful co-existence.*

5. A Vocation to both Support and Critique the State. *Whatever the current and future relations between the church and the state, Christians have a duty both to affirm what is of God and to challenge what is sinful in free obedience to every legitimate authority. Where we have concerns about the aims of some Muslims in Britain, we work with transparency within the democratic processes, recognizing that, while the majority of the population claim to be 'Christian' in some sense, we operate in a largely secularized society and that Christians should not seek to work from a position of power and privilege.*

6. Freedom of Religion. *We affirm the right of every person and community to freedom of speech and worship. According to the United Nations Declaration of Human Rights, this includes the freedom to practise, propagate and change one's religion. We therefore feel obliged to draw attention to the difficulties experienced by Muslims in different contexts who have sought to become disciples of Jesus and seek to support them in whatever way we can.*

7. Reciprocity. *We hope that both Muslims and Christians will seek to follow the Golden Rule in their relations with each other, treating those of the other community as they would themselves wish to be treated. For our part, we endeavour to speak about Muslims truthfully, to allow Muslims to interpret themselves and not to compare the best expressions of Christianity with the worst of Islam.*

8. Dialogue. *We want to engage in the 'dialogue of life', dialogue about social and political issues, and theological dialogue. We seek to develop genuine honesty and openness; we rejoice in all the areas of common ground where we can agree, and address honestly areas where we disagree. As we seek to establish relationships of trust and respect, Christians and Muslims can and must have the freedom to challenge and critique each other's beliefs and practices.*

9. Mission. *Because of our understanding of God's mission to the world, we want him to be known as he has revealed himself in Christ, and want others to have an opportunity to know about Christ. The Great Commission ('Go and make disciples of all nations . . .' Matt. 28:19²) stands as our mandate. We therefore believe that we are called to proclaim the good news about Jesus both in word and deed; and the outcome of our mission and witness is entirely in the hands of God. We recognize that Islam is as much a missionary religion as Christianity, and in neither can there be any place for pressure to encourage people to convert.*

10. Awareness of the World Dimension. *We see our relationships here in the light of relationships between Christians, Muslims, other faith communities and people of no religious faith in other parts of the world and in the light of local and international political issues. We are therefore aware both of situations where Muslims experience prejudice, discrimination or persecution from Christians and of situations where Christians experience the same from Muslims.*

We believe that this is an appropriate Christian response to Muslims and Islam in Britain today, and that it is well summed up in these words of the apostle Paul:

'Love is patient, love is kind. It does not envy, it does not boast, it is not proud. It is not rude, it is not self-seeking, it is not easily angered, it keeps no record of wrongs. Love does not

delight in evil but rejoices with the truth. It always protects, always trusts, always hopes, always perseveres.' (1 Cor. 13:4–7, NIV)

All enquiries to:
Global Connections, Caswell Road, Sydenham
Industrial Estate, Leamington Spa, CV31 1QF
www.globalconnections.co.uk

Appendix 2

Muslims in England – Statistics

Borough level: **Where are the Muslims in London?**

Top 3 boroughs: Tower Hamlets 36 per cent
                   Newham   24 per cent
                   Waltham Forest 15 per cent

Guardian **statistical maps from 2005:**
http://www.guardian.co.uk/britain/london/
0,,1394802,00.html
London by religion: http://www.guardian.co.uk/
graphic/0,5812,1395106,00.html
London by ethnicity: http://www.guardian.co.uk/
graphic/0,5812,1395103,00.html
Muslims in London: http://www.london.gov.uk/gla/
publications/equalities/muslims-in-london.pdf

Parish level: **Where are the Muslims in England?**

Top 3 parishes:
Purlwell: St Andrew (Batley, Kirklees, W. Yorkshire)   79%
Sparkbrook: Christ Church (Birmingham)   73%
Bradford: St Clement   71%

Church of England Presence and Engagement – Parish Statistics by Dioceses:
http://www.presenceandengagement.org.uk/pdf_lib/ 14_Parish_Statistics_By_Dioceses.pdf

Ethnic groups: **Who are the Muslims in England?**

Top 3 nationalities:	Pakistani	650,416
	Bangladeshi	254,704
	Indian	131,098

Communities and Local Government – Understanding Muslim Ethnic Communities:
http://www.communities.gov.uk/communities/race-cohesionfaith/research/understandingmuslimcommunities/

N.B. The Muslim population has increased since the 2001 census, which was a conservative estimate. All recent responsible estimates are around 3 million (Pew Survey, Office of National Statistics).

List of Contributors

John Azumah is Associate Professor for World Christianity and Islam, Columbia Theological Seminary, Atlanta, Georgia, USA. He comes from a Muslim background in Ghana, and has a doctorate in Islamic Studies from Birmingham University. His books include *The Legacy of Arab-Islam in Islam: A Quest for Inter-Religious Dialogue* (Oxford: Oneworld, 2001) and *My Neighbour's Faith: Islam Explained for Christians* (Grand Rapids, MI: Zondervan, 2002).

Steve Bell has lived in the Middle East for ten years where he studied Islamics and Arabic after teaching at multicultural British schools. He trains people to engage appropriately with Muslims. Currently National Director of Interserve – which has a team of twenty-eight working among British Muslims and Hindus and Sikhs – he is author of *Friendship First* (Milton Keynes: Kitab, 2010), *Grace for Muslims* and *Gospel for Muslims* (Milton Keynes: Authentic Media, 2006, 2004, 2006, 2011).

Colin Chapman is an ordained Anglican and a founder member of the CRIB network. He has worked for eighteen years in the Middle East and taught in theological and mission colleges and churches in the UK and the

Middle East. He is the author of *Cross and Crescent* (Leicester: IVP, 1995, 2007), *Whose Promised Land?* and *Whose Holy City?* (Oxford: Lion, 2002, 2004).

Emma Dipper lived in Central Asia for many years and works in the UK as an associate lecturer at All Nations Christian College. Her ministry is in equipping persecuted Christian women around the world and communicating with the British church about mission and issues relating to persecution and suffering.

Ida Glaser is the Academic Director of the Centre for Muslim-Christian Studies in Oxford. She has trained Christians and related to Islamic issues for many years. She has a doctorate in Islamic Studies from Durham University, and her books include *The Bible and Other Faiths* (Leicester: IVP, 2005).

Tim Green worked with Interserve for nearly eighteen years in Pakistan and Jordan. His particular focus is on disipleship and training, and these days he assists work in several Muslim countries from a base in Oxford, while also studying for a doctorate on conversion at the University of London.

Toby Howarth worked among Muslims for five years in India before returning to the UK to be the vicar of a church in a multicultural area of Birmingham. He is now Secretary for Inter Religious Affairs to the Archbishop of Canterbury and National Inter Religious Affairs Advisor for the Church of England. His doctoral thesis was published as *Pulpit of Tears: The Twelver Shiᶜa as a Muslim Minority in India* (London: Routledge, 2005).

Bryan Knell is currently the Church Relations Consultant for Global Connections. He has travelled extensively throughout the Arab world and has lectured on Islam in churches, colleges and at conferences for the last thirty years. He has been the chair of CRIB since it was launched in 1998.

Phil Lewis worked in Pakistan as a mission partner with the Church Mission Society, and for more than twenty years has been teaching at the universities of Leeds and Bradford. He is a specialist on Islam in Britain, and his books include *Islamic Britain* (London: I.B. Tauris, 1994) and *Young, British and Muslim* (London: Continuum, 2007).

Richard McCallum worked for some years in Tunisia before becoming pastor of the Community Church in Yeovil. He is at present working on a doctorate at the University of Exeter, studying responses to Islam among evangelicals in Britain.

Anthony McRoy lives and works in a multicultural area of east London and teaches at the Evangelical Theological College of Wales. His doctoral thesis was published as *From Rushdie to 7/7: the Radicalisation of Islam in Britain* (London: The Social Affairs Unit, 2005).

Ziya Meral is a Turkish Christian from a Muslim background who has studied at the London School of Theology and the London School of Economics. Until recently he was working on human rights issues with Christian Solidarity Worldwide, and is now studying for a doctorate at the University of Cambridge. He is the author of the 2008 CSW report *No Place to Call Home: Experiences of Apostates from Islam.*

Chawkat Moucarry is Syrian. He taught Islamic Studies at All Nations Christian College for twelve years before working with World Vision as director for inter-faith relations. He has a doctorate from Sorbonne University in Paris, and his books include *Faith to Faith: Christianity and Islam in Dialogue* (Leicester: IVP, 2001), *The Search for Forgiveness* (Leicester: IVP, 2004), and *Two Prayers for Today – the Lord's Prayer and the Fatiha* (Tiruvalla: CSS Books, 2007).

Bill Musk has worked in churches in Egypt and London, and is now based in Tunis as Assistant Bishop in North Africa for the Anglican Diocese of Egypt. He holds a doctorate in Islamics and has written extensively on Islam including *The Unseen Face of Islam, Touching the Soul of Islam, Holy War* and *Kissing Cousins? Christians and Muslims Face to Face* (London: Monarch, 1989, 2005, 2003, 2005 respectively).

John Ray OBE has been involved in education for more than forty years both in the UK and Kashmir, India, where he was head teacher of a Christian school. For the last twenty-five years he has lived in very multicultural areas of Birmingham and has been intimately involved in schools as a school governor and consultant on educational issues.

Julian Rivers is Professor of Jurisprudence in the School of Law at the University of Bristol. He is a prolific contributor to legal journals, and has authored books on the relationship between law, religion and human rights, including *The Law of Organized Religions: Between Establishment and Secularism* (Oxford: OUP, 2010); and *Institutional Reason: The Jurisprudence of Robert Alexy* (Oxford: OUP, 2011).

Andrew Smith is Director of Youth Encounter at Scripture Union, having worked among British Muslim children and young people for sixteen years pioneering a Christian-Muslim dialogue project for teenagers. His doctoral thesis was entitled *Faiths, Friendship and Pedagogy* and continues to write and advise churches on how Christians can disciple young people for a meaningful engagement with their Muslim peers.

Jay Smith is an American who has lived and worked in India, Senegal, France and the UK. He is the founder of the Hyde Park Christian Fellowship, and travels widely, teaching Christians about Islam and engaging in public debates with Muslims. His apologetic material has been distributed widely through the internet.

Richard Sudworth has recently been ordained in the Anglican Church and continues to work towards a doctorate in Christian-Muslim relations in Britain, at the University of London.

Martin Whittingham is the Director of the Centre for Muslim-Christian Studies at Oxford. He has a doctorate in Islamic Studies from Edinburgh University and lectures in various contexts on various aspects of Islamics.

References

Chapter 1: Steve Bell

[1] Lakoff, George and Mark Johnson, *Metaphors We Live By* (London: The University of Chicago Press, 1980), p. 4.
[2] Taylor, Jenny, *The False Consciousness of Western Civilisation*, Tuesday 30 November 2010, Lapido Media, www.lapido-media.com
[3] Bell, Steve, *Grace for Muslims – The Journey from Fear to Faith* (Milton Keynes: Authentic Media, 2003).

Chapter 2: Ida Glaser

[1] For an introduction to reading the whole Bible with its background of different faiths and today's multi-faith world in mind, see my *The Bible and Other Faiths: What Does the Lord Require of Us?* (Leicester: IVP, 2005).
[2] See my *The Bible and Other Faiths* (Leicester: IVP, 2005), chapters 9–12.
[3] I have tried to explore their thinking and ask where they went wrong in my 'Crusade sermons, Francis of Assisi and Martin Luther: What does it mean to "take up the cross" in

the context of Islam?' Crowther Centre Monograph No.14 (Oxford: Church Mission Society, 2010). For a range of Christian thinking about the cross in the context of Islam, see D.E. Singh, ed., *Jesus and the Cross: Reflections of Christians from Islamic Contexts* (Carlisle: Regnum/Paternoster, 2008).

[4] For a summary of the earliest records, see Hoyland, R., *Seeing Islam as Others Saw It: A survey and evaluation of Christian, Jewish and Zorostrian writings on early Islam* (Princeton: The Darwin Press, 1997). Translations of John of Damascus' and Mar Timothy on Islam can be found in N.A. Newman, *Early Muslim-Christian Dialogue* (Pennsylvania: Interdisciplinary Biblical Research Institute, 1993).

[5] Marshall, David, *God, Muhammad and the Unbelievers* (Richmond: Curzon Press, 1999), demonstrates this development on the basis of the Qur'an.

Chapter 3 – Bryan Knell

[1] Murray Williams, Stewart, *Post-Christendom* (Carlisle: Paternoster, 2004), p. 129.

[2] Lewis, Bernard, *The Crisis of Islam: Holy War and Unholy Terror* (New York: The Modern Library, 2003), p. 5.

Chapter 4 – Richard McCallum

[1] For a survey of American evangelical books see Kidd, Thomas, *American Christians and Islam: Evangelical Culture and Muslims from the Colonial Period to the Age of Terrorism* (Princeton, NJ: Princeton University Press, 2009).

[2] Green, Stephen, *Understanding Islam* (Surbiton: Christian Voice, 2005), pp. 3,17,18.

[3] Pawson, David, *The Challenge of Islam to Christians* (London: Hodder & Stoughton, 2003), pp. 7,86,8.

[4] Sookhdeo, Patrick, *Islam: The Challenge to the Church* (Pewsey: Isaac Publishing, 2006), pp. 66,68,33.

[5] Cox, Caroline and John Marks, *The West, Islam and Islamism: Is Ideological Islam Compatible with Liberal Democracy?* (London: Civitas: Institute for the Study of Civil Society, 2006, 2003), pp. 193,151,143.

[6] Orr-Ewing, Amy and Frog Orr-Ewing, *Holy Warriors: A Fresh Look at the Face of Extreme Islam* (Carlisle: Authentic Lifestyle, 2002), p. 103.

[7] Riddell, Peter, *Christians and Muslims: Pressures and Potential in a Post 9/11 World* (Leicester: Inter-Varsity Press, 2004), pp. 166,199,200,213,174.

[8] Nazir Ali, Michael, *Conviction and Conflict: Islam, Christianity and World Order* (London: Continuum, 2006), pp. 39,98,105.

[9] Bell, Steve, *Grace for Muslims* (Milton Keynes: Authentic Media, 2006), pp. 137,133,160.

[10] Moucarry, Chawkat, *Two Prayers for Today: The Lord's Prayer and the Fatiha* (Tiruvalla: India, Christava Sahitya Samithi, 2007), pp. 88,120,110.

[11] Chapman, Colin, *Cross and Crescent: Responding to the Challenges of Islam* (Leicester: Inter-Varsity Press, 2007, 1995), pp. 191,55,410.

[12] Musk, Bill, *Kissing Cousins?: Christians and Muslims Face to Face* (Oxford: Monarch, 2005) pp. 12,380,390.

[13] The latter position has been a particular feature of the work of Bishop Kenneth Cragg who has been accused of 'Christianizing Islam'.

[14] Murray, Stuart, *Post-Christendom: Church and Mission in a Strange New World* (London: Authentic Media, 2004).

Chapter 5 – Martin Whittingham

General surveys:

Daniel, Norman, *Islam: The Making of an Image* (Oxford: OneWorld, various reprints of 1960 original).

Gaudeul, Jean-Marie, *Encounters and Clashes* (2 vols.) (Rome: PISAI, 2000). Volume 1 is a historical survey of interaction, volume 2 is a selection of key texts in translation.

Goddard, Hugh, *A History of Christian-Muslim Relations* (Edinburgh: Edinburgh University Press, 2000).

Jenkins, Philip, *The Lost History of Christianity* (Oxford: Lion, 2008; New York: Harper Collins, 2008).

Specific works:

Mar Timothy, 'The Dialogue of Patriarch Timothy I with Caliph al-Mahdi' in *Early Christian-Muslim Dialogue*, N.A. Newman, ed. (Hatfield, Pennsylvania: Inter-disciplinary Biblical Research Institute, 1993). Entire text also available via http://www.tertullian.org/fathers

Luther, Martin, 'On War Against the Turk' in Luther's *Works*, vol. 43, Gustav Wiencke, ed. (Philadelphia: Fortress Press, 1968), pp. 215–41. Entire text available at http://www.godrules.net/library/luther/NEW1 luther_e10.htm

Glaser, Ida, *Crusade Sermons, Francis of Assisi and Martin Luther: What does it mean to 'take up the cross' in the context of Islam?* (Oxford: CMS: Crowther Centre Monograph, no. 14, 2010).

Ragg, L. and L., *The Gospel of Barnabas* (Oxford: Clarendon Press, 1907). Modern reproductions of this translation, lacking the critical introduction, are widely available. Entire text available at http://www.sacred-texts.com/isl/gbar/index.htm

Chapter 6 – Philip Lewis

[1] This can be downloaded from www.cis.cam.ac.uk/CIBP. html, p. 19.

[2] An important new study comparing American with European Christianity – Berger, Peter, Grace Davie and Elkie Folkas, 'Religious America, Secular Europe? A theme and variations' (Surrey: Ashgate, 2008) – indicates why American Christians finds it very difficult to understand European Christians and vice versa and is particularly illuminating in this regard.

[3] A useful chapter about the ordinary lives of Arabs in London can be found in Hopkins, Peter and Richard Gale (eds.), *Muslims in Britain: Race, Place and Identities* (Edinburgh: Edinburgh University Press, 2009).

[4] Pauly, R., *Islam in Europe: Integration or Marginalization?* (Surrey: Ashgate: 2004).

[5] Ahmed, Sughra, *Seen and Not Heard: Voices of Young British Muslims* (Leicester: Policy Research Centre, Islamic Foundation, 2009), pp. 39,40.

[6] See Open Society Institute 2005.

[7] See Ansari, H., *The Infidel Within: Muslims in Britain since 1800* (London: Hurst & Co., 2004), p. 200.

[8] Listed in Ameli's, S.R., *Globalization, Americanization and British Muslim Identity* (London: ICAS, 2002).

[9] The picture is not all rosy, however. See Singh, G., 'A city of surprises: Urban Multiculturalism and the "Leicester model"' in N. Ali (et al) *A Post Colonial People: South Asians in Britain* (London: Hurst & Co., 2006).

[10] For many such developments see my *Young, British and Muslim* (London: Continuum International Publishing Group, 2007).

[11] 'Whereas the Muslim population . . . is around 3%, the total, British Muslim population stands at 6%. If foreign Muslim prisoners are added to the total the figure actually

stands at 11%' see 'Contextualising Islam in Britain' (Cambridge: Centre of Islamic Studies, 2009), p. 22.

[12] See the Ouseley Report 2001 and *Kilo*, an award-winning novel by Alam, M.Y., (Wakefield: Route, 2002).

[13] Modood, Tariq, *Multicultural Politics, Racism, Ethnicity and Muslims in Britain* (Edinburgh: Edinburgh University Press, 2005), p. 160.

[14] See Samad, Y., *Media and Muslim Identity: Intersections of Generation and Gender* (London: Innovation, 11:4, 1998).

[15] For details see my *Young, British and Muslim*.

[16] See Ahmed, Sughra, *Seen and Not Heard*, pp. 42,43.

[17] See Ahmed, Sughra, *Seen and Not Heard*, p. 64.

[18] For details see my *Young, British and Muslim*, pp. 46-53.

[19] The quotations are taken from Saeed Khan's paper, 'The Phenomenon of Dual Nihilism Among British Muslim Youth' delivered at the Association of Muslim Social Scientists' Conference – 'Muslim Youth: Challenges, Opportunities and Expectations' – at University of Chester, 20–22 March, 2009. I am grateful to Saeed for sending me a copy of his paper.

[20] Badawi, Z., *Islam in Britain* (London: Ta Ha Publications, 1981), p. 27.

[21] Abedin, S.Z., Minority Crises, Majority Options, in Hashmi, T., and H. Mutalib (eds.) *Islam, Muslims and the Modern State* (London: Palgrave Macmillan, 1994), p. 36.

[22] Moosa, E., 'Introduction' to F. Rahman, *Revival and Reform in Islam* (Oxford: Oneworld, 2000), p. 26.

[23] Siddique, A., *Christian-Muslim Dialogue in the Twentieth Century* (London: Macmillan, 1997), p. 196.

[24] 'Fifty Years of Christian-Muslim Relations', Islamo-Christiana, 26, 2000, pp. 51–77. A promising initiative has just begun at Cambridge – www.cambridgemuslimcollege.org – whereby a course is being developed to address such lacunae. On its website a number of CMC Papers can be downloaded: No 1 is entitled 'Some Reflections on

Principles of Islamic Education within a Western Context' and itemizes the enormity of the challenges ahead.

[25] '*Takfir*' is to declare another Muslim a '*kafir*', non-Muslim – tantamount to declaring someone an apostate which can entail their execution, if they do not recant, or murder, where the outraged family takes the law into their own hands; '*Salafi*' refers to the movement that believes that Muslims should emulate the first three generations of Islam known as the 'pious forefathers'; this movement – literalist and intolerant of other Muslim traditions – is funded by the Saudi government. See Meijer, Roel, ed., *Global Salafism, Islam's New Religious Movement* (London: Hurst & Co, 2009).

[26] See Rahman, Tariq, 'Madrasas: The Potential for Violence in Pakistan?', in Malik, J. (ed.), *Madrasas in South Asia: Teaching Terror?* (Abingdon: Routledge, 2008), pp. 61–84.

[27] See Geaves, Ron, 'Drawing on the Past to Transform the Present: Contemporary Challenges for Training and Preparing British Imams', *Journal of Muslim Minority Affairs*, 28/1, April 2008, pp. 99–112.

[28] See Sageman, Marc, *Leaderless Jihad: Terror Networks in the Twenty-First Century* (Philadelphia: University of Pennsylvania Press, 2008) and Hussain, Ed, *The Islamist: Why I joined Radical Islam in Britain: What I Saw Inside and Why I Left* (London: Penguin, 2007). Since he left, Hussain and other ex-radicals have set up the Quilliam Foundation to de-legitimize, Islamically, the radical narratives underlining extremism.

[29] One has only to access the influential multi-lingual *Deobandi* website – (English, French, German, Spanish, Italian and Portuguese) www.inter-islam.org; its section 'prohibitions' is especially insightful, as is www.fatwaislam.com recommended by the influential Birmingham and Bradford *Salafi* networks – to see how out of step these are with such an egalitarian ethos. The latter simply rehearses

the opinions, in translation, of Saudi scholars who exhibit little familiarity with British culture, whether gender equality or democracy, both of which are deemed anathema.

[30] This report is the first, to my knowledge, which has engaged all Muslim schools of thought, Muslim academics and activists. Moreover, it pulls no punches in identifying some of the intellectual challenges facing the Islamic tradition in Britain, whether the need to reconnect Islamic law and ethics, why Muslims can and should affirm 'procedural secularism', a critique of utopian readings of politics undergirding much 'Islamism', to the need to move from a traditional discourse of submission and subject to one of citizen and responsibility.

[31] See Jalal, Ayesha, *Partisans of Allah: Jihad in South Asia* (Harvard: Harvard University Press, 2008).

[32] See some of the essays in *Muslim Spaces of Hope, Geographies of Possibility in Britain and the West* (Richard Philips, ed.; London: Zed Books, 2009). For one citywide example of Christian involvement see Philip Lewis, 'For the Peace of the City: Bradford – A Case Study in Developing Inter-Community and Inter-Religious Relations', in Stephen R. Goodwin, *World Christianity in Muslim Encounter* (London: Continuum, 2009). For a good overview of patterns of principled accommodation and cooperation between churches and mosques, Christians and Muslims see website for the Christian Muslim Forum www.christianmuslimforum.org

Chapter 7 – Tim Green

[1] In many countries hundreds of Muslims have turned to Christ, in some countries they number thousands, in at least four countries more than ten thousand, and in another three countries probably over one hundred thousand.

[2] Gaudeul, Jean-Marie, *Called from Islam to Christ* (UK: Monarch, 1999), p. 294.

[3] Kate Zebiri based her estimate of 15,000 British Muslim converts – *British Muslim Converts: Choosing Alternate Lives* (UK: Oneworld, 2008) – on Yahya Birt, who was drawing on 2001 statistics. But by 2010 she believed this figure to be 'too low for the present day' (personal correspondence, November 2010). Sarah Harris in http://www.timesonline.co.uk/tol/comment/faith/article7135026.ece (written 29 May 2010, accessed 9 September 2010) gave an estimate of 30,000. But she also cited Kevin Brice, of the Centre for Migration Policy Research, Swansea University, who believed this number may be closer to 50,000; he explained his reasons for this in http://www.bbc.co.uk/programmes/b00snm84

[4] http://www.ex-muslim.org.uk/ (accessed 13 March 2010). See also the website http://www.apostatesofislam.com which includes apostates from several countries including Britain.

[5] Is this perhaps why the *Oxford Mail* in September 2009 ran a special feature on four British converts to Islam, but did not take up a subsequent request to feature Christian converts from Islam?

[6] Channel 4 in 2007, and BBC Radio 4 in 2008, both had difficulty finding converts willing to be interviewed at all, let alone be identified. I refer to 'Unholy War' (Channel 4 Dispatches, broadcast 17 September 2007) and 'Could I Stop Being a Muslim?' (Radio 4, broadcast 22 April 2008).

[7] One article in one mainstream journal did appear in 2007, but its content and references were very thin. Khalil & Bilici, 'Conversion out of Islam: A Study of Conversion Narratives of Former Muslims', in *The Muslim World*, 2007, 97:11.

[8] Part of Kathryn Spellman's research was on Iranian Christians in London, see her *Religion and Nation: Iranian*

Local and Transnational Networks in Britain (Oxford: Berhahn Books, 2004).

[9] Two of these are by Des Harper and Tom Walsh, discussed later in this chapter. I also found, too late for discussion in this chapter, Tracey Messenger's 'The Conversion of South Asian Muslims to Christianity in the UK' (MA dissertation, University of Leeds, 1999).

[10] Biographies of those who converted before coming to Britain include *The Torn Veil* by Gulshan Esther and *Into the Light* by Steven Masood; conversion stories within Britain are found in *Persian Springs* by Pauline Selby, *The Imam's Daughter* by Hannah Shah and *Aisha My Sister* by Sally Sutcliffe.

[11] I have held brief discussions on this with several people, and in more depth with Revd. Bassi Mirzania, Anglican Chaplain to the Persian Community in the UK, in personal conversation on 8 September 2010. She travels widely and estimates that around 70 per cent of all converts from Islam in Britain are Iranian.

[12] The Channel 4 *Dispatches* programme broadcast on 17 September 2007 estimated 3,000 converts, though without explaining their basis for this figure. In any case, numbers have continued to grow since then. Thus in Britain today there are proportionally at least as many converts *from* Islam as converts *to* Islam, in relation to the Muslim and non-Muslim populations as a whole.

[13] This Hadith is in Sahih Bukhari, volume 4, book 52, number 260, found in http://www.usc.edu/schools/college/crcc/engagement/resources/texts/muslim/hadith/bukhari/052.sbt.html

[14] I have only given a brief summary. For more detail, see *Apostasy: An Overview* (Manchester: The Maranatha Community, 2006); Ziya Meral, *No Place to Call Home: Experiences of Apostates from Islam, Failures of the International Community* (UK: Christian Solidarity Worldwide,

2008); Patrick Sookhdeo, *Freedom to Believe: Challenging Islam's Apostasy Law* (USA: Isaac Publishing, 2009).

[15] 'Ala Mawdudi, Abul, *The Punishment of the Apostate According to Islamic Law*, Urdu *Murtadd ki Saza Islami Qanun Men* (1942), translated into English by Syed Silas Husain, publisher not given (c.1995).

[16] Further helpful detail is found in Chapman, Colin, *Islam and the West: Conflict, Coexistence or Conversion?* (UK: Paternoster, 1998), chapter 5, and Ziya Meral, *No Place to Call Home*, chapter 3.

[17] These names include Zaki Badawi, Ziauddin Sardar, Abdul Hakim Winter, Ruqaiyyah Waris Maqsood and Tariq Ramadan, all of whom have spoken clearly against the punishment of apostates. See http://apostasyandislam. blogspot.com for the full list and for their respective opinions.

[18] Reported in *The Muslim Weekly*, 21 September 2007, p. 2.

[19] The radio programme obtained this quote from the website www.muftisays.com but the particular individual is not named.

[20] 'Contextualising Islam in Britain' (Cambridge: Centre of Islamic Studies, 2009), p. 75, downloadable from www.cis.cam.ac.uk/CIBPReportWeb.pdf

[21] The ten guidelines are downloadable from www.christianmuslimforum.org/downloads/Ethical_Guidelines_for_Witness.pdf

[22] For more on attitudes and trends among British born Muslims, see Philip Lewis, *Young, British and Muslim* (London: Continuum, 2007).

[23] The account is given in Interserve's *Go* magazine, www.interserve.org.uk, 2010/1, p. 5.

[24] See www.news.bbc.co.uk/1/hi/england/kent/8380580 .stm, which reports the attack but erroneously states that the attackers were white.

[25] The information was reported to me by someone who knows them personally, and who told me that the police were investigating these attacks.

[26] His account appears in newspapers and in Sookhdeo, *Freedom to Believe*.

[27] For a March 2010 report on alleged intimidation by Muslim gangs in British prisons, see http://news.bbc.co.uk/1/hi/uk/8558590.stm

[28] 'South Asian' refers to those whose ethnic origins are from Pakistan, India or Bangladesh. The 2006 Maranatha report, p. 30, lists several cases of attempted murder of Pakistani females, and one actual case where the girl was sent back to Pakistan and shortly afterwards died in an improbable 'accident'.

[29] Thomas Walsh, 'Voices from Christians in Britain with a Muslim Background: Stories for the British Church on Evangelism, Conversion, Integration and Discipleship' (MA dissertation, University of Birmingham, 2005).

[30] Harper, Des (2004), 'Why South Asians in Britain come to Christ: Factors in the conversion to Christ of People of other Faiths', (MA dissertation, All Nations Christian College, 2004).

[31] 'Amal Farah' in the Council of Ex-Muslims website http://www.ex-muslim.org.uk

Chapter 9 – Anthony McRoy

[1] Ibn Shihab Al-Muwatta 45.5.18, 'The Messenger of Allah (peace be upon him), said, "Two deens [religions] shall not coexist in the Arabian Peninsula."'

[2] Manchester Online, http://www.manchesteronline.co.uk/news/content.cfm?story=106714 2002 (accessed June 2010).

[3] Vasagar, Jeevan, David Ward, Abigail Etim, Abigail and Matt Keating, '"No go for whites" in race hotspot', *The Guardian*,

20 April 2001, http://www.guardian.co.uk/Archive/Article/0,4273,4172796,00.html 2002 (accessed June 2010).

4 Clayton, Emma, 'Sheer Criminality is the Root Cause', *Bradford Telegraph & Argus*, http://www.thisisbradford.co.uk/bradford__district/bradford/riot/BRAD_NEWS 11.html 2002 (accessed June 2010).

5 Clayton, Emma, 'Sheer Criminality is the Root Cause'.

6 McRoy, Anthony, 'No More Cheeks to Turn: Bradford's Christian Minority', *Q-News*, no. 338, December 2001, p. 11.

7 Walsh, Sarah, 'Race-hate Mob Tries to Burn Church', *Bradford Telegraph & Argus*, 6 November 2001, http://www.thisisbradford.co.uk/bradford__district/archive/2001/11/06/brad_news01.int.html 2002 (accessed June 2010).

8 Stokes, Paul, Brownies Forced to Quit Church after 'Race Attacks', *Daily Telegraph*, 14 November 2001, http://www.telegraph.co.uk/news/main.jhtml?xml=%2Fnews%2F2001%2F11%2F14%2Fnbrad14.xml 2002 (accessed June 2010).

9 Alibhai-Brown, Yasmin, *When Muslims Behave Badly*, 28 January 2002, http://www.independent.co.uk/story.jsp?story=116691 2002 (accessed June 2010).

10 BBC, 'Priest Hurt in Faith-hate Attack', http://news.bbc.co.uk/1/hi/england/london/7297901.stm 15 March 2008 (accessed June 2010).

11 BBC, 'Police Protection for Clergymen', http://news.bbc.co.uk/1/hi/england/london/7400815.stm 14 May 2008 (accessed June 2010).

12 Rochdale Online, 'Gang of Youths Attack Pastor and his Church – Again', http://www.rochdaleonline.co.uk/news-features/2/community/19846/gang-of-youths-attack-pastor-and-his-church-again 6 February 2009 (accessed June 2010).

13 Petre, Jonathan, 'Minister Beaten after Clashing with Muslims on his TV Show', *Daily Mail*, http://www.dailymail.co.uk/news/article-1162039/Minister-beaten-clashing-Muslims-TV-show.html 15 March 2009 (accessed June 2010).

[14] BBC1, *The Koran and the Kalashnikov*, broadcast 23 January 2000.

[15] Chaudhry, Humayun, 'Islam on our Side', *Q-News*, no. 316, February 2000, p. 30.

[16] Colvin, Marie, Dipesh Gadher, 'Britain's Islamic Army', *The Sunday Times*, 17 January 1999, p. 15.

[17] Vasagar, Jeevan, Vikram Dodd, 'British Muslims Take the Path to Jihad', *The Guardian* (29 December 2000), p. 3.

[18] Vasagar, Jeevan, Vikram Dodd, 'British Muslims Take the Path to *Jihad*'.

Chapter 10 – John Ray OBE

[1] See springfieldproject.org.uk, thefeast.org.uk and youthencounter.org.uk

[2] In John Gray, *After Enlightenment*, 1984 (no further information available on source).

[3] Shah, Hannah, *The Imam's Daughter* (London: Ebury Publishing, 2009).

[4] Presence and Engagement is a consultation process which reflects the Church of England's determination to continue and extend practical service and witness to young and old in the many parishes where people of other faiths, mainly Muslims, are numerous. See their website as well as that of the 2011 Near Neighbours development, www.presenceandengagement.org.uk

Chapter 11 – Emma Dipper

[1] http://news.bbc.co.uk/1/hi/5411954.stm '"Remove Full Veils" Urges Jack Straw' (*BBC News*, 6 October 2006).

[2] Khiabany, Gholam, Milly Williamson, Veiled Bodies – Naked Racism, Race & Class Vol. 50:2, 69–88

http://rac.sagepub.com/content/50/2/69.refs.html (accessed 8 December 2010).

3 Asian community worker, interview by author (8 December 2010).

4 The role of women in Islam http://www.essortment.com/all/roleofwomenis_rhzn.htm (accessed 7 December 2010).

5 'Crimes of the Community: Honour-based Violence in the UK'. Centre for Social Cohesion Report 2010, second edition. Copies are available to download from their website www.socialcohesion.co.uk

6 'Crimes of the Community: Honour-based Violence in the UK', p. 6.

7 Bradby, H., 'Negotiating Marriage: Young Punjabi Women's Assessment of their Individual and Family Interests' quoted in Abdullahi An-Na'im, Charles Howard Candler, Professor of International Law at Emory University, USA, *Forced Marriage*, 2000, http://www.soas.ac.uk/honourcrimes/resources/file55689.pdf (accessed 13 December 2010).

8 Dorkenoo, Eflua et al., '*A Statistical Study to Estimate the Prevalence of Female Genital Mutilation in England and Wales*' (FORWARD, 2007), http://www.forwarduk.org.uk/key-issues/fgm/research (accessed 17 December 2010).

9 Ann-Marie Wilson, founder/director, 28toomany, interview by author (13 December 2010).

10 28toomany is a Christian organization set up to raise the awareness of FGM globally as well as in the UK. For further information see www.28toomany.org.

11 Abdel-Haleem Hamed, Sheikh Mohammed Abdel-Haleem Hamed, *How to Make Your Wife Happy* http://www.islamfortoday.com/how_to_make_your_wife_happy.htm (accessed 12 December 2010).

12 www.muslimparliament.org.uk/marriage

13 http://www.fco.gov.uk/en/travel-and-living-abroad/when-things-go-wrong/forced-marriage/

Guidelines and a leaflet are available to download from this site.

14 Taylor, Jenny, director Lapido Media – Religious Literacy in World Affairs. An interview with the author, 13 December 2010. For further information, see www.lapidomedia.com. Werner Menski is Professor of Asian Law at SOAS (School of Oriental and African Studies).

15 Nicholas, Sian, Interfaith practitioner and former mission partner working with Muslim women. Interview with author, 8 December 2010.

Chapter 12 – Julian Rivers

1 Williams, Rowan, 'Civil and Religious Law in England: A Religious Perspective', *Ecclesiastical Law Journal* 262, 2008. The phrase 'tranformative accommodation' is that of Ayelet Shachar.

2 Patrick Glenn, H., *Legal Traditions of the World: Sustainable Diversity in Law* (Oxford: OUP, second edition, 2004).

3 Brief introduction in Anderson, J.N.D., *Islamic Law in the Modern World* (New York: New York University Press, 1959); see also the essays in *Islamic Law and Legal Theory* (Ian Edge, ed.; Aldershot: Dartmouth, 1996).

4 Fyzee, Asaf A.A., *Outlines of Muhammadan Law* (New Dehli: OUP, fourth edition, 1974).

5 The fullest modern British treatment is David Pearl and Werner Menski, *Muslim Family Law* (London: Sweet & Maxwell, third edition, 1998).

6 Khaliq, Urfan, 'The Accommodation and Regulation of Islam and Muslim Practices in English Law', *Ecclesiastical Law Journal* 332, 2002.

7 Ainley, Michael, (et al.), *Islamic Finance in the UK: Regulation and Challenges* (Financial Services Authority, November 2007).

8 See Lord Phillips of Worth Matravers, 'Equality Before the Law', a speech given at the East London Muslim Centre, 3 July 2008, reproduced in various places including *Law and Justice*, 2008.

9 Yilmaz, Ihsan, *Muslim Laws: Politics and Society in Modern Nation States* (Aldershot: Dartmouth, 2005).

10 'Dispute Resolution in Family Law: Protecting Choice, Promoting Inclusion' (December 2004), http://www.attorneygeneral.jus.gov.on.ca/english/about/pubs/boyd/full-report.pdf

11 See Poulter, Sebastian, *Ethnicity, Law and Human Rights* (Oxford: OUP, 1998), chapter 6.

12 Samia Bano, 'In Pursuit of Religious and Legal Diversity: A response to the Archbishop of Canterbury and the "Shari'a Debate" in Britain', *Ecclesiastical Law Journal*, 283, 2008.

Chapter 13 – Richard Sudworth

1 http://www.micahnetwork.org/en/integral-mission (accessed 27 October 2009).

2 http://www.lausanne.org/covenant (accessed 27 October 2009).

3 Wright, N.T., *The New Testament and the People of God* (London: SPCK, 1992), p. 64.

4 Volf, M., *Exclusion & Embrace: A Theological Exploration of Identity, Otherness, and Reconciliation* (Abingdon: Nashville, 1996), p. 213.

5 For a very persuasive theology of religions that offers a basis for encounter with others that takes risks in order to be vulnerable yet encountering then in depth, their traditions with integrity, while maintaining differences, I am indebted to Michael Barnes' *Theology and the Dialogue of Religions* (Cambridge: Cambridge University Press, 2002).

Chapter 15 – Toby Howarth

[1] See Sobhani, *Ayatollah Jafar, Doctrines of Shiʿi Islam* (trans. and ed. Reza Shah-Kazemi; London: I.B. Tauris, 2001), p. 150.

[2] For an interesting example of a current popular level online debate between *Sunnis* about how to view *taqiyya* (which is seen as a *Shiʿite* doctrine), see www.yanabi.com/forum/PrintTopic147373.aspx (accessed 8 July 2010).

[3] 'The real reason Iran can't be trusted', in *The Christian Science Monitor*, 20 November 2009. See also the earlier and more academic writing by, for example, Dr Andrew Campbell, 'Iran's nuclear deception: *taqiyya* and kitman' in the Australian web-based journal *National Observer* (Council for the National Interest, Melbourne), no. 67, summer 2006, pp. 8-25, and his earlier article in the same journal, '*Taqiyya*, how Islamic extremists deceive the West', no. 65, winter 2005, pp. 11–23.

[4] See, for example the discussion on Daniel Pipes' blog, www.danielpipes.org/comments/138544, or the video, *Taqiyya Obama is no Christian*, on www.youtube.com/watch?v =_b_GanwbFl4 (both accessed 30 March 2010). According to a Harris poll of 24 March 2010, 32 per cent of Americans believed that Obama is really a Muslim.

[5] 'Implications of the Violent Hamas Takeover of Gaza' emailing from the Barnabas Fund, 21 June 2007.

[6] 'Report on the Teaching of Islam in Universities', emailing from the Barnabas Fund, 22 June 2007.

[7] See the official Common Word website, www.acommonword.com (accessed 30 March 2010). The assertion of *taqiyya* was made in 'Response to Open Letter and Call from Muslim Religious Leaders to Christian Leaders', 13 October 2007, emailing from the Barnabas Fund, 29 November 2007. It is not unusual in Islamic discourse for different messages to be delivered to the different audiences. This is permitted

by the Islamic doctrine of *taqiyya* (dissimulation) which allows Muslims to practise deception in certain circumstances.

[8] Sookhdeo, Patrick, *Islam: The Challenge to the Church*, and *Global Jihad: The Future in the Face of Militant Islam* (Three Rivers, MI: Isaac Publishing, 2006 and 2007 respectively).

[9] See www.fulcrum-anglican.org.uk/page.cfm?ID=380 and www.fulcrum-anglican.org.uk/page.cfm?ID=386 respectively (both accessed 8 July 2010).

[10] Exodus 1:15–21.

[11] Joshua 6:25.

[12] Sahih Muslim, Book 032, Number 6309. I have quoted this Tradition from the website of the University of Southern California's Centre for Muslim-Jewish Engagement as a widely used and easily accessible source: www.usc.edu/schools/college/crcc/engagement/resources/texts/muslim

[13] I am indebted to Martin Whittingham of the Oxford Centre for Muslim-Christian Studies for his help in this section, in finding, translating and evaluating some of the Arabic texts.

[14] *Taqiyya* is above all of special significance for the *Shiʿa*. (*'Taqiyya'*, Encyclopaedia of Islam, second edition article). At a popular level, see the standard Arabic-English dictionary by Hans Wehr (ed. J.M. Cowan) which translates the term as 'fear, caution, prudence; (in *Shiʿitic* Islam) dissimulation of one's religion (under duress or in the face of threatening damage).'

[15] The translation here (and elsewhere in this chapter) is that of Abdullah Yusuf Ali (Islamic Foundation, 1975) which interestingly is published with a commentary that steers the reader away from an interpretation in line with the doctrine of *taqiyya*. There is no permission in this for weakness or dissembling under torture or persecution. (p. 685).

[16] *'Takiyya'*, *Encyclopaedia of Islam* (second edition).

[17] This and the previous quote are from Mahmoud Ayoub, *The Qur'an and its Interpreters*, vol. 2 (New York: State University of New York, 1992), pp. 78,79.

[18] Sahih Muslim, Book 32, Number 6303 (from the USC website).

[19] Sahih Bukhari, Book 59, Number 369 (from the USC website).

[20] Al-Ghazali, from Book 37 of *Ihya Ulum al-din* (Cairo: *Dar al-bayan al-ᶜarabi*, 2005/1426), p. 5.

[21] Muller, Roland, *Honor and Shame: Unlocking The Door* (Bloomington, IN: Xlibris Corporation, 2001), p. 83.

[22] Al-Ghazzali, in an earlier book (Book 24, *Kitab Afaf al-Insan, The Evils of the Tongue*).

[23] The child abuse scandals in the church have been widely reported. Hannah Shah's autobiography, *The Imam's Daughter*, tells the heartbreaking story of how horrific abuse can be covered up in the name of protecting a family and community's honour (London: Rider, an imprint of Random House, 2009).

[24] In both *Global Jihad* and *Islam: The Challenge to the Church*, referred to above, the author puts the two concepts together as one, and labels it *taqiyya*. As he writes, 'It is important for non-Muslims to be aware that in classical Islam Muslims are permitted to lie in certain situations, one of which is war. This kind of permitted deception is called *taqiyya*, *Global Jihad*, op. cit., p. 196.

[25] Kingsley's assertion and Newman's response (from an appendix to his *Apologia pro Vita Sua*) are quoted here from chapter 14 of Paul J. Griffiths' excellent study, *Lying: An Augustinian Theology of Duplicity* (Grand Rapids, MI: Brazos Press, 2004).

[26] Bonhoeffer, Dietrich, *Letters and Papers from Prison* (ed. E. Bethge; London: SCM, 1967, third edition), p. 16.

[27] Bonhoeffer, Dietrich, *Ethics* (London: Touchstone, 1995), p. 359.

[28] For an exploration of the relationship between the United Kingdom Islamic Mission and the Jamaʿat-i-Islami party in Pakistan (and more widely), see Howarth, T., 'What do we do with Mawdudi?' in *Crucible: the Christian Journal of Social Ethics* (July-September 2008), pp. 27–36.

[29] Bonhoeffer, Dietrich, *Ethics*, op. cit. p. 364.

Chapter 16 – Jay Smith

[1] Riddell, Peter G., and Peter Cotterell, *Islam in Conflict* (Leicester: IVP, 2003), pp. 7,8.

[2] Riddell and Cotterell, *Islam in Conflict*, chapters 10–12, and page 193. Also a lecture by Riddell on the theme 'Muslim Views on the World' held at the London Institute for Contemporary Christianity and sponsored by the London Lectures Trust, 23 October 2003.

[3] *Sunday Telegraph*, 19 February 2006.

[4] 'US Image Worsens in Europe Poll', news release credited to AFP (Agence Francaise de Presse), Washington, *The Korea Times*, Seoul: 18 March 18 2004, p. 6.

Chapter 17 – Chawkat Moucarry

[1] See the official website for this document at www.acommonword.com

[2] To appreciate the significance of this fresh understanding of Sura 3 verse 64 by the letter's signatories, one needs to compare it with the interpretation of this text by Razi (d. 606/1209), a mainstream and highly respected Muslim exegete. He considers that this qurʿanic verse calls Christians to sign up to 'a fair statement', *kalimat sawaa*, with Muslims about their respective faiths. This statement, based on God's oneness, requires that Christians give up

three of their misguided beliefs and practices, namely i)
worshiping someone else than God, i.e. Christ; ii) ascribing
partners to God through their belief in the eternal Trinity
(Father, Son, Holy Spirit); iii) taking their leaders and
monks as lords, at least implicitly, through obeying their
human teaching, venerating them and believing that God
is infused in some of them (see Razi's *Great Commentary* on
3:64, Vol. viii, pp. 76,77).

[3] One noteworthy response was the statement issued by the
Yale Center for Faith and Culture (see www.yale.edu/
faith). Many Christians including this author have signed
this response.

Conclusion

[1] Newbigin, Lesslie, *Faith and Power: Christianity and Islam in
"Secular" Britain* (London: SPCK, 1998).
[2] Jenkins, Philip, *God's Continent: Islam, Christianity and
Europe's Religious Crisis* (Oxford: Oxford University Press,
2007).

Appendix 1

[1] NRSV.
[2] NIV.

Grace for Muslims

*The Journey from
Fear to Faith*

Steve Bell

'Why should an essentially "benign" religion turn some into "demons"?' asked a Muslim journalist. It is a question that is at the heart of the Islamic debate. Alarmist claims are made about these 'demons', while the possibility of a peaceful Islam is dismissed. Many are confused about the religion's contradictory faces.

Is it possible for Christians to relate to Muslims without being politically naïve or theologically liberal? Steve believes it is. He shares his own journey and reflects upon how he arrived at the crucial ingredient – grace.

978-1-85078-664-1

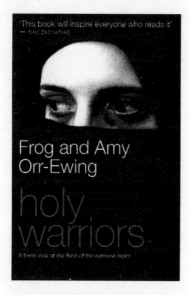

'This book will inspire everyone who reads it'
— RAVI ZACHARIAS

Frog and Amy
Orr-Ewing

holy
warriors
A fresh look at the face of the extreme Islam

Holy Warriors

A Fresh Look at the Face of the Extreme Islam

Frog and Amy Orr-Ewing

A scholarly and sensitive analysis of Islam and Islamism and a unique account of the Taliban.

'We write this account of the Taliban with probably a unique experience and perspective on them. We have a story that intertwines our lives with theirs long before the twin towers were destroyed and the appalling attacks on America had wreaked their havoc. For much of the Western press, the Taliban were just another fundamentalist regime, renowned for their treatment of women, and their ultra-orthodoxy. They are a group now ingrained upon the visual imagination of the western world.' – **Frog and Amy Orr-Ewing**

978-1-85078-460-9